Drag Racing's Quarter-Mile Warriors

THEN & NOW

DOUG BOYCE

CarTech®

838 Lake Street South
Forest Lake, MN 55025
Phone: 651-277-1200 or 800-551-4754
Fax: 651-277-1203
www.cartechbooks.com

© 2014 by Doug Boyce

All rights reserved. No part of this publication may be reproduced or utilized in any form or by any means, electronic or mechanical, including photocopying, recording, or by any information storage and retrieval system, without prior permission from the Publisher. All text, photographs, and artwork are the property of the Author unless otherwise noted or credited.

The information in this work is true and complete to the best of our knowledge. However, all information is presented without any guarantee on the part of the Author or Publisher, who also disclaim any liability incurred in connection with the use of the information and any implied warranties of merchantability or fitness for a particular purpose. Readers are responsible for taking suitable and appropriate safety measures when performing any of the operations or activities described in this work.

All trademarks, trade names, model names and numbers, and other product designations referred to herein are the property of their respective owners and are used solely for identification purposes. This work is a publication of CarTech, Inc., and has not been licensed, approved, sponsored, or endorsed by any other person or entity. The Publisher is not associated with any product, service, or vendor mentioned in this book, and does not endorse the products or services of any vendor mentioned in this book.

Edit by Bob Wilson
Design concept by Connie DeFlorin
Layout by Monica Seiberlich

ISBN 978-1-61325-133-1
Item No. CT528

Library of Congress Cataloging-in-Publication Data

Boyce, Doug, author.
  Drag racing's quarter-mile warriors : then & now / by Doug Boyce.
     pages cm
  ISBN 978-1-61325-133-1
  1. Dragsters–History. 2. Drag racing–United States–History. I. Title.
  TL236.2.B68 2014
  629.228–dc23
                          2014001337

Written, edited, and designed in the U.S.A.
Printed in China
10 9 8 7 6 5 4 3 2

Front Flap (top): This photo was taken at Bowling Green, Kentucky, in 2013, and yes, the headers got hot. The culprit turned out to be a defective shutoff valve. Sure made for a great photo op.

Front Flap (bottom): With Mark Schley behind the wheel of the Schley Brothers restored Lightning Bug Gasser, wheels-up 6.90 eighth-mile passes are the norm. Results prove that these guys aren't afraid to hammer on their VW as the times turned equal 1971 results. (Photo Courtesy Schley Brothers)

End Papers: The inaugural Pro Stock race at the 1970 NHRA Winternationals boiled down to the 430-ci Camaro of Bill Jenkins and the Hemi 'Cuda of Sox & Martin. Jenkins' aging Camaro trailered the 'Cuda with a 9.99 time. Sox turned in an off-pace 10.12.

Frontispiece: Jim and Julie Matuszak's Funny Car is one of two Ramchargers cars remaining today and was the last Ramchargers Funny Car built. Although the original block was "ventilated" long ago, the majority of parts found on the stretched-out Hemi are original to the car. Its best elapsed time (ET) was a 6.39 and the best MPH was 230.17.

Title Page: In a 2008 informal NHRA online poll, the Willys of Stone, Woods & Cook was voted fans' favorite race car of all time. Swindler II in the near lane later became Swindler B, and in 1965, both cars were painted an almost identical candy blue. The restoration of the near Willys to Swindler II status was chosen to not detract from Swindler A.

Contents Page: Today's Cobra Jet drag cars have nothing on the Georgia Shaker. This car looks flat-out mean and has performance characteristics to back it up. In its day, the match racer faced and defeated many top Chevy and Chrysler opponents.

Back Cover Photos: They're still out there if you're willing to look. Sam Auxier ran this Don Hardy Pro Stock Pinto between 1973 and 1975. The car was found in a Maryland field where it had been sitting since the mid-1980s. At this point, a total restoration is planned.

All photos courtesy Doug Boyce Collection unless otherwise noted.

Author note: Many of the vintage photos in this book are of lower quality. They have been included because of their importance to telling the story.

OVERSEAS DISTRIBUTION BY:

PGUK
63 Hatton Garden
London EC1N 8LE, England
Phone: 020 7061 1980 • Fax: 020 7242 3725
www.pguk.co.uk

Renniks Publications Ltd.
3/37-39 Green Street
Banksmeadow, NSW 2109, Australia
Phone: 2 9695 7055 • Fax: 2 9695 7355
www.renniks.com

Contents

- Acknowledgments 6
- Introduction 6

Chapter One: Diggers: The Top Dogs 8
- Tommy Ivo's Twin Engine 10
- England's First Dragster 13
- Mickey Thompson's *Assault I* Dragster 15
- *Hellzapoppin* A/Dragster 18
- VanRonk and Bumgarner *The Vagabond* 20
- *Syndicate Scuderia* 22
- Winkel, Trapp & Fuller *Magicar* 24
- Bobby Langley's *Scorpion V* 27
- Don Tognotti's *Bushwacker* 29
- Warren, Coburn & Miller 31
- *The Stone Age Man* 34
- D.A. Santucci's *Bubble Gum Car* 36
- Petersen & Fitz 38
- Stephens & Venables 40
- *Great Expectations II* 42
- Gary Cochran's Rear-Engine Dragster 43
- John Peters' *Freight Train* 45

Chapter Two: Funny Cars and Not So Funny Cars .. 47
- Dick Landy's AWB 1965 Dodge 48
- Gas Ronda's Long-Nose Mustang 51
- Pete Gates' *Gate Job* Comet 53
- Dave Koffel's Experimental Stock Barracuda 56
- *Ingénue* 1967 Buick Skylark 58
- Jim Kirby/Dick Harrell Camaro 60
- Ed Schartman's *Rattler* Cougar 62
- Jungle Jim Liberman's Twin Novas 64
- *Chi-Town Hustler* Charger 66
- Ramchargers 1972 68

Chapter Three: Rockin' Pro Stocks 70
- Al Joniec's Match-Race Mustang 71
- Don Nicholson's 1970 Maverick 73
- *Red Light Bandit* 1970 Challenger 75
- Sandy Elliot/Barrie Poole 1971 Comet 78
- Dutch Irrgang's 1972 Vega Wagon 81
- Bob Glidden's 1973 Pinto 84
- Wally Booth's AMC Brigade 86
- Sox & Martin 1973 Duster 88
- Dick Landy's 1973 Dart Sport 90
- Ronnie Sox's Hemi Colt 92
- *Grumpy's Toy XI* 1974 Vega 95
- The Mopar Missile That Wasn't 98

Chapter Four: The Wild Bunch 101
- Stone, Woods & Cook Willys 102
- *Jolly Dolly* C/Gas 1939 Chevy 105
- Moody-Jones C/Gas 1937 Chevy 107
- Gene Moody's D/Gas 1955 Chevy 109
- Jersey Jimmy's Altered 111
- *Lil Screamer II* 1934 Ford 113
- Dave Hales' S&S Race Team 1937 Willys 115
- Hugh Tucker's AA/SR Chevy 117
- *Mr. C* Competition Roadster 120
- *The Grove Boys* 1940 Willys 122
- Jack Merkel's 1933 Willys 124
- Kohler Brothers' *King Kong* 128
- Jim Oddy's AA/GS Austin 130
- Fred Hurst's A/GS Barracuda 132
- Mondello & Matsubara AA/FA 134
- Ron Bizio's AA/GS 1933 Willys Pickup 138
- George Montgomery's AA/GS 1969 Mustang 139
- Schley Brothers' *Lightning Bug* 141
- Kroona & Sandberg 144

Chapter Five: Door Slammers Galore 148
- Dave Strickler's *The Old Reliable II* 149
- Dave Kempton's Plymouth Fury 151
- Frank Sanders' Z-11 Chevy 153
- Osburn Trucking's Lightweight Ford 155
- Golden Commandos' Barracuda 157
- Sox & Martin 1967 Plymouth 160
- Al Joniec's Cobra Jet Mustang 162
- Larry Griffith's Super Stock 1968 Hemi Dart 164
- Anderson Oldsmobile's W-31 Cutlass 167
- *AMX-1* Super Stock 1969 168
- McMaster & Gunning 1957 Chevy 171
- Hubert Platt's Ford Drag Team Mustang 173
- Scotto & Blevins Chevy Nomad 175
- High School 1957 Chevy 177
- *Granny Goose II* 1969 Camaro 179
- Dianna & Ripes Corvette 181
- Stark Hickey's Super Stock Mustang 183
- Arlen Fadely's Super Modified Maverick 185

Epilogue: What Goes Around 189

Acknowledgments

A book this involved requires many helping hands and I am eternally grateful to all those who contributed their time and resources to help see it through.

A special thanks has to go to Dave Davis and Jim Handy. These guys have a deep passion for the sport and their contributions went well beyond all expectations. Carl Rubrecht has been a godsend. He has been involved in all of my written work, providing photos, leads, and support. It wouldn't be an exaggeration to say that I couldn't have done it without him.

Additionally, I'd like to thank Larry Anderson, Lyle Barwick, Tim Bass, Kevin Beal, Brian Beattie, Craig Blanton, Forrest Bond, Darren Boyce, Peter Broadribb, Robert Byrd, Robert Casado, John Cassiol, Mary & Carlos Cedeno, John Cesareo, Jack Chisenhall, Bill Crosby, Larry Crossan, Jeff Cryan, Bob Dastalto, Tom Fedrigo, Bob Fite, James Fullingim, Hank Forss, Pete Gemar, Robert Genat, Larry Griffith, Ken Gunning, David Hakim, Dave Hales, Valerie Harrell, Darr Hawthorne, Jerry Heasley, John Hilger, Scott Hoerr, Doug Huegli, Daryl Huffman, Marlin Huss, Paul Hutchins, George Hutcheson, Todd Hutcheson, Tommy Ivo, Chadly Johnson, Madonna Jones, Joyce Keller, Richard Kinistry, Arnie Klann, Dean Klein, Sue Koffel, Dave Kroona, Ivan Landry, Martin Libhart, Bruce Lindstrom, John Lipori, Pat Lobb, Jim Marlett, Jim Matuszak, Richard McKinstry, Michael Mihalko, Greg Mosley, Karpo Murkijanian, Thomas Nagy, Al Nosse, Ralph Norberg, Ron Normann, Ted Pappacena, Mark Pappas, John Peters, Bill Pitts, Andrew Popovich, Bill Porterfield, Clark Rand, Rick Riley, Robert Rohrdanz, Greg Rourke, Richard Rudolph, Clare Sanders, Tom Schiltz, Bobby Schlegel, Mark & Pat Schley, Joe Scotto, Charlie Seabrook, Dave Siltman, Mike Sleeth, Lee Smith, Nick Smith, Joe Spinelli, Arch Stanton, Mike Strickler, Geoff Stunkard, Brian Taylor, Nick Taylor, Tony Thacker, Karl Thiele, William Truby, Hugh Tucker, Mike Wales, Tera Wendland, Royce Wiley, Dan Williams, Wendy Ann Williams, Bob Wenzelburger, Todd Wingerter, Robert Wytosky, and Paul Zielsdorf.

Websites: Cacklefest, Dover Dragstrip, Drag Racing Imagery, Drag List, Drag Racing Online, HAMB, James Handy Photography, Mopar Max, Mustang Monthly, and World of Speed.

Introduction

Being a dyed-in-the-wool fan of quarter-mile pursuit and feeling a twinge of nostalgia, I began to look back on the history of drag racing and the cars and categories that have come and gone. Back to those glorious days of Slingshot Dragsters, the Gassers Wars, Factory Experimentals, and those wicked, wicked Fuel Altereds. There were categories galore and what seemed like an endless choice of body styles and configurations.

Compared to other forms of organized motorsports, drag racing is relatively young. The first sanctioning body, the National Hot Rod Association (NHRA), wasn't formed until 1951 while the Indianapolis 500, for example, was first run in 1911. The NHRA was the brainchild of Wally Parks and Robert Petersen. They formed it as a way to bring respectability to the growing hobby and to help prevent the kids from racing on the streets. Within a few years the NHRA had spread from its humble Southern California beginnings to engulf the nation, to the point that each state held its own regional meet.

The NHRA was quickly followed by the United Drag Racers Association (UDRA), American Hot Rod Association (AHRA), and International Hot Rod Association (IHRA). They all brought us plenty of first-rate action. As the 1960s unfolded, the popularity of drag racing exploded, in both fan appeal and participation. Drag racing continued to expand and saw enormous growth through the 1970s but as rules progressed and cars evolved, we said good-bye to a number of categories including Top Gas, Gas, Fuel, Altered, and Modified Production.

Cars that were so dominant and plentiful went the way of the dinosaur and were replaced with cookie-cutter cars. Mustangs and Camaros seemed to dominate the landscape as the 1970s wound down and drag racing became big business. Electronics crept in and drivers became passengers in cars that resembled traveling billboards. The cars that we once enjoyed were now relegated to the brackets, backyards, and barns.

In recent years, surviving, restored, and "tribute" drag cars have gained in popularity. I'm no Sigmund Freud but I'll bet dollars to donuts that it just may have something to do with wanting to turn back the hands of time to a period when drag racing had style, appeal, and characters.

While writing the books *Grumpy's Toys: The Authorized History of Grumpy Jenkins' Cars* and *Junior Stock: Drag Racing the Family Sedan* the question of where these drag cars are now kept popping up. If you enjoy drag racing as it once was I'm sure you have asked the same question many times. These early drag cars influenced thousands and brought celebrity status to the likes of Wild Willie Borsch, Grumpy Jenkins, and "Big Daddy" Don Garlits. Where did these cars go? In this book you'll learn the location of many cars. If you're like me, you'll be pleasantly surprised by how many remain.

This book covers the gambit from Rails to Stockers, legendary cars, and cars that left lasting impressions. Although not all the cars are of historic significance, each one does have its place in the history of the sport and contributed to its evolution. Each car is a true survivor with a story to tell. Even though plenty of tribute and cloned cars have been built over the years, this book focuses only on the real deals. These are the true survivors from yesterday.

They're still out there if you're willing to look. Sam Auxier ran this Don Hardy Pro Stock Pinto between 1973 and 1975. The car was found in a Maryland field where it had been sitting since the mid-1980s. At this point, a total restoration is planned.

CHAPTER ONE

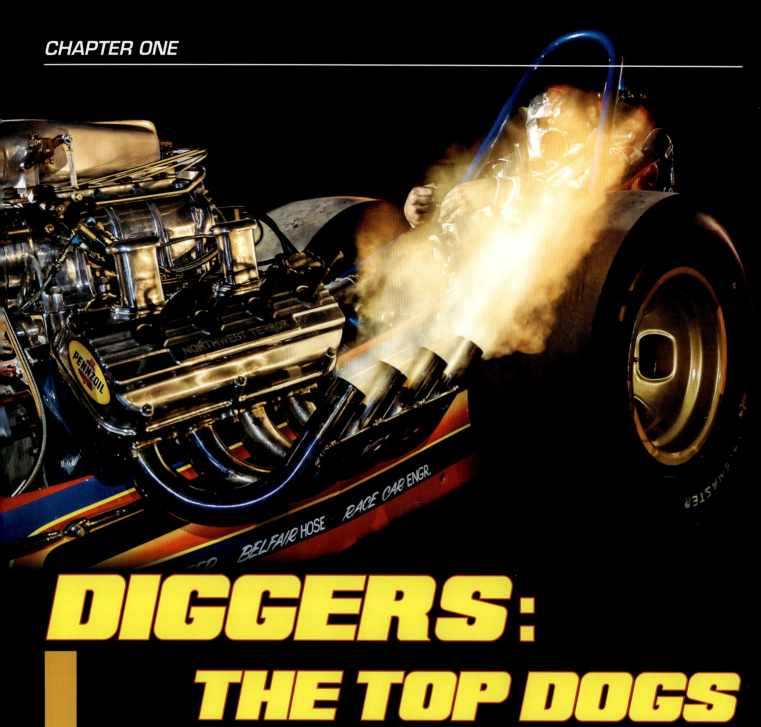

DIGGERS: THE TOP DOGS

Dick Kraft's *The Bug*, considered by most to be the first dragster, was assembled in 1950. Although Dick started with a '27 T rescued from his folks' West Coast orange grove, little beyond the original frame rails remained of the car once Dick was through with it. Powered by a flathead 8, *The Bug* was the first "rail" to top 100 mph when Dick accomplished this feat at the Santa Ana airstrip.

Dragsters were quick to evolve and by the mid-1950s, competitors were fabricating frames, bolting on blowers, and stretching the wheelbase. Mickey Thompson has been credited with developing the slingshot design, placing the driver behind the rear wheels as a way of optimizing traction.

INGENUITY REALLY WAS IN ACTION AS OUT OF THE WOODWORK CAME MID-ENGINE RAILS SIDEWINDERS AND TWIN-ENGINE DRAGSTERS.

Above: The current 392 in the Petersen & Fritz FED was built around a virgin block and features a 3/8-inch stroke increase, .030-over bore, Crower clutch, and 8.75 Chrysler rear end. (Photo By Doug Huegli, Courtesy worldofspeed.org)

When Don Garlits' front engine rail, *Swamp Rat XIII,* suffered a violent transmission explosion in March 1970, it led directly to Don designing and building his first rear-engine car. *Swamp Rat XIV* made its debut at the 1971 NHRA Winternationals where it won the event and changed Top Fuel forever. Today, all of Don's *Swamp Rat* cars are on display at his museum in Florida. (Photo Courtesy James Handy)

In 1957, the NHRA banned the use of nitromethane as an alternate fuel because of safety concerns. Gasoline became the only option and those hoping to maintain the same performance levels turned to unorthodox dragster layouts and configurations.

Ingenuity really was in action as out of the woodwork came mid-engine rails, sidewinders, and twin-engine dragsters. Classes and categories for the variance grew and, depending on the particular setup you wanted to run, dragsters were either placed in Top Eliminator, Top Gas, or even Comp and Street Eliminators by the end of the 1960s.

Until Don Garlits' infamous clutch explosion at Lions Drag Strip in 1970 when his dragster was blown in half, the basic slingshot layout changed little throughout the 1960s. Garlits' *Swamp Rat XIV* was the first successful mid-engine dragster and by 1972, the mid-engine rail had pretty much forced the slingshot design into obsolescence.

It was classified as a roadster in 1950 but Dick Kraft's *The Bug* is now recognized as drag racing's first dragster. Dick created the car from a weed sprayer that had been used in his parents' orange grove. (Photo Courtesy Pat Ganahl)

Tommy Ivo's Twin Engine

Tommy's twin Buicks featured Hilborn injectors and Isky five-cycle cams. The car was the first gas burner to run both 8- and 7-second quarter-mile times. Olds rear brakes and the first use of a Deist chute brought the car to a stop. Driving the push car is a young Don Prudhomme. "Don needed an engine built and I needed a car painted so we made a deal." Tommy's influence saw Don give up his show rod for drag racing. And, as they say, the rest is history. (Photo Courtesy Tommy Ivo Collection)

TV Tommy was born in Denver, Colorado, and had a natural talent for acting; his specialty was song and dance. At the age of seven, he hopped onto a bus with his mother and headed for the bright lights of Hollywood in search of his big break. While his father and Donald, his older brother, waited for word back home, Tommy's mother took him to auditions around town. He eventually earned his first key part in *Earl Carroll's Vanities*. Recalls Tommy, "My mother was 36 years old at the time and suffered severely from arthritis. In the warm, dry climate of California it all but disappeared. If it weren't for my mother's chronic arthritis, I probably never would have left Colorado and gotten into the movies." So, without the movies, there wouldn't have been TV Tommy the drag racer.

Tommy's car of choice was the Buick, a brand he became hooked on in the early 1950s. He bought his first one in 1952 because his girl thought it was pretty. Living in Southern California was all it took to pique his interest in drag racing and in 1955, with a new 322-powered Buick, he trekked out to Santa Maria and won himself a number of trophies. He had a desire to go faster; he was in his first rail in 1957, which, of course, was Buick-powered.

With the NHRA fuel ban in 1957, many Top Eliminator dragsters compensated for the loss of power by adopting either a blower or twin engines, in some cases, both. Tommy, influenced by Howard Cams' "Twin Bears" chose to go the twin, injected route and in 1959, bolted two Buicks into a Kent Fuller–designed chassis. Kent wasn't a fan of these twin-engine oddities and did his best to convince Tommy to go the single, blown-engine route. Kent felt the car would be quicker than a twin-engine rail but Tommy, being an engine builder and tuner, felt otherwise. He didn't want to go with a blower because he wanted to stick with his Buicks and knew that the small valves in his nailhead wouldn't work with a blower. As Tommy recalls, "At the time, blown cars were breaking a lot of parts."

To appease Kent, Tommy bolted a blower onto his Buick and proceeded to prove Kent wrong. Of course, Kent had no idea that Tommy had detuned the blown engine to make sure it ran like a slug.

Tommy's injected engines measured 464 inches and were based upon the standard 401 block. Both engines faced forward with the passenger-side engine running in reverse rotation. The engines were tilted outward so that the starter ring gears would mesh. Front and rear engine plates were fabricated to hold it all together. The twin ran a single clutch off the driver-side engine, which you had to slide (long before slider clutches) to make it all work. From the clutch, it was a direct drive to the offset quick-change rear end.

The old nail-valve Buicks ran on torque and as Tommy recalls, he may have been hitting 4,000 rpm going through the lights. The car wasn't necessarily quick but it was fast. The secret to making the car perform was the 2.90 rear gears, "and we had the right combination of tire and horsepower."

In 1960 Tommy became the first traveling professional drag racer when he took his rail match racing across the country. At Concord Drag-O-Way in North Carolina, the drag chute failed and to avoid damaging the car by running into the catch cables at the end of the track, Tommy made a hard right and ended up partway down an embankment. "I wasn't traveling very fast so I didn't do much damage. Don grabbed a rope, hooked it to the tow car, and pulled the car back from the brink. It could have been a lot worse." (Photo Courtesy Tommy Ivo Collection)

Tommy was always experimenting and at one point installed the blown Buick of good friend Tony Nancy. "The blower had a barn-door injector and the suction of the blower held it closed. It wasn't really throttle-able. It was either all open or closed. You couldn't slide the clutch so it took a quarter of the track for it to hook up. We ran the blower one weekend only and hit 179." (Photo Courtesy Tommy Ivo Collection)

The Kent Fuller chassis initially featured a 92-inch wheelbase but it never worked for the twin. "It never grabbed the ground very well so we started shorting it at 2-inch increments until we settled on 88 inches where the car seemed to hook the best."

And hook it did. The twin hit 169 when it debuted late in 1959 and became the first gas rail to hit 9.50s in the quarter-mile. It also became the first to hit the 8s and the 7s and the first to turn 170 and 180 mph.

Tommy became the first traveling professional racer, hitting the road in 1960 with a young Don Prudhomme. Referring to Don as his "tire wiper," the pair headed east and made 10 stops in three short months. The car was a huge hit. "The East had crowds like you wouldn't believe, and that sparked the idea for the four-engine *Showboat*. I figured that if they liked two engines, they'd like four better."

Like most drag racers, you sold one car to finance the next and that's exactly what Tommy did. In August 1960 while in Illinois wrapping up the tour he sold the twin to Ron Pellegrini and a group of his buddies. Tommy raced the car through the following winter, replacing the weak-link quick change with a Halibrand Champion unit. Pellegrini attempted to drive the car at the NHRA Nationals in 1961 but just couldn't get it to hook.

The car was sold again in 1963 to Billy Herndon who stretched the wheelbase out to 122 inches. The twin dragster's career came to an abrupt end when, failing to open the chute in time, Billy crashed the car into a tree. The wreck was hauled

This cutaway by Tom West shows the finer details of Tommy's twin. The car weighs 1,800 pounds with 618 of them resting on the front wheels. Those with a keen eye will notice only six pipes coming up between the two engines. The other two pipes exited below. (Photo Courtesy Tommy Ivo Collection)

to Don Garlits' shop where it was roughly repaired but never saw the track again. The car sat on an open trailer for the next 10 to 15 years behind Billy's house where inevitably it began to rust. Billy offered the car for sale and Garlits beat Tommy to the purchase, buying the car for $5,000.

Don did a quick cleanup and added it to his growing museum. There she sat until borrowed and restored by Tommy for a showing at the NHRA Museum. Tommy, with a great amount of help from Bill Larzerlere, spent three months pulling the car down to its last nut and bolt. She was in rough shape from the accident years before, "The engines were frozen from sitting outside all that time, and gears were misaligned when it was pieced back together after the accident."

Today, the car has taken its place in drag racing history as the most successful twin-engine car and once again resides at the Don Garlits Museum of Drag Racing.

This rear view shows the twin Deist chutes and push-bar extension. Tommy has a sense of humor and usually placed a wind-up key in the extension. The only time Tommy can recall losing his temper was at Bakersfield in 1960, "I had the field covered by a lot and was counting my chickens before they hatched. I lost in the final after pulling a giant wheelie." (Photo Courtesy Tommy Ivo Collection)

Tommy has never shied away from getting his hands dirty. Once the drag racing bug bit him, the movies were simply a means to an end. Here he is seen piecing together one of the 464-inch Buicks during restoration. (Photo Courtesy Tommy Ivo Collection)

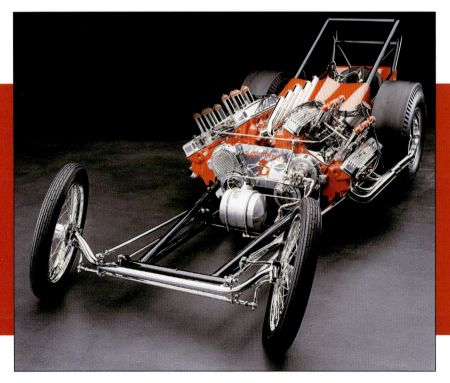

Tommy's twin-engine dragster lays claim to many firsts and has earned its place in drag racing's history books. Looking back on his 36 years in drag racing, Tommy says he had no idea that he was building a career when he first started, "I just wanted to see my cars in magazines." Tommy spent about $2,000 of his own money building the twin back in 1959. Care to guess what it would cost today? (Photo Courtesy Tommy Ivo Collection)

England's First Dragster

Sydney Allard at Goodwood 1962. In 1963 Sydney formed the British Drag Racing Association and match raced *Dante Duce* from the U.S. in Dean Moon's *Mooneyes* digger. (Photo Courtesy Bernard Gudge)

While rails were being built in America in 1950, the British were busy running Grands Prix and road races. Drag racing was slow to catch on in Europe and it wasn't until 1960 that the British Hot Rod Association was formed. Later the same year, multitalented Sydney Allard started work on the Allard Chrysler, Europe's first dragster.

Shortly after World War II, Sydney formed the Allard Motor Company and went to work building Ford V-8 conversions and selling performance equipment. Unfortunately for Allard, post–World War II import restrictions greatly limited U.S. performance parts from reaching his shores. These restrictions excluded "personal gifts" and friends at Edelbrock and Ardun (among others) provided parts and allowed Allard to have U.K. manufacturers reproduce them.

Sydney proved to be just as capable behind the wheel and in 1949 won the British Hill Climbing Championship, finished third at Le Mans in 1950, and in 1952 drove one of his own Allard cars to victory at Monte Carlo. By the late 1950s, Sydney's interest had been piqued by American drag racing. Using a photo of Chris Karamesines' *Chizler* as a reference, Allard, along with designer David Hooper and mechanic John Hume, went to work building the Allard Chrysler.

Those of us on the left side of the big pond had to adhere to the rules and regulations of the NHRA. Among other sanctioning bodies, those in Europe were forced to adhere to the much stricter Royal Automobile Club (RAC) rules. One of those rules was that all moving parts had to be covered. This explains the full body panels. For streamlining purposes, the choice was made to mount the GMC 6-71 blower to the front of the 354 Hemi rather than the top of the engine.

In 1963, the blown Hemi propelled the Allard to a record kilometer sprint time of 16.68 seconds. Top speed was pegged in the neighborhood of 160 mph. Based upon a mild steel 3 x 1.5 frame the Allard Chrysler featured an English Ford Pilot front beam axle along with a Pilot 2-speed transmission. An Allard quick-change rear end, which was based upon a Halibrand design, held 3.54 gears. The underslung rear was also narrowed and featured bearing retainers and safety hubs.

Per RAC requirements, the dragster runs both front and rear brakes with a twin master cylinder. As a precautionary measure, a chute was added to aid braking. However, it wasn't just any chute. An Irving aviation chute originally used on hydrogen bombs dropped by Vulcan bombers was bolted to the roll cage.

This photo shows Sydney Allard in the driver's seat along with David Hooper (designer) and John Hume (chief engineer) during the car's initial construction at Clapham Workshop. The build was well on its way to completion in early 1961 when this photo was snapped. (Photo Courtesy National Motor Museum, Beaulieu)

Chapter One: Diggers: The Top Dogs   13

This dramatic cutaway gives a detailed view of the Allard dragster's underpinnings. Allard fabricated many parts while American suppliers such as Moon Equipment donated numerous performance parts. (Photo Courtesy Tom West/Bruce Gordon)

Supporting the car are 15-inch Lotus magnesium rims up front and 16-inch steelie rims mounting Inglewood cheater slicks. During the restoration, Radir piecrust slicks replaced the original M&H tires; up front, the guys stuck with Dunlop tires.

After its retirement in 1964, the Allard dragster languished in a barn for a number of years. Eventually it ended up in the National Motor Museum in Beaulieu where it sat under cover until 2006, waiting for Brian Taylor to come along and blow off the dust. Brian, a drag racing historian and author of *Crazy Horse: The History of British Drag Racing* says, "I was aware that the car had ended up in Beaulieu but it was during my visits to the library that the idea to bring her back to life grew." Brian sought approval from both the Allard family and the museum and once that was received, restoration began.

Although the chassis and body were in excellent shape and for the most part complete, the Hemi was long gone, having been pulled and placed in Allard's second dragster. Brian knew he was going to need some help with this undertaking and so formed the Allard Chrysler Action Group, a group of likeminded enthusiasts who had the skills and funds to help see the job through.

An unmolested 354 Hemi was hunted down and sent to Booth-Arons in Michigan for a rebuild. Knowing the car was going to be a Cacklefest regular, the engine was built to make the most of it. The original Hemi produced 480 horses but the fresh mill knocked out 750. Big-block Chevy rods were pinned to RaceTec pistons with a final compression of 6:1. An original GMC blower, Hilborn two-port injector, and Potvin adapter were provided by Beaulieu and sent to Littlefield's in California for necessary modification. Steve Sanchez at Total Flow Research ported and polished the heads that relied on Manley for its severe-duty valves. Crower donated the camshaft and valvesprings. For crowd appeal, the camshaft was profiled to maximize exhaust flame rather than for cylinder efficiency.

The five-year restoration was completed in mid-2013 and the Allard Chrysler was handed back to the museum. The Allard Chrysler Racing Group led by Brian should be commended for breathing new life into this fascinating piece of British drag racing history. Plans call for a 2014 tour of the United States to commemorate the fiftieth anniversary of the American Racing Team's visit to the U.K.

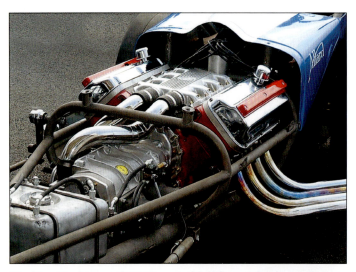

The Hemi features a 6-71 blower with Hilborn injection, a Vertex Magneto, and runs methanol for fuel. The Royal Automobile Club (RAC) rules (to which the car was built) required that all moving parts be covered. Allard formed an aluminum shell that is retained by Dzus fasteners. (Photo Courtesy Andy Wilshire)

The blue on the restored Allard is a custom blend by BASF matching what was believed to be a BMW color. (Photo Courtesy Bob Roberts)

Mickey Thompson's *Assault I* Dragster

Mickey used variations of Pontiac's V-8 to set both quarter-mile and land speed records through the early 1960s. Assault I *features a Don Borth–designed aluminum body, Dragmaster chassis, disc brakes, and magnesium Halibrand rims. (Photo by Doug Huegli, Courtesy worldofspeed.org)*

Much has been written about the illustrious career of Mickey Thompson. Anyone familiar with Mickey's exploits on the salt flats, drag strip, and in business knows that it would take volumes to tell the complete Mickey Thompson story. Few people have contributed more to the world of motorsports than Mickey Thompson. He participated in hundreds of motorsports events, setting nearly 500 speed and endurance records. This is more than anyone else in history; it includes 295 records at Bonneville alone. He invented stadium racing and contributed immeasurably to safety with, among other things, the invention of water-filled safety barriers.

Born on December 7, 1928, Marion Lee Thompson made his first trip to Bonneville in 1951 where he won the "Most Determined Effort" award after running his '36 Coupe to 141.065 mph. Mickey embodied the old cliché, "idle hands . . ." Mickey managed to find the time and energy to form and operate his own business, field a fleet of race cars, and manage Lions Drag Strip. At the same time he was working the nightshift as a pressman at the *Los Angeles Times* and raising a family with his first wife, Judy.

In 1954, Thompson developed what can be regarded as the first, purpose-built, slingshot-style dragster. He directly coupled the engine-transmission assembly to the rear axle and placed the driver behind the axle to focus the weight on the rear wheels. To aid directional stability, the front track was widened and the rear track narrowed as much as possible. It was a revolutionary design that was embraced by all chassis builders until the early 1970s.

On September 4, 1955, at San Fernando Drag Strip Mickey became the first to break the 150-mph barrier with a single-engine slingshot dragster. Driving the 300-inch Chrysler-powered slingshot of Ray Brown, Mickey cranked out a solid 151.26 mph in the cool Southern California air.

Mickey's next achievement was building a twin-engine dragster, which was followed by the four-engine *Challenger* that in 1960 became the first American car to top 400 mph. Powered by four Pontiac engines, producing an estimated 1,600 hp, Mickey clicked off a record 406.6 mph at the salt flats of Bonneville.

Meanwhile, Mickey continued drag racing using his favorite Dragmaster frames and a variety of Pontiac motors. One of his greatest victories was over Art Malone in Don Garlits' *Swamp Rat* at the 1960 Bakersfield Meet in March. On May 14, 1960, he took what was then the pale-blue painted *Assault I* to March Air Force Base near Riverside, California, in an attempt to rewrite the record books. Loading up the trailer with experimental Goodyears and three different Pontiac engines, Mickey set a dozen national and international Class A, B, and C records in the standing-start kilometer and mile categories.

History notes that the day began poorly when a wrist pin in the 292-ci "C" engine broke. Mickey and crew immediately went to work swapping in the big 502-ci "A" engine for the absolute record. First to fall was the kilometer record and then the mile record. Some

Chapter One: Diggers: The Top Dogs 15

observers noted that at some points in the run, the car was completely airborne, which directly led to two complete sets of rear axle bolts shearing off. However, in three runs Mickey had garnered eight new records. The now repaired "C" engine was reinstalled and Mickey set out again to break more records. By the end of the day, Mickey had set 12 new records, some of which had stood for more than 30 years.

A year later Mickey returned to the 8,000-foot runway of March to field a four-car record attempt.

Mickey's Assault *saw plenty of dragstrip action and made an appearance at the National in 1960. Running A/Dragster (minus its pontoon wheel covers), the rail could hit 140 in the quarter-mile. A legend in his own right, veteran Darrell Droke was Mickey's crew chief with his salt cars. (Photo by Doug Huegli, Courtesy worldofspeed.org)*

Mickey often referred to the streamlined Assault *as his favorite car. Powered by a blown 303-ci Pontiac V-8, the* Assault *competed at the 1960 NHRA Nationals. (Photo by Douglas Huegli Courtesy worldofspeed.org)*

Removing the aluminum wrap reveals a modified Dragmaster chassis and a destroked 303 measuring 293 inches. Contributing to the record runs were an Isky-supplied roller camshaft, Grant pistons, and Jocko-prepped cylinder heads. The block featured two-bolt mains with steel straps. B&M provided the Hydro Stick transmission while the rear was a locked Halibrand '48 Ford. (Photo Courtesy Dave Davis)

Compare this primitive blower chain drive to today's 3-inch (and more) polyurethane belts. A crank-driven pump circulated water through the tank (right), directly to the cylinder heads. (Photo Courtesy Dave Davis)

These included a Class F Dragmaster powered by a blown 2-cylinder Pontiac Tempest; the fully streamlined *Attempt* powered by Class D and E 4-cylinder engines; the blown 303 Pontiac-powered *Assault I*; and a 389-powered Pontiac Catalina. This time all of the cars were painted dark blue and despite the 109-degree heat Mickey jumped from car to car and drove to 14 of a possible 18 records.

The *Assault*'s 104-inch Dragmaster chassis was fitted with a bored and destroked 1957 Pontiac engine measuring 303 ci. The internals included Mickey's own forged connecting rods and pistons, roller cam, and other parts. Sitting on top of the block was a Hilborn-injected chain-driven 6-71 GMC blower that fed a mixture of methanol and nitro. Horsepower was pegged at 690 at 7,200 rpm. A Joe Hunt magneto sparked the Champion plugs, while the power was transmitted through a B&M Hydro Stick to the Halibrand quick-change with a final ratio of 2.7:1.

Mickey, wearing black leathers and a white open-face helmet, shattered the international and national Class C records, bumping Ed Cortopassi's kilometer record set in the *Glass Slipper* dragster from 116.43 mph to 123.902 mph. He also shattered German Bernd Rosemeyer's mile record of 123.3 mph with a 138.926. Mickey fared equally well with the rest of the fleet in classes D, E, and F. In the Catalina he also upped Chuck Daigh's National Stock Car Class B record from 73.15 mph for the kilometer to 81.497. In the mile run, he pushed the record from 84.02 mph to 95.571.

After the successful record runs of the early 1960s, Mickey refocused his energy on business and dragstrips. *Assault I* was loaned to Jim Nelson and Dode Martin of Dragmaster Chassis, who took the car on tour of dragstrips throughout the Midwest and the East.

The car was retired to Mickey's home collection in Bradbury Hills and was heavily damaged in the mid-1980s when a wildfire swept through. Despite doing his best to fight the fire, the building housing the cars was badly damaged. Tragically, not long after, Mickey and then-wife Trudy were brutally gunned down in their driveway. Eventually Jim Travis and Mickey's son Danny restored the cars.

For many years *Assault I*, *Attempt*, and *Challenger* resided at the Wally Parks NHRA Motorsports Museum in Pomona, California. In 2010, on the *Assault*'s fiftieth anniversary, Travis had it running and Danny drove the car in the Cacklefest parade at the California Hot Rod Reunion (CHRR). It was a fitting tribute to Mickey's record-setting achievements. In 2013, *Assault I* was acquired by the World of Speed as part of its permanent collection in Wilsonville, Oregon.

Jim Deist provided the 16-ring slot chute that helped bring **Assault** to a halt after record runs. Wheels are Halibrand front and back and the rear tires are 7 x 16 Goodyears. Jim Travis headed the beautiful restoration. Bob Berg is responsible for the outstanding body and paint. (Photo by Douglas Huegli Courtesy worldofspeed.org)

Hellzapoppin A/Dragster

Ron Abbott ran a couple of different **Hellzapoppin** Dragmaster rails and each was painted Honduras Maroon. Best times turned back in the day were a 9.60 at 161. The GMC blower was trialed briefly but proved to be too much for the drivetrain and the Hilborn injectors were reinstalled. (Photo Courtesy Bob Schlegel Collection)

The Dragmaster chassis supporting the *Hellzapoppin* A/Dragster typifies early slingshot design. California-based Jim Nelson and Dode Martin formed Dragmaster in 1959; in 1960 they earned plenty of accolades after taking top-speed honors at the NHRA Nationals with their twin-engine *Two Thing* dragster. Through 1964, the pair owned the market with their Dart Mark I, II, III, and IV chassis designs.

The *Hellzapoppin* dragster featured here runs a Mark II chassis and was built in 1960. It features a chassis of 1-1/2-inch mild tubing and a 95-inch wheelbase. Compared to the earlier Mark I chassis design, the Mark II was built with additional frame supports. New York–based Ron Abbott campaigned *Hellzapoppin* and, for power, relied on a 283 Chevy opened up to 301 inches. While performing the meticulous restoration, Bobby Schlegel stuck true to the original mill and bolted-on Hilborn injectors that feature 2-1/8-inch bores, a Vertex Magneto, large valve heads, a solid-lifter camshaft, and a compression ratio of 10:5.1.

The front suspension was designed by Jim Dode and consists of friction bars instead of shocks and a wishbone that trails to a crossmember below the Moon fuel tank. Hubs are by Chassis Research for Moon equipment. The spoked rims are original Moon; out back, American Traction replicated the 9-inch Hurst piecrust slicks, which are mounted on 15-inch magnesium rims.

Backing the Chevy mill is a 1938 Ford truck transmission and a 1940 Ford truck rear end containing 5:13 gears. Stopping power comes courtesy of 2-inch drum brakes out back.

Ron campaigned the dragster into 1962 before stepping up to a blown Dragmaster Mark III. A highlight for Ron was pulling Garlits at the 1964 NHRA Nationals.

The original *Hellzapoppin* dragster went to John Foley who campaigned the car into 1965. Finding the traction

John Foley, who built the engine for **Hellzapoppin**, became the second owner and painted the car yellow. A mishap at Dover saw the car bottom up in a ditch with a bent frame. (Photo Courtesy Bob Schlegel Collection)

Bob Long ran the dragster in nostalgia races until 2010 and installed the radiator to help keep things cool. Bobby Schlegel immediately removed the radiator, stating, "Dragsters don't have rads." (Photo Courtesy Bob Schlegel Collection)

at New York's Dover dragstrip more than ideal, John stood the dragster on its tail and bent the frame after coming down hard. Repaired, the dragster then passed through several owners before showing up on eBay late in 2010.

With Schlegel in the market for a front-engine dragster and this one being within driving distance of his New York home, he went to check it out. He knew at first sight that he had to have it. Bobby used to watch this car at Dover and states, "If there is one car that stood out and that people would remember, it was this one." And they do remember. Bobby is constantly approached by people who are more than happy to share their recollections.

Considering the number of hands the car had passed through, it was relatively complete and original when Bobby purchased it. In recent years, the dragster had been competing in the occasional nostalgia drag meet with a single 4-barrel Chevy engine. With the help of Rich Head, Steve White, and Bob LaRegina, Bobby spent five months resurrecting *Hellzapoppin*. The drivetrain was rebuilt and the body repainted a GM metallic red. A new cowl was necessary and headers were fabricated, replacing the long-gone originals.

In September 2010, Bobby debuted the restored *Hellzapoppin* at the Reunion at Dover Dragstrip, a long-defunct track the car used to call home. Many of the early Dragmaster rails survive today, although few have been restored as nicely as this one.

Dragmasters had the market cornered in the early 1960s. Customers could direct-order a complete chassis or a kit to assemble themselves.

A complete restoration was performed in Bobby's home garage. In this photo, the original second roll-bar loop has been reinstalled. John Foley had removed it in 1962 as it hampered him when getting in and out of the dragster. Original measurements came from Dragmasters' Dode Martin. (Photo Courtesy Bob Schlegel Collection)

Although the original restored chassis no longer meets NHRA requirements, the car is shown regularly and has proven to be a hit throughout the Northeast. It brings back plenty of fond memories for those who watched it race and sparks an interest in the younger crowd. (Photo Courtesy Bob Schlegel Collection)

VanRonk and Bumgarner *The Vagabond*

Gary Ormsby propelled The Vagabond *to drag racing's first 200-mph clocking, hitting the mark at Sacramento in June 1965.* The Vagabond *went through three different drivers before being sold (minus the engine) around 1969.*

Kent Fuller built *The Vagabond* in 1962; it was commissioned by Southern California residents Jim VanRonk and Roy Bumgarner. The two men filled their days driving trucks but had an overwhelming desire to go drag racing. Lacking the needed funds to fulfill the dream, the pair headed to the bank and each secured a home-improvement loan. Kent was happy to take their money and late in 1962 started building them a chassis. Measuring 121 inches, the rail featured Arnie Robert's bodywork and was powered by a blown and injected 392 Chrysler Hemi.

Larry "Shorty" Leventon initially took the seat but by the end of 1964 he had given way to greenhorn Gary "Wildman" Ormsby. It was Gary's first ride in a Top Eliminator car and by June 1965 he had gained enough experience behind the wheel to drive *The Vagabond* to drag racing's first-recorded 200-mph clocking. It proved to be an ideal day at Sacramento where he tripped the timers with an earth-shattering 201.34. *The Vagabond* continued to tear up California strips into 1969; it eventually hit the mid-6s with new driver Ken Machost handling the controls.

The exact date is unknown when the car passed to Glen Wild at B&N Automotive in Sacramento (minus the engine) but it was sometime in 1969 or 1970. Glen got as far as installing a late-model Hemi but never got around to racing it. The car spent many years sitting idle. The next owner, Harold Van Ryn, installed a small-block Chevy during the mid-1970s but like Glen, never got around to racing it. Through a later chance meeting with Harold, current owner Larry Anderson learned that the car had been sold to someone in Idaho. The car was raced by a father-and-son team before switching hands in 1980. The Shumways purchased the rail and spent the next 15 years bracket racing it with a big-block Chevy.

Larry's search for the car began in the early 1990s with phone calls, flyers, and an ad in *National Dragster*. He spoke with original owner Roy Bumgarner (partner Jim VanRonk died in 1967) but came up blank. Roy hadn't seen or heard of the car since parting with it back in 1969. By chance, he still had the original Hemi and told Larry that if he ever found the car, he could have it.

It seems that the Hemi had a sordid life of its own. Roy had used the engine in a few Bonneville cars that had set a couple of Salt Flats records. The next stop for the Hemi was in a fuel car driven by Howard Johnson. Howard was severely injured when the car crashed but he thankfully survived. Roy managed to save the engine, which found a new home in his nephew's sand rail and later in a tractor-pull truck before being retired in the mid-1990s.

Street Rodder magazine picked up the story of Larry's search for the dragster and it was through a Randy Fish article that he hit pay dirt. Idaho subscriber Duane Neary recalled seeing a similar car in a friend's garage and contacted Larry. Larry sent Duane original photos and, sure enough, it was the car.

The Shumways, who owned the dragster, were reluctant to part with it as they had grown attached to it themselves. Economics being what they are (the car needed to be brought up to date to continue racing), the family finally accepted Larry's offer. As Larry relayed through cacklefest.com, "We scrambled to come up with the money, borrowed a pickup truck and car trailer, and headed to Idaho. About 36 hours later, we pulled into our driveway with our dragster."

The next step was to call Roy, who stuck to his word and donated the Hemi. Larry borrowed the pickup truck once again and headed for Hanford, California, to retrieve the engine. "The car and engine each had very interesting lives and were now back together."

 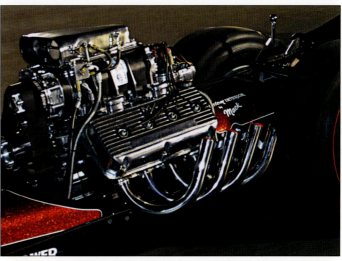

The Vagabond *originally measured 121 inches long and contained only the rear body panels. Not long after its 200-mph run, it was stretched to its current 142 inches. This photo was shot at Bakersfield in 2009 and also shows the period-correct push car. (Photo Courtesy Dave Davis)*

The Vagabond *went through a couple of engines back in the day. Today's engine is the last original engine that was placed in the car. It's a 1957 392 Hemi that features original pistons, rods, heads, Snider camshaft and intake manifold, and Enderle injectors. The blower and zoomies are new. The drivetrain consists of an original high-gear setup. An in-and-out box was added for safety. The rear end consists of original, non-Posi 3.20 gears. Airheart disc brakes in conjunction with a Simpson chute brought the car to a halt. Sponsorship came courtesy of Century Speed Center and B&N Automotive. (Photo Courtesy Dave Davis)*

A close examination showed the dragster to be surprisingly complete and original. Today, the front axle, wishbones, springs, and steering box are original as are the front wheels that Kent Fuller hand-made in 1962. The rear end, the hand brake, seat, upholstery, and even the front tires (1966 Avon Speedmaster Mark IIs) are original. The extent of modifications to the car over the years included an additional loop added to the roll cage and modifications to the body cowl and side panels; the frame was more than just tweaked. The car had been stretched to 156 inches and the rear end had been pushed back 3 inches to make room for a Powerglide transmission.

Larry reached out to Kent Fuller to restore the chassis to its 1965 configuration while Arnie Roberts was asked to redo the cowl and side panels. Although Arnie had retired, he did provide a number of photos to help the restoration. In the end, Kent did a beautiful job fabricating the needed panels and restoring the nose. Don Honstein laid the original black lacquer and red metalflake paint in 1965 and jumped at the chance to do it again. Bob Thompson, whom Larry met at the CHRR in 1994, spent three days duplicating the original lettering from old pictures.

Once the Hemi was installed, Larry and company began the search for period-correct engine parts, such as showerhead nozzles for the Enderle injector, shut-off

Even though the chassis of The Vagabond *is original, at one point the rails had been stretched even further to 156 inches and an extra hoop was added to the cage. Of course the modifications were undone during its restoration and the car is considered to be 90-percent original. Current owner Larry Anderson and* The Vagabond *are regulars at the Bakersfield reunion. (Photo Courtesy Dave Davis)*

valve, clutch-can, and Schiefer Magneto. Ron "Pro" Welty was a great help in hunting down a number of these hard-to-find pieces as were George Wulf (of Wulf & Van Dyke) and Rod Hynes. Some of the other required parts came from interesting places. The Goodyear Blue Streaks on American mags were found at a swap meet just 20 miles from Larry's home. The Airheart disc brakes came from longtime racer and good friend Bob Foster.

The Hemi fired in September 2000, the first time in five years and had its first shot of nitro since 1969. Larry was invited to participate in the Cacklefest to be held at the 2000 CHRR. "We weren't able to push-start due to the fact that we weren't 'hooked-up' [no driveshaft] so we were on the line during the memorial service, and then 'blower-started.' We were the first to fire up. Words really can't describe the totally awesome experience of being in the Cacklefest of 2000."

In 2001 the engine was pulled and rebuilt. At the same time, the guys installed a driveshaft so that they could push-start the car, once they learned how. The guys went out to Sacramento Raceway to learn how it was done. Once warmed up (on alcohol), they pushed her down the chase road. Taking her up to about 30 mph, they let out the clutch, brought up the oil pressure, turned on the fuel, light touch on the throttle, clicked on the mag, and the Hemi fired! Finally, after 32 years, *The Vagabond* was back and on the track under its own power.

Syndicate Scuderia

Jack regularly wowed the Northwest crowds with long smoky burnouts. Shown here in Washington in 1963, Syndicate Scuderia *warms the M&H slicks preparing for another 160-mph or faster blast. Stopping power came courtesy of a Deist chute and fabricated rear disc brakes. (Photo Courtesy Wendy Ann Williams)*

Jack Williams can be called one of hot rodding's true pioneers. Hailing from Vancouver, British Columbia, Canada, he built his first roadster in 1947 from a wrecked '27 Nash. Sixteen-year-old Jack cut the body off the Nash and installed his own hand-built body, swapped in a big Pontiac 6, and began to roam the streets. Jack was a man of many talents; it seemed he was a natural and he built many hot rods and customs with basic tools and torches.

He followed up the roadster with a hopped-up '34 Ford. The car featured a 1948 Mercury V-8 with twin carbs and finned-aluminum heads. He completed the car in 1949 and many have called it Vancouver's first hot rod.

Taking advantage of all of his talents, Jack dipped into the world of customs and built himself a highly modified '49 Ford. The car featured all the custom tricks of the day and a 1937 Cadillac V-12 for power. Garnishing top honors at the Pacific International Motorama, the Ford opened many eyes to Jack's skill level and soon the city youth were clamoring for his services. However, Jack's first love was hot rodding and in 1954, he built a twin flathead-powered dragster to compete at the local airstrip.

His next endeavor was teaming with Brian Devine and Gordie McDougall of the Syndicate Race Team. The three men rebuilt Brian's rail in the early 1960s as the famed *Syndicate Scuderia* you see here. The beautifully constructed dragster features an aluminum body covered in a pearl blue lacquer. The hand-formed Lexan canopy has a blue tint, which really adds to the car's overall appearance.

Power, now as then, comes courtesy of a 404-inch Chrysler Hemi. The original front-mounted Potvin blower was swapped in the mid-1960s for Hilborn injectors mounted on a GMC 6-71 running 18-percent

A 70-year-old Jack takes the wheel one more time, catching some good air with the restored car. Jack has always performed the majority of work on the car but left the custom pearl blue paint up to Fred Wesh and the gold leafing to Dave Johnstone. (Photo Courtesy Wendy Ann Williams)

overdrive. The Hemi internals include welded steel rods, a roller cam, and 7:5.1 compression. Backing the engine is an 11-inch dual-disc ceramic clutch, an in-and-out gearbox, and a 1948 Ford quick-change rear carrying 4.10 gears. The front suspension consists of a hand-formed chrome-moly axle, friction shocks, and four leaf springs. Rolling stock are American 12-spokes up front and 10 x 15 American magnesiums out back mounting M&H slicks.

In 1963, a change in team personnel saw Brian and Gordie replaced by Ron Lowe. Ron took on the role of crew chief while Jack handled the controls. The two decided to haul their rail south for the 1963 NHRA Winternationals but before doing so, they needed to put in a few warm-up runs. And what better place than a city street? Given approval by city officials and overseen by the local police, Jack let *Syndicate Scuderia* rip. He blasted the rail down the newly paved, unopened city street to the tune of 120 mph. With its 16-foot drag chute sailing in the wind, Jack was satisfied with the car's performance (as were onlookers) and prepared the car for his trip to Pomona.

Like any national event, competition at the Winternationals was tough. Jack served notice that he

Jack's Chrysler Hemi measures 404 ci and is more than capable of laying down the numbers. Today, Jack's daughter, Wendy Ann, handles the controls at nostalgia events. (Photo Courtesy Wendy Ann Williams)

It's no surprise that Syndicate Scuderia won Best Engineered Car at the Pacific International Motorama three years in a row during the 1960s. (Photo Courtesy Rolf Norberg)

meant business, opening up with a run of 8.83 at 169.17 mph, an unofficial Top Gas record. Yup, things were looking good; that is, until mechanical issues caught up with them and the car fell prematurely during eliminations. Not to go home empty-handed, the rail walked away from the event with the Best Appearing Car award. Jack later captured the A/Gas Dragster record "officially" when he turned out a 168.22 clocking at Arlington.

After *Syndicate Scuderia* was retired in 1967, it sat dormant for close to 20 years before coming out of mothballs for Expo 1986. A revitalized Jack took the car on tour of the West Coast nostalgia meets. During a race at Freemont the car was nearly destroyed when it crashed at the end of a run. Jack sustained some serious injuries and the car needed some repairs. It wasn't until the early 1990s that Jack got around to restoring it. In 2001 Jack celebrated his 70th birthday and it was time for both him and *Syndicate Scuderia* to retire. But not until after one more pass. To the delight of thousands of onlookers, Jack made his last full-throttle pass down the airstrip in Sechelt, British Columbia, Canada.

The car was an invited guest to the 50th anniversary of the NHRA Winternationals. With his daughter, Wendy-Ann, at the wheel and Jack riding shotgun in the push vehicle, the *Syndicate* once again made its way down the Pomona tarmac, push-started just like it was 1963 for this very special Cacklefest. It's hard to imagine what was louder, the car or the applause of the crowd.

Winkel, Trapp & Fuller *Magicar*

A young guy named Gerry Glenn became the third driver of Magicar, replacing Gerald "Jeep" Hampshire in the spring of 1965. Although this was Gerry's first trip down the quarter-mile, in anything, he made a good showing of himself making a license pass of 9.08 at 168. Five years later in another car, Gerry "The Hunter" Glenn became the NHRA's Top Fuel Champion.

I guess one could say that the Kent Fuller chassis under *Magicar* exemplifies how quickly dragster chassis design evolved in the mid-1960s. Kent built his first chassis in 1956 and by the early 1960s had earned a reputation as one of the nation's best. Clientele included Tommy Ivo and Tony Nancy.

Over the years Kent has been involved in building plenty of Top Fuel and Funny Cars (and the occasional Pro Stock); *Magicar* stands out as one of the more innovative of the bunch. Even though the car failed to meet performance expectations, it was unique and an instant standout and a key in the evolution of the dragster. While most rails of the day relied on a solid-mounted rear end, *Magicar* used a coil-spring suspension mounted on a sub-frame.

In the September 1965 issue of *Drag Racing* magazine, the chassis setup was described this way: "Basically the whole power train is mounted in a separate sub-frame, which is suspended on coil springs within the main chassis. The engine then is an isolated, cushioned component. Its horrendous vibration isn't transferred directly to the car's main structure and its weight is allowed to shift rearward slightly for added bite coming off the line."

The current owner, Bill Pitts, referred to the rear suspension as the heart of the car, "the magic in the *Magicar*." And after all these years, the suspension has remained intact.

The drivetrain of *Magicar* is solidly mounted to the subframe, which in turn is bolted to the main frame just to the rear of the engine. Under acceleration, the engine would lift back and the live rear axle would aid the car in loading the slicks. At the same time, the roll cage would lift, and the front end would plant. Up front, rubber biscuits were incorporated in place of the typical leaf spring or torsion bars used by most dragsters of the day. From the steering box, the main link passed along the passenger's side of the car, hooking to a tie rod that passed

Here are the Magicar's team members during the car's debut appearance at the Pond. Left to right are Ron Winkel, Kent Fuller, Dennis Winkel, and driver Gary Casaday. The rail is sans paint at this point.

across the nosepiece bolting to a single radius rod that held the axle in place.

Lacking paint, the bare-metal *Magicar* made its debut at San Fernando in October 1964. Partner Kay Trapp, who was track photographer and worked for *Drag News,* ensured the car received plenty of ink. He described the anticipated debut of *Magicar* to *Drag News* readers, "The area surrounding the starting line suddenly resembled the first annual convention of chassis builders. Woody Gilmore of Race Car Engineering, Roy Steen of Race Car Specialties, and the Maestro behind those Fuller chassis, Kent Fuller himself. Why were they here? What was about to happen? Tonight was the unveiling of the long rumored Fuller-Trapp-Winkel 'Magic Car.'"

After all of the hype and publicity, the debut proved to be a little anticlimactic. *Magicar* performed well but failed to meet the unrealistic expectations. Hampering the car's ongoing development was the fact that three different drivers took the controls during the first season. Gary Casaday was the first to take the wheel but found the car a handful and relinquished the seat to Gerald "Jeep" Hampshire. Jeep was an experienced driver who, at the 1964 NHRA Winternationals, had set the low elapsed time (ET) of 7.85 behind the wheel of the Stellings/Hampshire *Red Stamp Special*.

Transplanting the *Red Stamp* engine into *Magicar*, Jeep laid down the car's best time of 7.62 at 204.08 mph. By the season's end, *Magicar* had won three Top Eliminators and grabbed top speed at meets in Freemont and Los Angeles County. By the end of 1965, *Magicar* was back in builder Kent Fuller's shop. In Kent's eyes, the car was a success, having proven a few of the ideas that had been kicking around in his head.

The car was sold to Ray Monteago, lengthened by 2 feet, and raced as *Uptight Out A Site*. With driver Jimmy Lynn taking the wheel, the dragster clocked 7.0 times at 168.

The dragster stayed in Monteago's possession until the late 1970s when enthusiast Louie Poole discovered it hanging from the rafters in Monteago's shop. Louie purchased the car and with the help of Roy Brizio he reassembled the dragster. He restored the front suspension, which had been converted to a standard torsion bar at some point.

At the Sixth Annual Spring Championship at Freemont, Jeep Hampshire propelled the Magicar *to a semifinal finish by turning in a best of 7.62. Here Jeep picks up the laundry after a successful run. Note the Don Garlits rig in the background. Don fell in the final to Mike Snively. (Photo Courtesy Bill Pitts Collection)*

It's the summer of 1990 and Bill Pitts becomes the proud owner of Magicar. *John Barrett did a lot of the restoration around 1980 with guidance from Kent Fuller himself. John brought the car from Kansas to trade for Don Prudhomme's Shelby Super Snake that Bill had initially purchased out of an old trailer in Santee, California. (Photo Courtesy Bill Pitts Collection)*

In the beginning, the car went through a series of engine changes and injector changes also. They first started with an Enderle "bird catcher" injector. Note the addition of an Enderle Barn Door injector on the blower. That Tony Nancy air scoop was quite the fashionable item in those days. The scoop was covered in gold leaf and it's believed to have been used only for shows.

Gary Cochran supplied the 392 that mounts a 6-71 blower and an Enderle bug catcher. Rick McDonald rebuilt the engine and is responsible for keeping the 1,500 to 2,000 horses in tune. (Photo Courtesy David Phillips)

He also restored the original wheelbase and lowered the modified roll cage so that the tail panels once again fit.

For the next couple of years, Louie had a great time touring nostalgia events of Central California before he sold the car to Oklahoma's John Barrett. Current owner Bill Pitts entered the picture in 1990. After seeing the car at a National Dirt Racing Association (NDRA) event, he struck up a conversation with John. At the time Bill owned the unrestored Baney/Prudhomme dragster and knew he didn't have the financial means to restore the car. It was during his conversation with John that the pair came to an agreement to swap rolling chassis. Bill was in his glory: He had the dragster of his dreams.

Bill had grown up watching *Magicar* and had fallen in love with the gold beauty back in 1965. Almost immediately, restoration began. He first had to find a suitable 392 Hemi, and got lucky with an engine that had been assembled and that suited his application. As the car was to be restored to its 1965 status, it would no longer meet the NHRA's strict safety standards. This didn't bother Bill; he had no intentions of racing it. Instead *Magicar* became a showpiece and a regular cackle car. Local enthusiast Tom Morris took an interest in the car and lays claim to the fantastic repaint; the renowned Roy Potter took care of the lettering.

In 1992, the rebirth of *Magicar* was complete and ready for its debut at the inaugural CHRR. On hand were Ron Winkel, Kay Trapp, and Jeep Hampshire. After 33 years, Jeep once again took the driver's seat to the obvious delight of a sea of onlookers. As the *Magicar* cackled to life, many eyes were watering and I doubt it was from the exhaust fumes.

In early 1992, the car received its gold paint job from the late Tom Morris and lettering by Roy Potter. During the car's race days with Ron Winkel, Trapp, Fuller, and Ray Monteago, the car went through three body changes and three paint jobs. All of those changes are reflected in the car's current appearance. (Photo Courtesy David Phillips)

Bobby Langley's *Scorpion V*

Bobby Langley lights them up in March 1965 at the U.S. Fuel and Gas Championships at Bakersfield. By trade, he was a machinist with General Dynamics in Forth Worth and on the weekends his racing took him as far away as Minnesota, Georgia, and California. Bobby was one of the first racers from east of the Rockies to travel to California to race. (Photo Courtesy Bill Crosby Collection)

Bobby Langley, a name long synonymous with Texas drag racing, campaigned the *Scorpion V* dragster from 1964 to 1966. Although his first *Scorpion* rail may well be the most recognized of his cars, and has been re-created, *Scorpion V* is just as beautiful and deserves to be recognized as the real deal. It was Bobby's second-to-last rail and features a 142-inch Don Garlits chassis. Bobby was known for his beautifully crafted bodies and *Scorpion V* was no exception. Like its namesake, the dragster took on a scorpion theme with a "finned tail climbing the roll cage."

Like all Bobby's *Scorpion* cars, number five performed as good as it looked and won the AHRA Nationals at Green Valley, Texas, in 1964. Bobby turned in the top time of the meet with a 197.36. His final go was against Art Malone, whom he trailered with a 7.84 at 195.22 versus a 7.90 at 194.80. Even though he was based in Texas, Bobby gained national recognition in the late 1950s. He was one of the first to take his show on the road, match racing the *Scorpion I* as far away as the Northeast. He took in Bakersfield in 1958 and the first annual March Meet in 1959. His wife was his regular companion and for a time, his only crewmember. As his children got older, they joined Mom and Pop at the track when it didn't interfere with school.

Bobby was a tool-and-die maker by trade and until *Scorpion V*, he was in the habit of building his own cars. The chassis of *V* is a unique Garlits/Connie Swingle design, one of four built specifically to allow more flex. Unlike other Garlits cars, the main roll cage hoop of *V* does not extend to the bottom frame rail. The chassis is also wider and rides lower. When the car was discovered in 2004, the modified hoop was one of the telltale signs that the car was the actual *Scorpion V*.

Current owner Bill Crosby recounts, "The car disappeared in 1966 after Bob sold it to George Fields and its whereabouts was unknown. I do know that Bob kept the engine for use in *Scorpion VI* and that George purchased the car on a payment plan. The car's disappearance remained a mystery until 2000 when it showed up at a swap meet in Texas. Minus an engine and its unique tinwork, *Scorpion V* appeared to be just another rail. Robert Cassels purchased it, dropped a blown Chevy in it, but did nothing with it."

The car then went to Arlington, where collector Charles Duran used it for display purposes. A friend, Don Ross, told Charles that he thought it was *Scorpion V*. In

Bobby is on the return road (going the wrong way) at Green Valley Raceway at the 1964 AHRA World Championships. This image was shot just after he was presented with the trophy for his elimination win. Green Valley Raceway is now a housing complex. (Photo Courtesy Bill Crosby Collection)

Chapter One: Diggers: The Top Dogs

There's nothing like the roar of a nitro-fed Hemi and the scent of burning rubber to get the heart pounding. Bobby was quite the showman, loved by fellow racers and the fans. He is credited with perfecting the fire burnout, prompting Garlits at one point to ask how he did it. (Photo Courtesy Bill Crosby Collection)

As discovered, Scorpion V *was little more than a frame, suspension, and miscellaneous parts. At this point it's far removed from the 1964 AHRA World Champion that it once was. (Photo Courtesy Bill Crosby Collection)*

2004, Charles attempted to have Garlits identify the car but Garlits was unsure. A trip to Bob Langley's residence was in order. Bobby took a look around the car and it was confirmed: it was his old ride.

It wasn't long after that that Bill Crosby entered the picture. Bill paid a visit to Don's shop; he was looking for someone to build him a front-engine chassis. Don was in the midst of building *Scorpion II* and had numerous photos of the *Scorpion* cars. Bill pointed out an image of *Scorpion V* and told Don that it was always his favorite. To Bill's surprise, Don said that he knew where the car was and that it could be purchased. Needless to say, Bill jumped at the opportunity.

As Bill relayed through cacklefest.com, upon seeing the car for the first time in 40 years, "It was red, not black, and looked kinda shabby with a small-block Chevy bolted in it. The gothic body was gone, replaced with a composite body (tin and aluminum) fastened in place with 10,000 pop rivets. But beneath all this you could see the unmistakable loop of the roll bar, the single-radius rods, and the bracket for the steering idler arm that gave the original car that 'broken in the middle' look.

"I began to think I could do this project, and then I quickly came to my senses. Paul and I shook hands . . . the deal was done. I owned the car that had lived in my memory for 40 years! I had no trailer to move it, no room in my garage to keep it, no tools left to work on it. My wife was out of town and didn't know anything about it. Was this *cool,* or what?"

Bill's in seventh heaven, wheeling the car he admired so much in his youth. His crew consists of son Blake, Jimmy Garritson, and Paul Adams. (Photo Courtesy Martin Libhart)

Bill hit up Don Ross to do the restoration but with a backlog, Don wouldn't be able to start on the car until 2006. In the meantime, Bill started dismantling what he had and began the search for what he needed. The restoration would include replacing rotted rails and forming new body panels. Craig Huls applied the high-gloss black paint while Daniel Gay did the deed when it came time to replicate Bobby's original pinstriping. Danny Greenshaw came out of retirement to stitch up the interior.

Power comes from a 1957 392 Hemi built by Tinker Faulkner. The current engine uses JE pistons, which are forged aluminum with flat-tops swinging from aluminum NOS Howard rods. The heads contain stainless steel 2-inch intake and exhaust valves and O-rings are used for seal instead of head gaskets. Bobby used stock Chrysler rocker arms; they have been installed on the fresh engine with no problems.

The cam is an Isky, of course, but the grind is unknown. Says Bill, "I guess that is between Bobby and Ed. When building the engine, Bobby called Ed and told him he wanted the car to have an Isky cam and that it was going to be a cackle car. Ed told him he had just the cam and sent it."

The blower is a GMC 6-71 on an Edelbrock manifold with port injectors. The injectors are Hilborn with eight nozzles fed by a 175 Hilborn pump. Spark comes courtesy of a Schiefer magneto reconditioned by Tom Cirello. The clutch is an 11-inch Hays dual-disc and has a Lenco high-gear shaft. The shaft is coupled to the Olds rear end through a Don Ross sliding coupler. The coupler allows Bill to disconnect the engine from the differential directly from the driver's seat. The fuel used is a high percentage of nitromethane. Of course the cackle crowds love it as it gives up maximum flame.

The car debuted in 2007 at the National Hot Rod Reunion in Columbus, Ohio, and you can bet Bobby was all smiles when it was his turn to take the seat once again. We lost Bobby in 2011 but thanks to guys such as Bill Crosby, Don Ross, and the countless others who have dedicated their time to the restoration of these cars, the legends will live on.

This photo was taken at Bowling Green, Kentucky, in 2013, and yes, the headers got hot. The culprit turned out to be a defective shutoff valve. Sure made for a great photo op. (Photo Courtesy Tera and Max Cackle)

Don Tognotti's *Bushwacker*

The freshly painted AA/FD Bushwacker *made an early appearance at the Smokers meet in Bakersfield. Lyle Kelly held the reins and pulled wrenches for Don Tognotti. Don Garlits looked at it and said, "You guys might have something here." Not long after, he started to play with streamlining. Note the zoomie headers rather than the earlier weed burners. (Photo Courtesy James Handy/jameshandyphotography.com)*

The term "cookie cutter" used in the context of the automobile has come to mean multiple cars built in the same manner. It would be easy to say that today's cars fit this description. With the rules and regulations in place today, it is difficult to break free of the mold. Ingenuity used to be big and in the early days of drag racing, there was plenty of it. There was room for experimentation, which led to plenty of unique cars.

Bushwacker debuted in 1964 at the Oakland Auto Show under the name Goldfinger. It featured a subdued copper paint and additional tinwork that was later reworked. It took a while to work the bugs out of the Ron Welty hemi; initial outings produced bottom-8-second times at 196-mph times. The engine featured fabricated headers, GMC 6-71 blower, Joe Hunt magneto, Engle 440-5 roller cam, Donovan rocker assembly, four-bolt main caps for added bottom-end strength, and O-ringed block to help with the seal. This photo was shot at the 1965 March Meet at Bakersfield. (Photo Courtesy James Handy)

Don Tognotti knew how to build unique cars, whether it was showstoppers such as his *Green Voodoo* '57 Thunderbird or his *Avenger* that debuted in 1960 and gained him national recognition when it appeared in the pages of *Car Craft* magazine. In 1964, Don debuted both his *King T* Ford and a front-engine dragster at the Oakland show and came home with the award for America's Most Beautiful Roadster and first place in the competition category. The latter award was really no surprise, though, because when Don chose to go drag racing it was a means of promoting his growing Tognotti Speed Shop: The car was going to be a knockout.

The full-bodied dragster debuted under the Ian Flemming–inspired name *Goldfinger* and carried the competition number 007. In 1966, the car was repainted and christened *Bushwacker*. Based upon a Peter Ogden 156-inch–wheelbase chassis, *Bushwacker* was a visual knockout. The beautifully formed Arnie Roberts aluminum body popped with Don Honstein–applied candy pearl lemon and lime green lacquer. Adding appeal was candy gold lacquer, which was used for shadowing. Equally impressive was the gleaming 354-inch hemi that was built by Ron Welty with parts coming from Mickey Thompson, Engle, Hilborn, and Cragar. The power passed through a Weber clutch assembly directly to a solid-mounted Olds rear end that carried a Mickey Thompson magnesium center section. Bringing the car to a halt from 200 mph were rear disc brakes and a 16-foot Simpson cross-form chute. Rounding out the

An early Top Eliminator win at Sacramento Raceway Park saw Bushwacker clock an 8.13 at 196-mph time. This photo was shot during the Bakersfield March Meet in 1966. It's an annual event that's still going strong today. (Photo Courtesy James Handy)

The restoration of Bushwacker was finished in 2007 . . . well, almost. The engine was a fiberglass dummy; everything else was real and connected. The dragster was built to plug Tognotti's Speed Shop in Sacramento, California. Don opened the shop in 1964 and today his son operates it in the same location. (Photo Courtesy James Handy)

suspension was a tube front axle with Anglia spindles and a P&S steering box. The tires were Michelins up front and Goodyears out back. The rims were Kellison spokes with American magnesiums on the rear.

Ron campaigned the car for a couple seasons before selling it to Mark Danekas (Danekas blowers), who ran the car himself briefly before putting it on the market once again. Where the car went is unknown but in 2006, the neglected dragster showed up in Tulsa, Oklahoma.

Larry Crossan received word from Ron's son Dean that the owner had contacted him, but he, Dean, couldn't afford to buy the car himself. Larry, who had been searching for a unique early dragster for some time (with hopes of finding *Bushwacker*), called the owner, and within 10 minutes, the car was his. He took delivery of the dragster at the National Hot Rod Reunion in 2006 and spent the next year restoring it.

Although the car was almost complete, the years hadn't been kind. When Larry purchased the dragster, the front showed some damage and the tin forward of the engine had to be replaced. While Larry headed up the restoration himself, he relied on John Dearmore to build a fresh Hemi and Don Honstein to match the paint he had laid in the mid-1960s. Upon completion of the restoration, Larry and *Bushwacker* were invited to the 60th anniversary of the Oakland Car Show where, once again, the car proved to be an instant hit with the crowds.

Original American five-spoke mags mount Goodyear Blue Streaks. Disc brakes and a Simpson chute brought the car to a halt. Painter Don Honstein was called in to redo the paint, graphics, and pinstripes that he had originally applied back in 1965. The car had been sitting for some time when it was found and was pretty rough. Nestled in its engine bay was a Ford engine. (Photo Courtesy James Handy)

Warren, Coburn & Miller

The story goes that when Warren and Coburn made their way south from Bakersfield, other competitors posted lookouts on the highway off-ramps to see which ramp they took. Once it was determined which track they were headed for, the competition headed in the opposite direction. (Photo Courtesy James Handy)

For those not familiar with the California freeway system, the section of Interstate 5 from Bakersfield to San Fernando is affectionately known as The Ridge Route. In the 1960s and 1970s, the top fuel team of James Warren and Roger Coburn made the journey most every weekend. Racing at the many

Chapter One: Diggers: The Top Dogs 31

The Warren, Coburn & Miller car was originally built with a short body but debuted at the 1969 NHRA Winternationals with a full skin. The guys switched back to the short body in 1970 to save weight and because Roger found that the full pieces made the car difficult to work on. (Photo Courtesy James Handy)

Southern California strips, the pair took no prisoners and became known as The Ridge Route Terrors.

The two young men from Bakersfield decided to pool their resources and joined forces in the late 1950s. Warren, a graduate of the dirt tracks, drove while Coburn built the engines. The pair debuted a twin-engine dragster before switching to a more conventional hemi-powered rail. In 1968, friend and successful Bakersfield businessman Marvin Miller joined the team as the major sponsor. His company, Rain For Rent, supplied irrigation equipment to many local farmers and provided the money for Warren and Coburn to order a new, 180-inch Woody Gilmore chassis. Next came a full body from master metal man Tom Hanna and eye-popping gold-leaf lettering by Tom Kelly. The partnership lasted well into the late 1970s and struck terror into the hearts of the competition whenever they ventured south.

What exactly did the team of Warren, Coburn & Miller accomplish? Here's a short list:

- April 16, 1967: First to top 230 mph, hitting 230.17 backed up with a 226.70
- 1968: Top Fuel win at NHRA Winternationals, Pomona, California
- 1973: Final-round win over Don Garlits at Orange County (6.41/229.00 to a losing 6.43/229.00)
- 1976: Top Fuel win at NHRA Gatornationals, Gainesville, Florida
- 1975–1977: Top Fuel wins at March Meet, Bakersfield, California
- 1972–1976: NHRA Division 7 Top Fuel Champion

Don Garlits once stated in a *Los Angeles Times* interview that James Warren was the toughest driver that he ever faced when he toured on the West Coast. At the 1968 NHRA Winternationals, Coburn defeated Big Daddy in the final go to take all the marbles. At the same time, he lowered the class record with a 6.86 at 230 mph.

The restored Warren, Coburn & Miller car seen here is the real deal and retains its original 1968 Woody Gilmore (Race Car Engineering) chassis. Coburn and Miller sold the car in 1971 to finance the team's first mid-engine car. Although little is known of the car's post-1971 history, for a time it did run as an NHRA Super Comp car. In 2001, Dave Beck came across a photo of the car at the Pomona swap meet and set out to contact the owner. The dragster was in San Jose and, after striking a deal with the

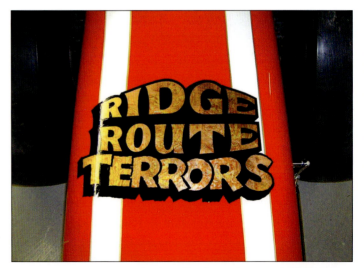

Before being tagged as the Rain For Rent *dragster in the 1970s, Warren, Coburn, and Miller were referred to as the "Ridge Route Terrors." They owned West Coast Top Fuel having taken the Division 7 championship five years running. Tom Kelly completed the fancy gold-leaf lettering originally in 1968; he was called upon to duplicate it in 2006. (Photo Courtesy James Handy)*

owner, Dave hauled the car home to Arizona to begin the restoration.

All reasonable efforts were made to keep the car as period correct as possible. The heart of the dragster is a 392-ci Hemi that retains its stock crank and heads. Actuating the valves is an Isky 505 experimental camshaft given to Dave by Ed Iskenderian himself. The Enderle fuel injection sits atop a 6-71 blower, which was rebuilt by engine man Don Waldschmidt and is fed fuel by way of a Hilborn pump. The rear end is a Ford 9-inch capped with original Airheart disc brakes. Many parts of the chassis required rework because the previous owner had modified or eliminated items to suit his taste and 1970s NHRA rules.

Once the chassis was complete, it was coated in gloss-black paint. To protect the paint while the Duane Dixon body was installed, the chassis was wrapped in Saran Wrap. The body panels were painted in place to get the colors and stripes in perfect alignment. Doug Jerger of Squeeg's Kustom Paint in Chandler, Arizona, covered the body in candy tangerine accented by pearl white scallops. The next stop was Tom Kelly's Crazy Painters shop in Bellflower, California. Tom Kelly is a living legend in Southern California, having apprenticed under Von Dutch and Ed "Big Daddy" Roth. Tom did the original lettering and striping on the car in 1968 and agreed to do the car a second time. As you can see, the lettering is perfect, thanks to Tom and his son Mitch.

The car made its debut at the CHRR in 2006. Today the car is still in the Phoenix area and under the care of Mike Aaby.

Restorer Dave Beck gathered all the period-correct parts for the 392 and engine man Don Waldschmidt brought it all together. The 6-71 blower was a swap-meet find rebuilt by Don while the Enderle injection came courtesy of Stu Hilborn. (Photo Courtesy James Handy)

The Ridge Route Terrors car retains its original Woody Gilmore chassis, skin, Tony Nancy interior, and suspension components. Credit goes to Dave Beck, Don Waldschmidt, Tom Homburg, and Duane Dixon for bringing it all together. The paint on this legendary car matches the original candy tangerine. (Photo Courtesy James Handy)

The Stone Age Man

The Stone Age Man *was built at a time when Top Fuel cars were as much about show as they were about go. Bill Carter was called upon to re-create the paint he originally applied in 1968. Gold, candies, and pearl make this car one of the more attractive vehicles to ever make a pass down the quarter-mile. Larry Crossan gets credit for doing* George *and* The Stone Age Man *justice. (Photo Courtesy Todd Hutcheson)*

Southern California, birthplace of the sport we all love, has provided us with a fair share of drag racing celebrities, but few as popular as George "Hutch" Hutcheson. George is drag racing's finest ambassador and he knew how to entertain. You want to know what drag racing use to be like? The fan appeal and the camaraderie? Then look no further than George's career.

The Stone Age Man wasn't just a name on a dragster; it was the whole persona. The drag racing bug has been in George's blood since the early 1960s when he first climbed behind the wheel of a Top Fuel car. He earned his license in Mike Tingly's car and exclaimed, jumping from the cockpit that, "I gotta get me one of these." He purchased a 392-powered Frank Huszar dragster from Tingly and chose to name it *Mistral*. A mistral is a strong wind that picks up speed as it blows through the valleys of the Rhone and Durance rivers of France. It seems like an appropriate name for this hard-charging dragster.

At about this point in George's career he had a vivid dream in which he saw a helmet similar to that of a Roman Centurion. Affixed to the helmet were 24 tall red plumes. Over the next couple weeks, George went to work building the helmet, which became part of *The Stone Age Man* persona.

George Hutcheson purchased his dragster from Mike Tingly and ran it through 1967 as Mistral. *In 1967 George chose to convert the car to a full body and had Kenny Ellis form new tin. Here Hutch is seen firing the stroked 392 hemi on the rollers at Lions Drag Strip. The RCS chassis was unique in that George's legs passed under the rear end rather than over it. (Photo Courtesy Todd Hutcheson)*

In 1967 George chose to convert *Mistral* to a full-body car and called upon Kenny Ellis to form the tin. With a Hemi borrowed from longtime friend Frank "Rootbeer" Hedge, he headed for Irwindale with the still unpainted car and his newly fashioned helmet in hand. It's hard to say what drew more attention, the newly skinned dragster or the unorthodox helmet. Adding to George's growing popularity was his habit of talking to the car as if it were an animate object.

Rootbeer's old Hemi had served him well through 15 or 20 runs and was what he referred to as his "stone age man." George won the Irwindale meet but, in the process, blew the Hemi. Frank tried his best to put on a straight face exclaiming, "You killed the stone age man!" The stone age man? George liked the name and told Frank that he was going to paint it on the car.

Bill Carter had the honor of painting the dragster, not once but twice. He initially sprayed red roses over pearl white but after George had scratched it up during a sideways slide through the dirt, he asked George if he could redo the paint. This time, Bill painted the car with red roses on one side and blue roses down the other. Highlighted in gold was the name *The Stone Age Man*. To

this day, *The Stone Age Man* is still considered one of the most beautiful dragsters to run the quarter-mile.

George's popularity grew with the fans and he was always accommodating. In the pits, people thronged to the car and kids clamored to sit in it. One such kid was Billy Pink. Unknown to George, Billy was the son of legendary engine builder Ed Pink. Billy brought the two men together, introducing Ed to George one afternoon.

The two legends became lifelong friends after Ed offered the use of one of his Hemis to George before a Las Vegas Invitational race at Stardust. Ed joined George's engine man, Doug Fisher, in the pits during the race and the three men prepared to take on Mike Snively in *Hawaiian*, Rick Ramsey in *Howard Cams Rattler*, Leroy Goldstein in *Der Wienerschnitzel*, and Larry Dixon in *Fireside Inn*. While Ed and Doug went through the pre-race details, George walked the track and studied the Christmas tree. He was one of the best at reading the tree and was rarely beat out of the gate.

The Invitational was a great race but one by one the big names fell until there was just *The Stone Age Man* and

Those old enough to remember *The Stone Age Man* **couldn't forget the helmet. The idea came to George in a dream one night and when he debuted the plumes at Phoenix a couple weeks later, they were an instant hit. George was forced to attach a brace to the roll bar to help hold the helmet in place. During his first run, the helmet slipped over George's eyes and he could only see a couple feet ahead. (Photo Courtesy Dave Davis)**

Howard Cams Rattler remaining. Now the betting money had to be on *The Stone Age Man*, which Ed and Doug had tuned to perfection. George was in the zone; both he and the car had been running consistently all day and George wasn't about to let the guys down. A pep talk with the car before the final go and he was ready to hit the line.

From a fan's perspective, nothing beats night drags; the cars are running their best in the cool, crisp air, flames popping from the zoomies . . . does it get any better than that?

Each driver pre-staged and then staged, the Hemis rattled their tune as the amber bulbs blinked down and at the hint of green, each car exploded off the line. George, with a slight lead, stretched it as both cars disappeared into the black night. Fans struggled to see through the darkness and only by the flash of the scoreboard did they know that George had won. The crowd went wild; the favorite had won with a 7.14 at 225.61 to Ramsey's trailing 7.20 at 222.60.

George moved on from this race, taking over the controls of the *Rat Trap* AA/FA, a car once thought unmanageable. Although cast aside, *The Stone Age Man* was never forgotten and remained George's favorite ride. He drove *Rat Trap* to speeds of 226 mph at a time when no one thought it would ever reach the expected 200 mph. George had a habit of taming these wild beasts.

Although George later tamed the Rat Trap *Fuel Altered and* U.S. Turbine 1 *exhibition cars, he is best remembered for* The Stone Age Man. *The car holds his fondest memories. From any angle, the car and plumes are unforgettable. (Photo Courtesy Dave Davis)*

His next stint was in the *U.S. Turbine 1* exhibition car. Driving flat on his back, he regularly took the *Turbine* to speeds in excess of 250 mph. At the time of his retirement, George and the *Turbine* were drawing crowds of more than 25,000.

Through all this, *The Stone Age Man* lay dormant, and in 1972 the car was loaned to Ventura College with the stipulation that George could re-claim it at any time. The car remained there, all but forgotten for the next 35 years. In 2008, the school was preparing for some renovations and the time came to part with *The Stone Age Man*. George got wind of the growing interest in *The Stone Age Man* and knew he had to act fast to retrieve his car. In March 2009 he went to the school. The Dean had been waiting for George to show up and was happy to honor the agreement.

Eric Bowman helped George retrieve the car from the rafters of the auto class and was the one who initiated the restoration. Even though the old car had been stored indoors and was for the most part complete, she was still in pretty rough shape. Eric had his work cut out for him. The Hemi (a shadow of its former self) was seized, the body tin was rough, and the RCS frame sagged. Late in 2009, as the restoration proceeded, an unexpected financial setback forced the sale of *The Stone Age Man*. George and Eric agreed that the car couldn't go to just anyone and when they showed the car at the CHRR in Bakersfield, they found the ideal buyer in Larry Crossan.

Larry had previously completed the Gingrass & Dearmore car along with the Tognotti Speed Shop *Bushwacker*. He knew what he was doing and came highly recommended by Kent Fuller. Larry spared no expense ensuring that *The Stone Age Man* was done right. Randy Ayers took on the responsibility of restoring the tin, which Bill Carter and his son Andy covered in pearl and lace roses just as Bill had done in 1968. Nat Quick was called upon to complete the pinstriping and lettering, which he copied from old photos.

Before putting on the restored tin, Dave Thornhill gave the RCS chassis some much-needed attention. John Dearmore built the fresh 392, which features a Donavon gear drive, Crower cam and lifters, heads prepped by Valley Head Service, and Venolia pistons that swing from Howard rods. A Hays two-disc clutch runs directly to an early-Olds rear end.

The goal was to build the car and engine as close to period correct as they could. It looks as if the guys accomplished their objective.

D.A. Santucci's *Bubble Gum Car*

D.A. Santucci had a banner year in 1969 taking Top Gas at the NHRA Nationals and winning a couple AHRA events. He hailed from Coraopolis, Pennsylvania, and took the division on points championship in both 1966 and 1971. He was an ambassador for Top Gas and pushed hard to "Keep Top Gas For 1970." (Photo Courtesy Bill Truby)

Drag racing is full of behind-the-scenes stories that never fail to amuse. It seems that every national event has its share, whether it's taking place in the pits, at tech, or on the track. One such event took place at the 1969 NHRA Nationals and involved Top Gas racer, Domenic Anthony "D.A." Santucci. D.A. had graduated from running Altereds to rails in 1965 after building a front-engine dragster that showed immediate success at his home tracks of Quaker City and Keystone. In 1966, D.A. won enough meets to earn the Division 1 points championship. His success carried into 1969 when he opened up with a win at the AHRA Spring Nationals, The momentum carried to Indy for the NHRA Nationals where D.A. had to have been a favorite to win his category.

Celebrating his low qualifying 7.58 the night before the finals, D.A. joined fellow racers in hopping from one sponsor's suite to another, taking in a nightcap or two. D.A. wasn't much of a drinker and by the time he

With the death of Top Gas at the end of 1971, D.A. went into a short-lived retirement. The rail was sold to parts unknown and reappeared in 1996 hanging from the rafters of a speed shop. By 1971, D.A. had the hemi cranking out a consistent 200 mph that clocked in the mid- to low-7s. (Photo Courtesy Bill Truby)

The rail was painted yellow when Ken Nishwitz purchased the car from an owner who had no idea what he had. The original green metalflake interior was cleaned and reinstalled during the restoration. The Hemi featured direct drive to an early-Olds rear end. (Photo Courtesy Bill Truby)

found his way back to his room, he was feeling no pain. Morning came too early for D.A. and he had to rush out the door to make class runoffs. Suffering from a little "cotton breath," D.A. popped a stick of gum into his mouth. However, before his run, D.A. forgot to spit out the gum.

When he nailed the throttle on the green light, the piece of gum lodged in his windpipe. No panic for D.A. as he figured when he popped the chute after his 7.66 run, it would dislodge the gum. Well, it didn't quite work out that way; when the chute came out, the gum stayed put. D.A. brought the car to a quick halt and with fading consciousness, alerted track officials that he was in dire need of assistance. He was quickly loaded into an ambulance and rushed to the hospital; upon arrival, he was unconscious. Doctors removed the gum and held D. A. overnight for observation.

The next day, D.A. returned to defeat Dick McFarland in the class final turning in a 7.65 at 193.94 to McFarland's 7.77 at 192.71. The choking episode was an ongoing gag for all involved and years later D. A. made light of the incident. Running Funny Car into the 1990s, D.A.'s wife, Barb, tossed bubble gum to the crowds. The Top Gas dragster, fondly referred to as the *Bubble Gum Car*, disappeared in 1971 when D.A. briefly retired.

It was unknown what had become of the car until 1996 when it was bought from Outlaw Performance, where it had been hanging in the rafters. Karl Nishwitz then bought the car in 1997 after answering an ad in *National Dragster*. He went through the painstaking work of restoring the car only to be forced to sell it in a divorce settlement. For Nishwitz, the story does have a happy ending. The dragster's new owner, Ron Leslie of Kenz & Leslie Funny Car fame, was forced to sell the dragster in 2012. There to pick it up was Karl Nishwitz and friend Greg Swenson.

The dragster is now back home in Pennsylvania and, weather permitting, is shown regularly. And you can believe that a dish of bubble gum isn't too far away.

Karl Nishwitz was a body and paint man for more than 20 years and his abilities show in the **Bubble Gum Car**'s metallic green paint. The car was a regular at Quaker City and Keystone between 1966 and 1971. D.A. went into retirement before returning in 1978 to run the **Black Magic Vega Funny Car**. He retired for good in 1992. (Photo Courtesy Bill Truby)

Petersen & Fitz

In the late 1960s and the early 1970s the Washington-based Top Fuel team of Herm Petersen and Sam Fitz was one to be reckoned with. The pair barnstormed up and down the West Coast dragstrips and rewrote track records along the way. (Photo by Doug Huegli, Courtesy worldofspeed.org)

Herm "The Northwest Terror" Petersen has seen more than his fair share of drag racing excitement. One bit he could have done without was the fiery crash that nearly cost him his life. In July 1973, Herm was making a qualifying run in his mid-engine rail at a PDA meet at Orange County. Not long into the run, an axle snapped, forcing the car into a quick right turn. Herm corrected the wheel and grabbed the brake, which caused the car to flip over as it careened down the track.

Reports noted that the resultant fire caused third- and fourth-degree burns over 55 percent of Herm's body. Never a man to give up easy, Herm spent the next four months going through extensive skin grafts and painful rehabilitation. Herm knew full well that, God willing, he'd be back behind the wheel. He had come a long way and I'm sure the downtime gave him plenty of opportunity to reflect.

Herm took in his first drag race in the late 1950s. After graduating from high school in 1961, he hooked up with the Handlers Car Club and built himself a B/Gas Willys. The small-block Chevy–powered sedan served him well before he pieced together a modified production Chevy. Within a few short years, Herm had become the car club's business manager and part of his responsibilities included managing the Bremerton race track. In late 1967, while making calls to entice Top Fuel drivers to a race, which paid $400 to win, Seattle driver Jerry "The King" Ruth demanded an extra $100 "under the table" just for showing up.

"Back then," said Petersen, "you couldn't have a race without Ruth so I reluctantly agreed to pay." That call was a turning point in Herm's career: "That conversation just didn't sit right with me. I had been racing my C/Modified Production '57 Chevy for a $12 trophy [his biggest payday had been $25 for winning a fairly large race in Seattle] and this guy gets a hundred bucks just for showing up."

Shortly after, Herm purchased a used Top Gas chassis from Olympia's Terrell Poage and a used Hemi short-block and an injector from Ruth. He picked up new cylinder heads and a blower from Ed Donovan in Los Angeles. Herm made his first appearance at Bremerton in 1968 and was immediately hooked. At the end of the season he and his wife, Sandy, headed back to Los Angeles to purchase a new, 188-inch-wheelbase chassis from Woody Gilmore's Race Car Engineering. The chassis featured Woody's torsion-bar front suspension, bell-crank

The fire burnout was all the rage in the early 1970s and added enormously to the fan appeal. Petersen is seen here in 1971, lighting the night sky after igniting his brew of flammable liquid. Drivers used anything from straight gasoline, to thinning glues, or their own hodgepodge potions. The NHRA banned the fire burnout at national events after a fiery show at Indy in 1971. (Photo by Doug Huegli, Courtesy worldofspeed.org)

A trip to the 2004 CHRR rekindled Petersen's interest in his old rail, which led to him tracking the car down in Iowa and bringing it home for restoration. The original George Carney paint was matched by Mark Dalton and covers the original Tom Hanna body. The dragster now resides in the World of Speed museum in Portland, Oregon. (Photo By Doug Huegli, Courtesy worldofspeed.org)

steering, and was covered by a Tom Hanna body. The 392 featured all the standard goodies of the day and today houses Arias pistons, Crower roller camshaft, Donovan rocker assembly, and tunnel port heads. Sitting on top of the Cragar manifold is a Hampton 6-71 blower and Enderle bug catcher.

The car debuted at the 1969 NHRA Winternationals and did well in Division 6 competition, winning its first race at Woodburn in Oregon. Herm and the car closed out the season holding down second place in the division behind the King himself, Jerry Ruth.

It was around this time that Herm was approached by Sam Fitz who was looking to get involved and wanted to sponsor the car. Sam was an original founder of the Handlers club and owned three restaurants at the time. Recalled Herm, "It started as a $2,000 sponsorship but it went so much further." The two friends formed a solid partnership: Fitz was ahead of his time in terms of lining up additional sponsors, obtaining parts, and the car. Petersen was a meticulous mechanic and a fearless driver. In 1969 he was hitting the national record, turning 6.54 ETs at his home track of Bremerton.

The pair raced the dragster through 1971 when

The current 392 was built around a virgin block and features a 3/8-inch stroke increase and a .030-over bore. Backing the Hemi is a Crower clutch and an 8.75 Chrysler rear end. Herm was lucky in his restoration: The Race Car Engineering chassis and Tom Hanna skin remained intact. (Photo By Doug Huegli, Courtesy worldofspeed.org)

they joined the exodus away from the slingshot-design dragster and purchased a new rear-engine Gilmore chassis. The old car was sold to help finance the new one, which showed great success into 1973, winning the NHRA Gatornationals before that fateful day in July. The team came back strong in 1974 and, with a new Woody Gilmore car, won the Division 6 points championship. Herm retired from racing in 1976 but as the old racers' saying goes, once it's in your blood, it stays forever.

In 2004 Herm made the pilgrimage to the CHRR where he was offered the seat of Chris "The Greek" Karamesines' AA/FD during the Cacklefest activities. That's all it took to rekindle the flame in Herm. Once home, he began the search for his old front-engine car, and it didn't take him long to find it. The car had passed through many hands over the years and ended up in Bonners Ferry, Idaho, where Herm bought the car from Kelly Albino.

The dragster carried a different paint scheme and housed a big-block Chevy and Powerglide transmission but little else had changed in more than 30 years. The car had never been cut up and still retained all its original Tom Hanna skin. Compared to what some folks have to go through during a restoration, Herm got off pretty easily. The original multicolored George Carney paint was a knockout and was duplicated by Mark Dalton of Dalton Motor Graphics and Tim Piecuch of Kingston Collision & Glass. The engine, of course, was assembled by Herm himself using a Velasco billet crank, Arias pistons, Crower cam, and Mondello heads. It was a potent combination that proved to be one of the loudest cackle cars on the track.

Today, the Petersen & Fitz front-engine dragster is part of the World of Speed Collection in Wilsonville, Oregon.

Chapter One: Diggers: The Top Dogs   39

Stephens & Venables

With Steve Stephens behind the wheel, the Stephens & Venable rail could easily hold its own. The pair dominated the South and in 1971 alone, won the Bayou Championship in Houma, the IHRA Texas Open, and the AHRA Labor Day Nationals. In this 1971 photo, you can see the unpainted new rear body panels; a clutch explosion had damaged the original sheet metal. Brian Hildebrand painted the car; it features pearl white and candy red and blue with gold-leaf lettering. (Photo Courtesy James Fullingim)

The Bucket List. We all seem to have one and if yours is anything like mine, there's that one seemingly unobtainable thing that will remain long after everything else has been crossed off. Rip Wiley has a Bucket List and for the longest time, an original front-engine dragster held a spot on it. That is until 2003 when a fateful trip to the National Hot Rod Reunion at Bowling Green answered that dream. You see, building or even buying a front-engine car isn't cheap and Rip had enough sense to realize that an original dragster was out of his reach. Life's priorities were holding him back, until one day in Kentucky.

Wandering the grounds with his wife, Natalie, Rip spotted an old Junior Fueler for sale that sported its original Tom Hanna skin. It was a real-deal 1960s dragster and the price seemed to make it doable. Rip spent the remainder of the day convincing himself and his wife that, one, they could afford it and, two, he must have it. Weighing their options, home renovations or dragster, the pair set their priorities and came to the same logical conclusion: They could afford the dragster by putting the home renovations on hold.

The next morning Rip approached the owner, Bob Gibson, with an ear-to-ear smile on his face, "Well, we're ready to buy" but with a crashing thud, Bob informed him that he had missed the boat as the car had sold earlier that morning. You could have knocked Rip over with a feather. Old dreams die hard and being so close to owning the car of his dreams, Rip spent the good part of the day in a funk. However, as his wife reminded him, things happen for a reason.

As the day went on Rip began to cheer up. Things got even better when Bob approached him with the news of another car for sale. Of course, Rip was all ears. It was a full-body car with a 205-inch wheelbase. Because of the "Don't Mess With Texas" sticker attached to it, it was believed to have run out of Texas. As the price was in his ballpark, Rip jumped at the opportunity and, sight unseen, made arrangements to purchase the car.

Rip was told that the dragster featured an Al Swindahl chassis but this proved to be incorrect. Stumped as to the

In this 1971 photo, shot at the pair's home track of Amarillo, Venables has just completed a burnout and is waiting to be pushed back to the starting line. The cockpit is unpainted thanks to a recent replacement following a clutch explosion. A new paint job came free of charge as a prize for another event win. (Photo Courtesy James Fullingim)

The Lester Guillory chassis (under the Stephens & Venables full-body rail) measures a sleek 205 inches. The car served the pair faithfully through 1972 before joining the increasing number of front-engine cars on the sideline. This one was retired to the rafters of Dick Venables' shop. (Photo Courtesy Bob Fite)

At the 2009 Bowling Green National Hot Rod Reunion, Dick Venables was more than happy to take the wheel during the parade. Wiley and Natalie Royce of Tennessee poured everything into the restoration and came out with a real winner. In its day, the 392 propelled the rail to a best of 6.52 in the quarter-mile. (Photo Courtesy Paul Hutchins)

car's origins, Rip contacted every chassis builder he could think of. It wasn't until Dave Tuttle led him to Ed Mabry that Rip finally discovered whose car it was. The car was built by legendary Louisiana chassis builder Lester Guillory in 1970 for the team of Steve Stephens and Dick Venables. The car was raced by Stephens & Venables through 1972 and was very successful in Division 4.

Powering the car was a Rahn Tobler–tuned, blown, nitro-fed 392 Hemi that propelled the car to a best of 6.53 at 225 mph. For those unfamiliar with Rahn, he later married Shirley Muldowney and was her crew chief during her three NHRA National Championships. He later headed up Don Schumacher's crew.

The engine today is very close to the one that Steve and Dick ran during the early 1970s. It is an aluminum-rod 392 Chrysler Hemi with a Reath crank and 354 heads. A GMC 6-71 blower with an Enderle fuel injection supplies the 85- to 90-percent nitro while a Cirello magneto lights the fire. Preston Davis and Eddie Wilbanks built the current engine while Mike Kuhl supplied the cam and fuel system. The valve covers, cam cover, valley cover, magneto, pulleys, and idler bracket all came from Dick Venables, who had held on to the parts all these years. A Schiefer clutch and pressure plate sends the power to an 8.75 Chrysler rear end.

Eddie Wilbanks had a hand in just about every aspect of the restoration. He assisted with the engine, massaged the body panels, and helped with the frame repair and parts fabrication. Eddie also laid out the paint design after George and Brandon Barker prepped the body. Ricky and Michael Neal did the paint and lettering. Today the car is approximately 90-percent original.

A footnote for you trivia buffs: The dragster, driven by Stephens, gets credit for being the last front-engine car to win an IHRA national event. On October 31, 1971, Stephens defeated the Jenkins/Swain car at the Texas Nationals held at Dallas International Motor Speedway. The car amassed an impressive win/loss record as it traveled the country, winning 10 races, playing runner-up at four more, and finishing with one early elimination. Stephens & Venables raced the car through 1972 before joining the mid-engine crowd.

After Stephens & Venables switched to a rear-engine car, this dragster was placed in the rafters of Dick's shop for a time and then eventually sold. The car's history after leaving Dick's hands is murky at best and is one for the cold case files. There seems to be a 30-year gap in its history until Bob Gibson showed up with it. The Wileys spent four years restoring the dragster and debuted the car in 2008 at Bowling Green. It was a family reunion of sorts; both Stephens and Venables were on hand for the unveiling.

How tempting it must be for the driver to fire it up before rolling through the water. We know the Hemi is good to go; it's just a shame that most of these restored cars don't meet current NHRA safety regulations. This one is about 90-percent original. (Photo Courtesy Paul Hutchins)

Great Expectations II

Tom Raley warms the M&H hides during a 1970 meet at Englishtown, New Jersey. Brian Beattie, the photographer, had no idea that he would own the car 34 years later. (Photo Courtesy Brian Beattie Collection)

Jim and Allison Lee's *Great Expectations II* has been referred to as the most correct Top Fuel restoration to date. Knowing the competition, that's saying a lot. Currently owned by Brian Beattie, the car was campaigned by the Virginia-based Lees between 1969 and 1973. With Tom Raley behind the wheel, the dragster dominated East Coast action capturing the Division 1 points championship in both 1969 and 1970 and set the class record three times. In 1970, Tom won six WCS points meets.

The dragster debuted at the 1969 NHRA Nationals where Tom defeated Steve Carbone in one of the closest side-by-side races at that time. Tom squeezed out a 6.51 to Carbone's 6.54. He made it to the semi-finals before falling to eventual category winner, Don Prudhomme.

Without a doubt, though, a career highlight has to be joining the Salute to Motorsports crowd at the White House in 1971. The Lees' colorful dragster held President Nixon's attention throughout the gala, which was attended by Sox & Martin, Richard Petty, Mario Andretti, and others. Closing out the 1971 racing season, the husband-and-wife team was awarded for their efforts by being voted onto the *Car Craft* all-star team as Top Fuel Crew Chiefs of the Year.

The 185-inch-wheelbase chrome-moly chassis was built by one of the West Coast's best, Don Long, while the just-as-talented Tom Hanna was relied on to do the tinwork. George Cerny applied the strikingly beautiful paint and the interior was stitched up by Tony Nancy. Power for the dragster came courtesy of an Ed Pink–built nitro-fed 392 Hemi. As you can see, no expense was spared and it showed in the car's on-track performance.

Brian Beattie was the track photographer at Englishtown in the 1960s and even though he remembers the car well, he never thought that someday it would be parked in his own garage. In 2004, he got lucky. Brian received a call from a gentleman who was hoping that he had photos of a dragster his father had once driven. Even though Brian couldn't help with the dragster photos, he did have photos of an Altered that the gentleman's dad had raced. Brian delivered the photos and enjoyed his visit talking about the old days. The conversation naturally turned to front-engine rails and Brian mentioned how he'd love to own one. Then the gentleman mentioned that he knew the location of *Great Expectations II*; it was located just 20 minutes from Brian's home in New Jersey.

The Lees sold the dragster in 1973 and it was campaigned by the new owners (Cottrell & Speelman) in Top Alcohol. The car passed through three more owners before Brian came along. Gaining the confidence of the owner, who was a little reluctant to sell, Brian snapped a number of photos of the car and sent them to the Lees to confirm that it was indeed *Great Expectations II*. In the meantime the owner decided to sell the car, but only to Brian.

A highlight of the Lees' career was a trip to the White House in September 1971 where Great Expectations II *held President Nixon's attention. Here, Nixon is seen chatting with Mario Andretti and Jim Lee (back to the camera). (Photo Courtesy Brian Beattie Collection)*

Restored to its 1969 configuration, the dragster received nothing but praise at its CHRR debut in 2009. Brian discovered the car in 2004 parked in a New Jersey garage. Along with the purchase came a spare chassis, a trailer, and enough parts to build two 392 engines. The dragster features the original Don Long chassis, Tom Hanna tinwork, and Tony Nancy stitching. (Photo Courtesy Joyce Keller)

Brian initially had the 392 built in his home state of Pennsylvania but it wasn't done right and set the project back a few months. The engine was then sent to California where car restorer Bruce Dyda built it correctly. Here Great Expectations II *is seen at the 2011 NHRA Gatornationals where it was a special guest. (Photo Courtesy Joyce Keller)*

Restoration of the nearly complete car began in 2005 with Brian scrounging swap meets and online auction sites for needed parts. Once everything was gathered, the car headed west to Bruce Dyda in Gardena, California, who faced the task of bringing it all together. He started by stripping the Long chassis, which required an extensive amount of work because of years of neglect. The frame had to be sawed apart to restore it back to its original length and trueness.

As the car was to be relegated to shows and Cacklefests, the kidney bars were removed and the roll cage was returned to original. A number of the original Tom Hanna body panels showed wear and were replaced before Richard Stannard (under the name Estrus) matched up the original Carney paint and Dennis Jones (under the name Jones) did the lettering. After a failed attempt to have the Hemi rebuilt in Pennsylvania, Brian had Dyda go through it and do it right.

The restored car fired for the first time in late 2009, and made its debut at the CHRR at Bakersfield to the delight of family and friends who made the trek west for the event.

Gary Cochran's Rear-Engine Dragster

Gary Cochran purchased the second rear-engine chassis produced by SPE. The dragster was a regular at Irwindale and clocked a best elapsed time (ET) of 6.40 before its retirement in 1976.

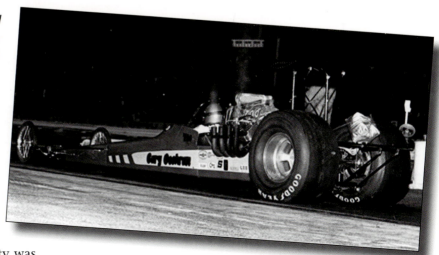

The mid-engine dragster wasn't a new idea in 1970 but by the time the new decade rolled around, drag racing was finally ready for it. With the increase in horsepower and what seemed like an increasing number of blower and clutch explosions, safety was

The aluminum Donavon measures 450 inches and is capable of producing 5,000 hp. The engine will run on a 90-percent load of nitro. Donavon never produced many of these blocks and this one carries the period-correct number 8. (Photo Courtesy Dave Davis)

Yeah, you know Gary Cochran is all smiles behind the wheel of his one and only rear-engine dragster. The 2013 CHRR was a memorable one as two of Gary's former rides were in attendance. Don Nosse helped restore the car. (Photo Courtesy Dave Davis)

finally taking precedence. Garlits' famous clutch explosion at Lions in 1970 was the turning point and by 1972, there were no threatening front-engine cars left in competition.

Southern California's Gary Cochran saw the writing on the wall and by 1973 had traded in his once-dominant SPE front-engine car for one of SPE's 210-inch mid-engine rides. The car was a beauty that featured Tom Hanna paneling and oriental blue paint by Tom Stratton. Motivation came courtesy of an aluminum Donavon engine featuring tunnel port heads and a Danekas 6-71 blower.

Gary competed with the car through 1976 and ran a quick 6.40 at 245. However, the face of Top Fuel was quickly changing and without a wealth of sponsorship money to pay the bills, you were dead in the water. Gary chose to sell his car rather than go broke and hitched a ride at someone else's expense.

After a career that spanned 30 years, he finally hung up his helmet in 1984 after competing in Bob Melville's AA/FC. Gary sold his Top Fuel car to Woody Duke, who ran it briefly as an A/Fueler before passing it down the line. Eventually the rail ended up in the hands of Larry Crossan. Larry had had his hands full restoring a number of dragsters and found out pretty quickly that he didn't have time for another car.

Current owners Kathy and Al Nosse came across the car in 2011 after reading of it while attending the CHRR. The car was shipped to their home in Ohio where the restoration began in January 2012. Amazingly, the dragster was approximately 85-percent complete by Larry's best guess but the all-important Donavon hemi was missing. With the help of Mike Cook, Al was able to procure a good used aluminum block from BRE. A little machine work and the block was as good as new.

Even though Don Garlits paved the way in the new age of rear-engine cars, Cochran and others followed suit and could still show him the way home. Don hated coming west to Division 7 where he had to face the likes of Cochran. (Photo Courtesy Dave Davis)

Al then assembled the engine using period-correct parts. Helping the Donavon produce upward of 5,000 horses are tunnel port heads, Venolia pistons and rods, and an original-profile camshaft. Original parts returned to the engine included the Cragar manifold and blower along with a rare Camico gear drive. Backing the hemi is a Hays two-disc clutch inside the original SPE bellhousing. A Mark Williams disconnect helps transmit the power to a Ford 9-inch rear end. Goodyear blue-streak slicks wrap Halibrand 16 x 13 rims that were block sanded to remove ripples. Topping the restored Tom Hanna tin is a House of Kolor oriental blue over a pearl-white base applied by Mark Tambarino and Dave Lindemuth.

Al debuted the dragster at the 2013 CHRR and was happy to give the seat to special guest Gary Cochran.

John Peters' *Freight Train*

By 1971, the cry in Top Gas was, "If you can't beat them, join them." It seemed that's what the competition was doing in an attempt to bring down the Freight Train. Drag News *columnist Judy Thompson pegged the car* Freight Train *after watching it defeat the competition by a train's length. Driver Bob Muravez made more than 1,300 runs in* Freight Train *and at one point went 28 consecutive rounds before a loss. (Photo Courtesy James Handy)*

Top Gas was borne out of the NHRA fuel ban in 1957 and remained a popular category until the end of the 1971 season. At that time, the NHRA made the decision to eliminate Top Gas. It's really too bad since it was also the death knell for one of the most famous cars in drag racing. John Peters and his *Freight Train* were and are the first and last name in Top Gas; they dominated the category for close to 10 years. When the category folded, John chose to retire the car.

The first *Freight Train* was built in 1959 by John and then-partner Nye Frank. It was an age of innovation and the original *Freight Train* had its share. Powered by twin small-block Chevys, the first *Train* featured a single front-mounted 6-71 blower that fed both engines through one long intake duct. The pair quickly picked up on the advantage of running twin blowers and, in short order, each engine housed its own top-mounted blower. The twin blowers were connected via a "driveshaft" with the front blower running the rear blower. There was only one blower belt; it was on the front engine, which allowed Peters to couple the engines closer together.

The car continued to evolve and in 1962 picked up its first major win, grabbing Top Gas at Bakersfield while being driven by Bob Muravez (aka Floyd Lippencotte, Jr.). Bob's story is interesting. He came from an affluent family who frowned heavily on his interest in drag racing. They were shocked to hear of his involvement and forbade him from driving. To avoid disownment by his parents, Bob relinquished the driver's seat and stood on the sidelines watching driver after driver fail to match his driving abilities.

According to John, the car went from top qualifier to non-qualifier in five short months. In John's eyes, there was only one way to rectify the situation and that was to get Bob back into the driver's seat.

To keep it a secret from his family, Bob initially raced under John's name to avoid recognition. When the team took Top Gas at the NHRA Winternationals, defeating Connie Kalitta, it was John Peters who was recognized as the driver and who stood in the winner's circle. One night in 1963 at San Gabriel, track announcer Mel Reck and track manager Steve Gibbs gave Bob the moniker Floyd Lippencotte, Jr.

John Peters (right), owner of Freight Train, never drove the car; instead, he preferred to build and direct the action. In 1966, the engineer outfits earned the crew best appearing honors. This photo was shot at the Bakersfield March Meet in 1965 and speaks volumes of the way drag racing used to be. (Photo Courtesy James Handy)

It's been reported that the alias was made up on the spot; "Lippencotte" was borrowed from Gibbs' college professor. Floyd, I mean Bob, explained his family situation to photographers, announcers, and competitors at each track where he raced and all agreed to keep his secret. In a previous interview, Bob went on to say that if a headshot was needed, the photographer had to wait until he had his goggles and helmet on. It was the NHRA's best-kept secret that I know of. In 1966, the NHRA went as far as issuing Floyd a license, with no photo.

It's sad to learn that in 1967, after Bob's Springnationals win, his father did find out and, true to his word, disowned him. Bob's father never spoke to his son after that day in 1967; he passed in 1993.

However, Bob/Floyd continued to rack up the wins for Peters, including six national events. In 1967 he set the class record at a UDRA meet at Lions with a 7.31 at 200.44. History has recorded this as the first 200-mph blast by a Top Gas car. Freight Train has a long list of accomplishments: it was the first Top Gas car over 190, the first Top Gas car to run a 7-second time, and the first to run a 6-second time. The Peters team won the Division 7 points championship five out of seven years and in 1967 were low qualifiers at every meet they ran.

There were three Freight Train cars; the final one was built in 1968. In 1970, John hooked up with Walt Rhodes and the small-block Chevys gave way to a pair of Chrysler Hemis. Walt drove the car to a Gatornationals win in 1971, which proved to be the Freight Train's last gasp. When the category died, so did John's desire to race.

With the growing popularity of nostalgia cars and cackle events, John pulled Freight Train from the rafters and in 1993 began a restoration. Today the car can be seen at cackle events and Hot Rod Reunions at both Bakersfield and Bowling Green.

A four-port injection-mounting configuration on a pair of 4-71 blowers and twin stretched-out small-block Chevys did the deed to the competition. In its final 1970–1971 configuration, Freight Train was sporting a pair of Hemis. (Photo Courtesy Dave Davis)

Freight Train went through many iterations and a few drivers. It was initially white and was given the nickname "The Great White Steamship" by Tommy Ivo. In its heyday the car was the top twin-engine gas dragster in the United States and still holds track records at some venues. The "cow catcher front wing" made it easy to recognize through smoky burnouts. (Photo Courtesy Dave Davis)

CHAPTER TWO

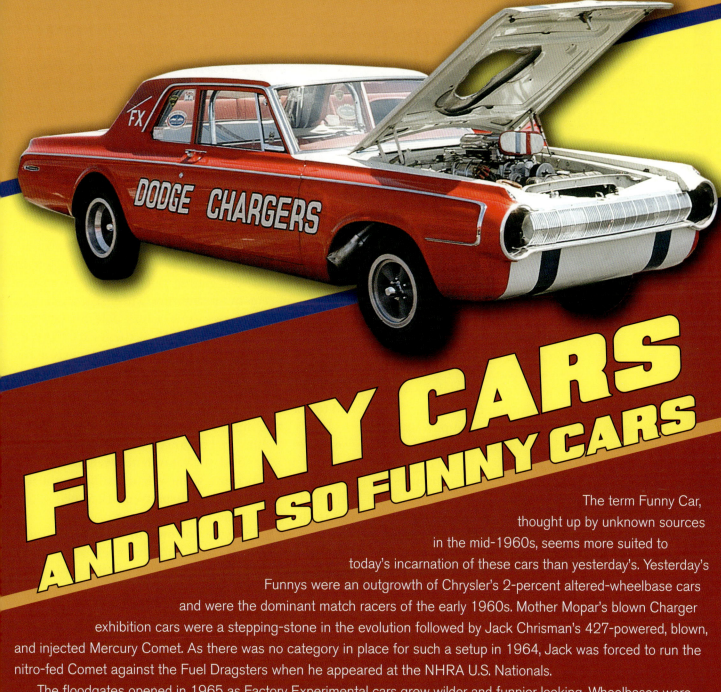

FUNNY CARS
AND NOT SO FUNNY CARS

The term Funny Car, thought up by unknown sources in the mid-1960s, seems more suited to today's incarnation of these cars than yesterday's. Yesterday's Funnys were an outgrowth of Chrysler's 2-percent altered-wheelbase cars and were the dominant match racers of the early 1960s. Mother Mopar's blown Charger exhibition cars were a stepping-stone in the evolution followed by Jack Chrisman's 427-powered, blown, and injected Mercury Comet. As there was no category in place for such a setup in 1964, Jack was forced to run the nitro-fed Comet against the Fuel Dragsters when he appeared at the NHRA U.S. Nationals.

The floodgates opened in 1965 as Factory Experimental cars grew wilder and funnier looking. Wheelbases were stretched and shuffled, engines were set back, and cars saw an increase in fiberglass paneling. Mercury created a handful of flip-top Comets in 1966, which led directly to the Funny Cars we see today.

THE FLOODGATES OPENED IN 1965 AS FACTORY EXPERIMENTAL CARS GREW WILDER AND FUNNIER LOOKING.

Above: Is this the grandfather of today's Funny Car? Many people feel that the three Dodge Chargers, built by Jim Nelson and Dode Martin of Dragmaster, is where it all started. When they were introduced in early 1964, the 480-inch blown and injected max wedge Chargers did not fit in any existing drag racing category so one was created for them: Supercharged/Factory Experimental. Today, just one of the three (almost) identical cars remains; and has been restored. (Photo Courtesy Richard McKinstry)

Dick Landy's AWB 1965 Dodge

More times than not, Dick Landy's Dodge left the line with its front wheels high in the air, just as this Darr Hawthorne photo depicts. Years later, Dick confirmed the Dodge as his old car by noting the message "This Side Up," which he had written on the underside of the car.

While Southern California's Dick Landy campaigned a countless number of memorial Mopars, he called the altered-wheelbase (AWB) Coronet his favorite. It was understandable, as during 1965 he dominated AHRA action by winning five events, played runner-up at the remaining two, and proved to be nearly unbeatable on the match-race circuit by winning 39 out of 40 matches.

Like so many, Dick had come up through the Stocker ranks starting in 1956 at age 18 with a Ford pickup. He stuck with Fords until 1962 when Mopar unleashed its Max Wedge 413. Dick was offered a deal by Plymouth and, realizing just how quick the new cars were, jumped at the opportunity. In an earlier interview, he had stated, "They brought a car out and I ran it, and I realized that in dead-stock tune it was going almost as fast as we were going with our highly modified 'stock' cars at that time. I was just shocked. I had to switch. The performance is what I liked. At that time, I said 'Yeah, let's do it.' So, they furnished me with a Plymouth, and I raced that all through 1962."

A Stage II car followed in 1963 before a switch to a factory-sponsored Hemi Dodge in 1964. Dick competed in SS/A with the car through Labor Day but shortly after, he was one-upping Chrysler and their 2-percent altered-wheelbase cars, pushing his Dodge's front wheels forward 6 inches and rear wheels up 8 inches.

In the meantime, the Chrysler folks wanted to have their new 1965 altered cars homologated for NHRA Factory Experimental competition. Having pushed the front and rear wheels forward 10 and 15 inches respectively, these new cars made the previous 2-percent cars look, well . . . stock.

Of course the NHRA took one look at these funny-looking cars and said no way! The sanctioning body, seeing the situation in Factory Experimental getting out of hand, chose this time to reel 'em in by limiting wheelbase alterations to 2 percent. The news came a little late for Chrysler as they had already prepared 11 of these cars. Chrysler then rush-built four new 2-percent cars to compete at the NHRA Winternationals while the 11 outlawed cars were dished off to capable owners to run AHRA competition and to match race.

Dick's acid-dipped Coronet (one of six built) was flown to him in Los Angeles in November 1964. Completely assembled, the car weighed well under 3,000 pounds with 56 percent of the weight resting on the rear wheels. Limited to the availability of 10.5-inch slicks, this really aided traction.

Chrysler really went to town in their bid to build the ultimate FX car, incorporating fiberglass fenders, doors, hood, front bumper, and even the dashboard.

Outlawed by the NHRA, Dick's injected Hemi Coronet dominated AHRA action and the booming match-race scene in 1965. After a month of twin Holleys and a cross-ram intake, he switched to injectors and alcohol. The tall Hilborn stacks measure 13.25 inches, reducing horsepower but increasing torque. A step up to nitromethane followed shortly after.

During an early afternoon of testing and tuning, Dick is seen here chomping on his Victory cigar, which he never actually smoked.

Thanks in large part to Dick's chassis prep and a full roll cage added by the third owner, the acid-dipped car remained fairly true all these years. To aid weight transfer, Dick had installed 2.5-inch raised front spindles. A pinion snubber against a homemade crossmember helped plant the tires. Rear gears ranged anywhere from 4.56 to 5.12. (Photo Courtesy Nick Smith)

The all-business interior retains its full cage and the single factory-installed A-100 Dodge seat. Dick was restrained by a lap belt only. Gauges include water temperature, oil pressure, and tach. (Photo Courtesy Nick Smith)

The windows were replaced with plexiglass while a stainless steel front crossmember was installed. Initial power for the Coronet came by way of a twin 4-barrel aluminum-headed Hemi. Dick used this setup to knock out 10.24 at 138.20 times while winning the Fuel and Gas Championship held at Bakersfield.

Ah, but a rolling stone gathers no moss, and the wheels in Landy's head were churning. Within a month, the Hemi was sporting Hilborn injectors and feeding on a healthy dose of nitromethane. Mid-9-second times became the norm for the Dodge and at the West Coast's first annual U.S. Super Stock Championship, Dick walked away with the win after turning in a 9.53 at 142.40.

Further accolades came with the distinction of being the first unblown stocker to crank out 150-mph quarter-mile times. Dick accomplished the feat while running injectors and a Torqueflite transmission. To crank out these speeds, the Hemi engine relied on an Isky camshaft and valvesprings in conjunction with a blueprinted factory bottom end. There was a lot of development and trial and error when it came to the new setup and, with a switch from gas to nitro, Dick burned through a few engines. But the Dodge kept winning!

Dick took the car on a three-week West Coast Factory Experimental tour and completely dominated, defeating Ronnie Sox, Dave Strickler, Hayden Proffitt, Butch Leal, Malcolm Durham, and others. Dick raced the car in 35 different states during 1965 and between running his Automotive Research speed shop and preparing a new car for 1966, it's no wonder that 16-hour workdays became a common occurrence. He ran the Coronet into 1966 before debuting his lighter stretched-nosed Dart. This blown Hemi car, which featured direct drive that eventually ran 8.20 times, brought us a step closer to modern-day Funny Cars.

The Coronet was sold to Landy employee, Jim Wetton, who had his own success running the car out of Studio Dodge. As the years passed, the Dodge saw a number of owners before finally being restored in 2010 by Ed Strzelecki. Today, only five of the eleven altered cars initially built remain. Of these, Dick's car is considered to be the cleanest and most original.

No expense was spared ensuring that the Landy Dodge was done right. Like most race cars, changes were always taking place and Dick's Dodge is no exception. Later in 1965 he tinted the windows blue and, at the recommendation of Chrysler's PR man, replaced the single headlights with duals so that the car looked more like a showroom model. (Photo Courtesy Nick Smith Collection)

Lee Smith's *Haulin' Hemi II*

Lee Smith was the recipient of one of the six acid-dipped altered-wheelbase cars produced by Chrysler in 1965. A number of these cars made their debut at the AHRA Winter Nationals where they were forced to run Ultra Stock. This Plymouth had been acid-dipped to within an inch of its life. This was something Lee discovered when he left the ballast in the trunk of his car while transporting it.

The ballast, along with the car bouncing on the trailer, caused cracks in the quarter panel. As Lee recalled, "It opened it up like a tin can." He had also discovered that if he opened the door and bounced on the rocker panel, it caused the roof to buckle. When he arrived home in Illinois, he stiffened the car by tying the chassis front to back and adding additional tubing to the roll cage. (Photo Courtesy Geoff Stunkard)

Of the six lightweight Plymouths produced, Lee's is the last one remaining. This can be attributed to the extra effort he put into reinforcing the chassis. Note the additional roll cage supports. Sponsorship was courtesy of Learner of Rock Line, Illinois, a dealership that moved a lot of expensive Imperials, which made Chrysler happy. The Plymouth called Cordova Dragway home and supported AHRA and UDRA competition. Low-10-second runs were the norm for the car. Today the Plymouth resides in the small but significant collection of Kathy and Greg Mosley. (Photo Courtesy Geoff Stunkard)

Lee picked up his Plymouth from the manufacturer in December 1964. He raced it from 1965 through 1966. The car was raced by the next two owners and then sat in a barn for "a decade or two" after that. It's lucky that the car was rescued when it was because the barn burned to the ground shortly after. The added roll-cage tubing runs to the spring perches; Lee added them after the 1965 AHRA Winter Nationals. (Photo Courtesy Geoff Stunkard)

The heart of the restored Haulin' Hemi II is a correct injected 426 Hemi assembled by Lee himself. As he recalls, the Hemi started the 1965 season carbureted before he switched to injectors late in the year. Although he never ran nitro through the engine, he does recall adding 30-percent toluene to his fuel to boost octane. Lee repeated his 1964 Cordova World Series win in 1965 taking the "Bonanza One" victory. (Photo Courtesy Geoff Stunkard)

Haulin' Hemi II has had nine different owners since leaving the factory. The car was fairly complete when found but it was rough. The third owner had cut open the firewall to set the engine back and opened up the rear wheel wells for larger tires. Lee ran fiberglass fenders and hood that were glued together by a previous owner to make a one-piece front end. The guys at Hot Rod Innovations and Mo-Par City can take most of the credit for the top-notch restoration. (Photo Courtesy Geoff Stunkard)

Gas Ronda's Long-Nose Mustang

Gas Ronda's ties with Ford put him behind the wheel of the long-nose Mustang in 1966. The contracted driver was required to pay $1 for his Mustang. Gas went to work as a salesman for sponsor Russ Davis Ford in mid-1964. Within his first year, sales of performance parts had increased 1,000 percent. (Photo Courtesy Nick Smith Collection)

Gaspar "Gas" Ronda started drag racing in the 1950s, taking up the hobby as an escape from the dance school he operated in San Francisco. Initially he bounced from one automotive brand to another before settling on Ford in 1961. He hooked up with Les Ritchey of Performance Associates in 1964 and his track record landed him in the manufacturer's good books. A Russ Davis–sponsored factory ride came in the form of a 427-powered Thunderbolt.

A car driven by Ronda at the NHRA Winternationals defeated Butch Leal in the all-Thunderbolt Super Stock final. A Holman & Moody–built SOHC, A/FX Mustang followed in 1965. One of eleven built, the Mustang dominated and won the AHRA World Finals and set both ends of the AHRA class record with a 10.43 at 134.73 mph.

Ronda's stretched-nose 1966 Mustang (seen here) is one of six produced by Holman-Moody for the Ford Motor Company. These cars were an integral part of the Funny Car evolution and could be looked at as the bridge between the early 1960s Factory Experimental cars and the full-blown, tube chassis, floppers that first appeared in 1966. The six cars were an extension of the two steel-bodied Factory Experimental cars Ford built in 1965 but taking things a step further, these six bodies were laid up in fiberglass. The wheelbase was shuffled north and extended from the stock 108 inches to 112. This was accomplished by sliding the front wheels forward 14 inches and the rear wheels back 10 inches. A 2 x 3 chrome-alloy chassis was fabricated along with a unique twisted quarter-elliptic leaf-sprung front suspension. At 2,400 pounds, the lightweight Mustangs were approximately 1,000 pounds lighter than a 1965 A/FX Mustang.

In January 1966, in an attempt to quash Chrysler's domination of the Factory Experimental category, Charlie Gray of Ford's Special Vehicles tried but failed to have these six cars homologated to run NHRA A/FX.

The cars were forced to run C/Fuel Dragster at the NHRA Winternationals where Gas and his Mustang took class. He backed that up by grabbing all the marbles at the AHRA winter meet. At the Smokers meet in Bakersfield, the Mustang became the first unblown Funny Car to turn in an 8-second time when Gas put away the Sox & Martin Barracuda with an 8.96 at 155.97. By late summer the Mustang was cranking out 174 mph in the rare air at Lions Drag Strip. To produce these numbers, Gas relied on Les Ritchey's Performance Associates to prepare the SOHC 427, which pumped out approximately 660 horses.

This late-1965 Holman-Moody construction photo shows that, in true Funny Car fashion, there is 15 inches between the engine and the front spindle line. (Photo Courtesy Nick Smith Collection)

You don't need to be Superman to hoist this fiberglass shell. The total vehicle weight of Ronda's Mustang was eventually pared down to 2,180 pounds. (Photo Courtesy Nick Smith Collection)

Gas sold the Mustang in late 1967 to his neighbor Pat Mahnken. Pat ran it as Psycho II *and then bracket raced the car for a couple years with a twin 4-barrel 427 wedge. The car ran as* Lady Bug, *but was then lost in a divorce and disappeared. The Mustang's historical significance was long forgotten, until the layers of paint started to come off. (Photo Courtesy Nick Smith Collection)*

Internal goodies for the SOHC engine included .586-inch-lift Crane cams, Mickey Thompson rods, and 12:1 compression. Topping the mill were 13-inch Hilborn injector stacks feeding a healthy dose of nitro. A Scintilla magneto with 32- to 38-degrees advance lit the Ford's fire. Initially, a Toploader 4-speed backed the potent mill but it proved to be a handful. Since consistency was the name of the game, a new-for-1966 C-6 automatic transmission was swapped mid-season. Shift points came at 8,000 rpm. Filling the 9-inch rear were 4.10 or 4.30 gears spinning 10.5-inch Goodyears. For stopping power, the Mustang relied on rear brakes only and a Deist chute. Long traction arms of unequal angles helped with preload along with multiple spring positioning locations.

Referred to as "Dollar Cars" because each car was sold to a member of the Ford Race Team for $1, the Mustangs were said to cost $30,000 apiece to build. Gas ran his car through 1967, hitting lower-8-seconds in the quarter-mile before parking it for a factory-backed Super Stock Cobra Jet.

As the car is prepared for paint you get a good view of the torsion-spring suspension and the cage used to support the extended front clip. As there were only six of these cars built, changes were incorporated on the fly. The motor mounts are unique to this car, as the other Mustangs' mounts were modified for clearance. The firewall in this car is one of the few non-original parts. (Photo Courtesy Nick Smith Collection)

The SOHC 427 Ford was originally designed to compete against Chrysler's Hemi in NASCAR competition but when the Hemi was banned, so was the 427. Estimated horsepower of the Ronda engine was well in excess of 600 thanks to Crane Ramsonic camshafts, Hilborn injectors, and 40-percent nitromethane. (Photo Courtesy Nick Smith Collection)

Although the history of this Mustang is a little sordid, we do know that it was sold to Pat Mahnken, who campaigned it through 1969 as *Psycho II*. Mahnken lost the car to his wife in a divorce in the early 1970s and then the car was run as *Lady Bug* well into the 1970s. The Mustang was discovered years later and it wasn't until a few layers of paint were peeled back that it was discovered that the car was Gas Ronda's old ride.

Restoration commenced in December 2006 by Erik Lindberg with the help of Ralph Whitworth and the guys at Hite Auto Body in LaGrange, Indiana. Today the historic car is in the lightweight collection of Nick Smith.

The restored interior features the original tinwork, a single fiberglass re-covered seat, and Mustang shifter. Mounted on the far side of the tunnel is a fire extinguisher. (Photo Courtesy Nick Smith Collection)

The folks at Hite Restoration did the final body prep and the poppy red paint on the restored Mustang. It matches the original color perfectly. Gas ran the car in A/XS at the 1966 Nationals and B/XS at the 1967 NHRA Winternationals where he lost class to Dave Strickler's stretched Corvette. Gas was a dominating force through the 1960s; in 1967 he earned AHRA's Driver of the Year honors. (Photo Courtesy Nick Smith Collection)

Pete Gates' *Gate Job* Comet

When the revolutionary flip-top Comets appeared in 1966, they had an easy .3 up on the competition. Gate Job was a late bloomer, debuting in December 1966. Pete and the Comet had no problem mowing down match-race competition.

Lincoln-Mercury's release of five revolutionary flip-top Comet Funny Cars in 1966 set the match-race world on its ear and overnight deemed obsolete everything that came before. Al Turner and the head of Lincoln Mercury's race division, Fran Hernandez, knew what it took to win. As removing weight is akin to adding

Gate Job was assembled in Pete's home garage and shared space with the 1965 A/FX Comet, which he had previously purchased from Dyno Don. Pete was never a contracted Ford driver but did enjoy plenty of back-door support.

This is the freshly lettered Comet, ready for action. The Earl Wade–built 427 produced in the neighborhood of 1,000 hp and propelled the Comet to mid-8-second times. For stopping power the car carries rear drum brakes and a Simpson chute. Shocks and springs are Autolite while the wheels are Halibrand, front and rear. (Photo Courtesy Daryl Huffman Collection)

horsepower, the Mercury guys commissioned Plastigage Custom Fabrication of Jackson, Michigan, to lay up the bodies in lightweight fiberglass. At the same time, the Logghe brothers were called upon to build a matching number of stock wheelbase tube chassis. With a SOHC 427 nestled between the rails, these bombs weighed less than 1,900 pounds. Once the cars hit the track, their ETs were .3 to .4 second quicker than their fading competition. Is it any wonder their win percentage approached 90?

Pete Gates' Comet may not have been the first flip-top Funny Car built but it is the last survivor of the original batch. All of the other cars were destroyed in track-related incidents. Pete's car was a leftover 1966 body that he was able to secure late in the year from Mercury with the help of fellow racer Don Nicholson. Pete had previously purchased Don's old A/FX Comet and, with the help of Earl Wade, went about putting his name on the map by using the car to win the Super Stock Nationals in 1966. Remarkably, this win was Pete's first race in Don's old Comet.

Earl continued to play crew chief for Pete through 1966 and helped build and tune the 427 for his new "flopper." The race-bred engine featured Crane Camshaft's pistons, rods, and injector by Mickey Thompson; Jardine headers; and a Mallory magneto to light the 80-percent load of nitro. Backing up the potent mill was an Art Carr–prepped C6 that fed power to a 9-inch rear end. The Ron and Gene Logghe Stage 1 chassis, which is believed to be the brothers' first, was fabricated from 1.5-inch round tubing and features a four-point roll cage, tube straight axle, and a ladder-bar rear-end setup. He was never a factory-contracted racer, but Pete was well connected and did enjoy some back door support.

Gate Job made an early appearance at the 1967 NHRA Winternationals where it lasted a couple rounds in Supercharged Experimental Stock (although the car wasn't supercharged) hitting mid-8-second times. While out West, Pete had an escape hatch cut into the roof of his Comet and is credited with being the first Funny Car owner to incorporate this safety feature.

Pete, who hailed from Wayne, Michigan, never enjoyed the taste of a national event victory. He did have plenty of success match racing the Comet, defeating Arnie Beswick, Dyno Don, Jungle Jim Liberman, and others. The Comet received a face-lift in the spring when Pete added a 1967 Comet grille and taillights. The beautiful sunset gold and cinnamon pearl paint, which was laid on by Paul Shidlick, remained intact. Pete swapped bodies during the summer of 1967, bolting on a new fiberglass Comet shell. It lacked the visual appeal of the first, but the lighter shell helped put Pete into the 7-second zone for the first time.

By the late 1960s, the cost of drag racing a Funny Car was becoming more and more prohibitive. Pete's parents owned a successful furniture store and he enjoyed their support through 1969 before they pulled the plug. Pete's drag racing career came to an end after campaigning a Cougar Funny Car. The demise of the 1966 Comet came in mid-1967 when Pete received his new Comet body.

Pete used his existing chassis with the new body while the old Comet shell was left to collect dust in the corner of his shop. When his Cougar entered the scene, the Comet bodies and the chassis were sold to Wayne Gapp. Wayne bolted a Mustang body onto the chassis and sold the Comet bodies.

Years later when a friend of *Gate Job*'s restorer, Daryl Huffman, discovered the cut-up Comet body about to be torched, he snatched it up and passed it on to Daryl. Daryl always wanted an early Funny Car and immediately set out in search of the original parts and the missing original chassis. It took him a year and a half to hunt down the chassis, "I spent a few hundred dollars placing ads in all the trade papers and finally got a response from the owner when I placed a $3 ad in the *Cleveland Times*." When Daryl purchased the chassis, it still retained the Mustang body that Gapp had installed along with the original Halibrand front wheels that Pete installed.

Restoration began in 1993 with the hunt for a period-correct SOHC 427 engine and parts. As you can imagine, finding parts for this nonproduction engine was like finding the proverbial needle in a haystack. Eventually Daryl was able to scrounge up the parts through numerous sources and by the time the car passed through Barrett Jackson in 2010, the only things missing were the correct short Hilborn injector stacks.

Once the restoration of the Logghe chassis was complete, the process of piecing the body together proceeded.

Extensive fiberglass work was required to put the puzzle back together and to undo modifications that had been made years ago. Once that was done, the original painter, Paul Shidlick, was called upon to replicate his work from 40 years earlier. Paul Hatton completed the pinstriping and lettering on all five of the original Comets and, once again, he repeated his work on the lone survivor.

Unlike Humpty Dumpty, the handful of Comet pieces were put back together again. The cut-up Comet was discovered by Steve Ziebold and passed to his good friend, Daryl Huffman. Another year and a half was spent hunting down the chassis, which was thankfully located intact. The wheels, steering, front suspension, and tinwork are original to the car. (Photo Courtesy Daryl Huffman Collection)

By early spring 1967, Pete's '66 Comet incorporated a '67 Comet grille and taillights. Elapsed times in the early 1960s were hampered by the lack of bite but as you can see, by 1967, tire compounds had greatly improved. (Photo Courtesy Daryl Huffman Collection)

Piecing together the Comet was a chore as numerous modifications had to be undone. The '67 Comet taillights made way for the original 1966 units while holes in the tail panel were filled. The "Don Who?" was in reference to Dyno Don and his Eliminator 1 Comet. (Photo Courtesy Daryl Huffman Collection)

To complete the Comet's restoration, then-owner Daryl Huffman brought in partners to help out financially. Part of the agreement they made was that once the restoration was complete, the Comet would be sold. Crossing the block at Barrett Jackson in 2010, the happy new owner picked up a bargain, paying $160,000 for the Comet. (Photo Courtesy Daryl Huffman Collection)

Chapter Two: Funny Cars and Not So Funny Cars 55

The restoration of the Comet was a major undertaking; the car's historic significance dictated that it had to be done. Daryl brought in partners to ensure the car received the attention it deserved and part of their agreement was that the car would be sold when completed. It was a bullet that Daryl was willing to bite to ensure the restoration did the car justice. The photos show that justice was done.

Pete Gates' Comet was the last of the original cars to hit the track and the last one surviving today. The Hilborn injectors are longer than the originals used but the search is on for proper shorties. (Photo Courtesy Daryl Huffman Collection)

Dave Koffel's Experimental Stock Barracuda

Dave was as smart as he was quick and in short order he had caught the eye of Chrysler. Factory backing came in 1965. His degree in metallurgy and physics led to him joining the Chrysler engineer group in 1968. At Chrysler's insistence, the Experimental Stock Barracuda was retired at the end of the 1968 season, and thus Dave's drag racing career ended. (Photo Courtesy James Handy)

The list of Dave's automotive accomplishments is nearly endless. If you don't believe me, just ask your friendly neighborhood Moparphile. Dave worked alongside the Ramchargers, developed the B-1 cylinder head, and in the 1970s, worked in conjunction with Tom Hoover to bring us *Lil Red Express Truck*. You may recall that the *Express Truck* was the fastest straight-line domestically produced production vehicle of 1978.

Dave's dragstrip accomplishments began in the mid-1950s while he was a member of the Akron, Ohio–based Cam Jammers Car Club. He drove a C/G '37 Chevy powered by a 302-inch GMC 6 and was a bit of a terror around Akron. He made his first trip to the NHRA Nationals in 1959 and, driving a Chevy-powered '32 Ford roadster, took runner-up in B/SR. Somewhere along the line Dave's automotive preference took a turn off the beaten path and he purchased a Packard. It wasn't his first oddball; back around 1957 he had a blown small-block-powered Studebaker.

His Packard was a work of art and, with the help of newfound friend Harvey Crane, the 4,400-plus-pound *Flyer* could run a half second under the E/G class record. Dave set the mark in 1962 with a 13.33 at 104.04 clocking. Dave followed up in 1964 with an equally impressive 1959 Studebaker Lark before hooking up with Bob Cahill and Mother Mopar in 1965.

A couple Super Stocks and a Factory Experimental car were next, followed, in 1967, by a Barracuda built to run A/XS. Experimental Stock ran under the Modified

56   Drag Racing's Quarter-Mile Warriors: Then & Now

Dave's Packard was a killer in E/G during the early 1960s and is seen here at the 1962 Nationals where he took class with an ET of 13.71. Susie Koffel painted the lettering and Freddie Flintstone graphic on the trunk. The *Flintstone Flyer* name came about when one of Dave's crew said that the Packard looked like something right out of Bedrock. (Photo Courtesy Richard McKinstry)

Says Susie Koffel, "Only we could love it." After restoring the Packard, the Koffels wondered what had they gotten themselves into. Even though the acid-dipped Barracuda looks pretty rough, it was, for the most part, complete and the extensive restoration to come was worth it. (Photo Courtesy Susie Koffel)

Eliminator category and was where you found the predecessor of the Funny Car. Dave, with the help of Ron Tiestze, started off with an acid-dipped body and a tube frame designed by Chrysler's structural engineers. Motivation for the Barracuda came courtesy of an injected 392 Hemi, which was backed by a B&M ClutchFlite and Dana 60 rear end. Filling the void between engine and transmission was a 60-pound flywheel and a 10.5-inch Chrysler green clutch.

Dave and his third *Flintstone Flyer* came close to winning his only national event in 1968 when he faced the '57 Corvette of Sam Gianino. Who knows how that race would have turned out; it was over before it started. The line lock on Dave's Barracuda failed, causing the car to roll out of the lights.

Koffel's *Flyer* held the A/XS class record numerous times throughout 1968 and as Dave recalls, the quickest times were in the 9.20s at well over 160 mph. The last hoorah for the Barracuda came in September 1968 when Dave took on Al Joniec's *Bat Car* in a match race at Pennsylvania's Maple Grove Dragway. The *Flyer* went out on top, taking Joniec in three straight.

Later that month, Dave sold the car to John Moore of Poquoson, Virginia. John had his fun with the car before he blew the engine and parked the remains. And there she sat, eventually ending up at the shop of Ed Miller,

Lunar module? This was the day that the chassis and body became one. The chassis and engine were hauled from John Nickel's shop in Port Clinton, Ohio, to Custom Auto Body in North Canton, Ohio. Dave originally received help with the build from Ron Tiestze of Custom Auto Body. Almost 40 years later, Ron's son Randy was on hand to help with the restoration. (Photo Courtesy Susie Koffel)

The stout 392 Hemi was built by Dave and replicates the original engine, which recorded a record 9.23 at 164 mph in 1968. The 1967 Barracuda body is original acid-dipped steel while the fenders, hood, and front pan are one-piece fiberglass. (Photo Courtesy Susie Koffel)

The Flintstone Flyer *Barracuda carried Koffel to many A/XS class wins including the 1968 NHRA Winternationals, Indy, and a number of NASCAR drag races. The restoration involved Scott Koffel and Randy Tiestze, sons of the original builders. (Photo Courtesy Susie Koffel)*

looking more than a little worse for wear. Collector Steve Atwell pried the car from Miller but it appears he did little with it before Koffel once again took possession of the Barracuda. The restoration was completed in 2008 and was headed by John Nickel in Port Clinton, Ohio.

Dave and his son, Scott, built the engine that features the original block and Hilborn intake.

This Barracuda has spanned the generations. Scott was involved and so was the son of the original painter, Randy Tiestze, who laid on the House of Color candy apple red, duplicating the color his father, Ron, had applied in 1967. The restoration just wouldn't be complete without the graphics that were applied by Jim "Dauber" Farr.

Unlike the Koffel-restored Packard, which is race ready, the restored Barracuda is for show only as the original chassis just isn't up to snuff. Dave is lucky enough to have three of his original race cars in his collection. He retired from Chrysler and opened his own shop, Koffel's Place, in 1980 with his sons Scott and Rich. (Photo Courtesy Susie Koffel)

Ingénue 1967 Buick Skylark

The Buick made its debut at Englishtown in May 1967. The car had its most success with the third driver, Bruce Bohen, behind the wheel. Bruce turned a best of 7.79 at 191 mph. In the 1990s the car was on the verge of being modified and raced with a big-block Chevy. (Photo Courtesy John Lipori Collection)

Such was the 1960s Funny Car scene when one could battle the Hemis and Rat Chevys with a better-built Buick. Long dismissed as a car for the Geritol set, Buick entered the muscle car scene late in 1965 and over the next half dozen years, proceeded to turn that image around. Jerry Lipori and business partner Steve Malise did their part in shaking up the troops when, in 1967, they dared to meet the competition head-on with their all-Buick fiberglass Funny Car.

These so-called Funny Cars were all the rage in 1966 and Steve, owner of Brooklyn's Mid-County Buick, was itching to get in on the action. To ease the financial burden of fielding a Funny Car, Steve convinced 19 area Buick dealers to chip in $1,000 each to help finance the project. As Buick performance parts were rare, it was necessary for Jerry and Steve to fabricate many of the parts that went into the car. No big deal for

The World's Quickest Buick in 1967 belonged to Jerry Lipori. The Wildcat 430 retained its stock bore and stroke; it also featured drag racing's first GMC 8-71 blower and dry sump oiling. Enderle injection fed the nitro while Mickey Thompson pistons squeezed out 8.8:1 compression. Like many of the parts, the headers were owner fabricated. (Photo Courtesy John Lipori Collection)

The fiberglass Buick shell is thick and weighs around 600 pounds. This probably saved it from delaminating after all these years like so many older, thinner Funny Cars. It takes three men to hoist the body just to install the prop rod. Future plans call for a thorough restoration and Cacklefests. (Photo Courtesy Hollywood Hank/H. Forss)

the two as they shared ownership of Brooklyn Speed and Machine and had every tool imaginable at their disposal.

Ron Pellegrini at Fiberglass Limited in Chicago was asked to mold two fiberglass skins using a showroom-fresh GS400, which he borrowed from Palmer Buick. Ron retained the second body and campaigned a funny Buick himself. Unlike *Ingénue*, which was a true-blue Buick with a 430-inch Wildcat engine, Ron's Skylark relied on a Chrysler Hemi for motivation. Sometime in the late 1960s, Ron loaned the car to a pair of racers who changed it up by replacing the Hemi with a big-block Chevy. It's believed that the only other fiberglass '67 Buick was wrecked long ago and no longer exists.

Excluding the body and candy paint, Jerry and his partner built the *Ingénue* Buick completely in-house. The 120-inch-wheelbase chrome-moly chassis was a Logghe knock-off laid out by Jerry and Tig-welded by Steve. Getting the power to the pavement was a hefty Buick rear end that carried 3.90 gears inside its Mickey Thompson magnesium center section. A liberal amount of chrome coated the rear end and ladder-bar suspension.

Working your way to the front of the car, a Vitar-prepped Turbo 400 received power from the GMC 8-71 induced 430. Gasser legend Jack Merkel prepared the stock bore-and-stroke engine that received aftermarket

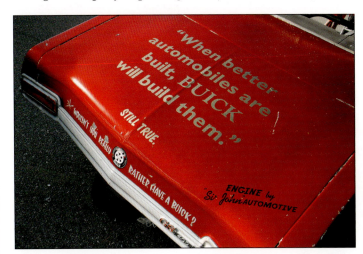

When better Buicks are built, it will be guys like Jerry Lipori and Steve Malise building them. Sir John Automotive on Long Island, New York, helped the guys out with balancing engine components. (Photo Courtesy Hollywood Hank/H. Forss)

The body, chassis, wheels, rear end, and front tires are original to the car. Even though the interior is complete, the previous owner replaced some of the tinwork. (Photo Courtesy Hollywood Hank/H. Forss)

goodies: Mickey Thompson supplied the rods and pistons and Crane helped out with a camshaft and valvetrain pieces. Jerry had the lathe working overtime as he fabricated an intake for the blower and a bottom-end girdle for added strength. Installing the 8-71 blower caused instant interference issues with the vertex magneto, which necessitated the fabrication of a custom timing cover and magneto that drove off the front of the camshaft.

The front suspension consisted of a '66 Corvair steering box, a straight-tube axle, and typical torsion shocks. Bringing the 2,005-pound bullet to a stop were rear-mounted Hurst Airheart disc brakes and a Simpson chute.

During its brief quarter-mile existence, *Ingénue* went through three different drivers. "Coney Island" Ralph Landolfi drove the car during test sessions and once during its initial outing at which he defeated Gary Dyer's *Bronco Buster*. Ralph had previously gained success running a Gasser but had suffered a bad accident that unnerved him. When *Ingénue* popped a blower during its initial outing, it was enough for Ralph and he wouldn't drive the car again.

Rapid Red was next to occupy the driver's seat. Red installed a Hemi from the Dead End Kids' AA/FD but drove the car just once. With nothing to lose, the reins were turned over to Brooklyn Speed and Machine manager Bruce Bohen. Bruce invested some of his own coin into the car and got it running respectable times. He raced the car into 1970 and posted a 30-percent win record before selling the Buick to someone long forgotten.

It's believed the car sat in a New Jersey warehouse for the next 20 years before turning up at an Englishtown swap meet. Nick Hardie purchased the car and restored it to a "barn find" appearance by prepping the body and coating it with a flattened candy red and original-style lettering. Jerry Lipori's son, John, purchased the car from Hardie in 2009 and at this time is working with his father and original crewmembers on a thorough restoration.

Current owner John Lipori, the son of the original owner, purchased the Buick from Nick Hardie who can take credit for reproducing the car's original lettering. Nick, a graphic artist, repainted the car. He chose to go with the "barn find" look that included dull candy red paint and unpolished magnesium rims. (Photo Courtesy Hollywood Hank/H. Forss)

Jim Kirby/Dick Harrell Camaro

The Don Hardy crew built four Camaros in 1968 with Jim receiving the third. Ron Pellegrini's Fiberglass Limited of Chicago provided the fiberglass bodies to Don Hardy; they were formed using showroom models. Halibrand wheels grace the car. The fronts are original to the car while the rears are period-correct replacements. (Photo Courtesy Bill Porterfield)

Like the decade that bore them, drag racing's Funny Cars were evolving quickly. What had started as altered-wheelbase door slammers in 1964 had grown into full-blown, tube-chassis, fiberglass wonders by the middle of the decade. In 1968, if you were trying to compete with anything less it left you out in the cold. Dick Harrell and Don Hardy were a couple of guys who realized this. Don, with backing from Kelly Chadwick, went into the chassis building business in 1968 and built four all-glass, tube-chassis Camaros. The cars went (in order) to Dick Harrell, Mike Burkhart, Jim Kirby, and Fritz Callier. Jim raced his car in AHRA competition beginning in early 1968.

Jim Kirby ran a bright gold injected 427 Chevy and won numerous matches through August. In the meantime, Dick Harrell, AHRA champion driver and record holder, was finding that between regular AHRA events and a grueling match-race schedule, he just couldn't keep up with the demand. He needed a second car and found one by adding Jim Kirby and his nearly identical Camaro to the Harrell Performance team. Jim's Camaro received one of Dick's potent, blown 427 engines along with a new Cadillac Firemist Plum paint job.

The first time Jim launched the car with the new Harrell engine, he enthusiastically exclaimed, "It was awesome." He shared driving duties with Harrell and Charlie Therwhanger through the remainder of 1968. Driving Jim's car, Dick won the "King of Kansas City" at the Kansas City International Raceway.

In 1969, Dick rebodied his 1968 chassis with a 1969 shell and both cars received matching candy apple red paint and gold-leaf lettering. At the same time, Jim's Courtesy Chevrolet sponsorship ended and was replaced by Boemler Chevrolet of Missouri. It was a busy year for Harrell Performance, which culminated in Dick winning the AHRA Championship and Driver of the Year honors.

In 1970, Jim and Dick parted ways. Some say it was because Dick chose to go the Hemi route while Jim wished to stick with his Chevy engine. The Boemler sponsorship

Early Funny Car bodies rarely survived the tests of time. This one wears original Halibrand front wheels and period-correct Halibrand rear wheels. The front and rear spoilers note, "Chevrolet Power Not an Imposter." Some say that this is in reference to Dick Harrell's switch to hemi power in his own Camaro. (Photo Courtesy Bill Porterfield)

ended for Jim and the dealer logo was replaced by "Super Rat" graphics. Jim continued to match race the car through 1972 when it was retired and put into storage. There she sat until 2003 when he put the car up for sale.

Matt Murphy, owner of the GMMG Registry, procured the car and set about restoring it. Matt rebuilt the chassis and 427 in 2006 and relettered the car with its original Boemler and Harrell graphics. Matt realized that a car, or paint job, is original only once and chose to leave the candy paint and gold-laced panels as is: nicks, scratches, patina, and all. Thankfully, Bill Porterfield, who purchased the car in 2009, agreed and left the paint alone.

The car's 427 retains its original Cragar intake manifold, 6-71 blower, Enderle pump, vertex magneto, and zoomie headers. The original Turbo 400 transmission has been replaced with a built Powerglide as future plans call

This is the last remaining Dick Harrell team car that retains its original Harrell team colors. The car retains its rare Eelco "bullet tanks" while the fuel system has been updated. On 95-percent nitro, the 427 semi-hemi produces about 3,000 horses. Approximately 95 percent of the Don Hardy tin is original. (Photo Courtesy Bill Porterfield)

Chapter Two: Funny Cars and Not So Funny Cars 61

for the occasional eighth-mile jaunt. Farther back is the original 1959 Oldsmobile rear end carrying 4.30 gears.

In preparation for those quick jaunts, the rear Airheart brakes have been replaced by Wilwood discs and a Stroud three-point fire system has been installed behind the seat. In 2010, Bill took the Camaro and his period-correct 1968 Chevy ramp truck to the Muscle Car Reunion at Kansas City International Raceway. It was a coming home of sorts. Kansas City was always one of Jim's favorite tracks and it was where Harrell won the King of Kansas City race driving Jim's car.

On hand was the Bruce Larson '68 Camaro as well as Valerie Harrell, Elaine Harrell, and original crewmember Mike Kausch. To the delight of onlookers, the pair of cars staged. With cameras popping on each side of the track the two blown Chevys cackled their way down the track, nitro flames spewing from the zoomies lighting the twilight.

Jim got his chance behind the wheel when Bill trailered up to his shop with the completed car. As Bill recalled, Jim was strapped in and the 427 was fired. Jim's grin was ear to ear and was the icing on the cake for Bill. With the 427 now running on 100-percent nitro, keeping the memories alive, Bill is preparing the car for burnouts, launches, and eighth-mile passes. Stay tuned!

The Jim Kirby Funny Car isn't the only Dick Harrell car that exists today. Dick's rebodied '68 Camaro received the 1969 shell with the beginning of the new season. Today, the Camaro belongs to Dick's daughter Valerie. This staged photo represents what might have been in 1969: Jim Kirby facing off against "the Boss," Dick Harrell. (Photo Courtesy Craig Blanton)

Ed Schartman's *Rattler* Cougar

At the Super Stock Nationals in 1968, "Fast Eddie" played runner-up to the Super 'Cuda after he launched the blower in the final. In the semi finals, Ed had trailered the Camaro of Dick Harrell, reportedly driven by Chuck Therwhanger. (Photo Courtesy Ted Pappacena/dragracingimagery.com)

It seems Ed was destined to spend his life on the race track. His father ran sprints and from an early age, Ed showed a keen interest. He gravitated to Henry's finest and built his first hot rod during his early teens: a flathead-powered '40 Ford. It seems Ed was a natural at this drag racing thing and terrorized tracks around his home in Cleveland, Ohio. In the late 1950s, he'd earned the B/Gas class record in a '55 Chevy. In 1963, he bounced back and forth between his own Jackshaw-sponsored Z-11 Impala and Dyno Don Nicolson's '62 Bel Air. Contracted to drive for Don in 1964, he drove the 427-powered A/FX Comet wagon around the competition to win the winter meet of NASCAR's short-lived drag racing division.

The nickname "Fast Eddie" came about during the mid-1960s when his factory-backed '66 Comet won the first NHRA Funny Car meets defeating teammate Don Nicholson. His win rate hovered around the 90-percent mark into 1967 when he became an S/XS terror by taking major wins at Orange County, Irwindale, and Freemont. His 1968 Cougar (pictured here) ensured he would carry on his winning ways, doing most of its damage match racing.

The new car centered on a Logghe 120-inch-wheelbase chassis, which was home to a 1,500-horse SOHC 427. Backing the potent mill was a C-6 transmission and 9-inch rear end that carried 3.50 gears. Not surprisingly, the Cougar carried suspension components supplied by key sponsor Air Lift. Ed raced the car into 1969, cranking out 7.50 times at a shade over 190 mph. Always moving

The Air Lift Rattler sticker adorned Fast Eddie's Funny Car. Smaller copies were passed out to fans and many appeared on quarter windows of street rats. Air Lift was best known for air bags designed as suspension aids for cars and trucks hauling loads. Today, the company is the top name in air-ride suspensions.

Eddie replaced his 1967 Comet Experimental Stock car in the spring of 1968 with this Fiberglass Limited Cougar and carried on his winning ways. The Cougar weighs 2,050 pounds and recorded a best of 7.50 at 196 mph. Unlike today's Funny Cars, you can tell the make of this one from any angle. (Photo Courtesy Ted Pappacena)

forward and looking to stay ahead of the pack, Eddie had a new Logghe Cougar built for 1969 and the old Cougar was sold minus engine and transmission.

Syd's Automotive of Brooklyn, New York, became the new owner of the 1968 Cougar in 1970 and raced the car as *The Panic Cougar*. They changed out the original Logghe chassis and opted for a new, narrow Funny Car chassis. Into the new chassis went a Ramchargers 426 Hemi and a Torqueflite transmission. The Cougar clocked a best of 7.89 at 189 mph before being retired in late 1971.

The car's history is unknown after 1971 and seemed to have been all but lost until it appeared for sale in *Hemmings* in the 1990s. The ad stated little more than "1968 Cougar Funny Car" but it caught the eye of a gentleman in Atlanta, Georgia, who positively identified it as Fast Eddie's *Rattler* and purchased it. Sadly, he passed away and his estate sold the Cougar as well as a couple of Mustangs and several Boss 429 parts. The buyer purchased *Rattler* as part of the group but had little interest in old Funny Cars and sold the Cougar to current owner Kevin Beal. Fortunately the original Logghe chassis and all the original components came with the purchase.

Today, the car is all original except for the engine and transmission. The body remains just as Fiberglass Limited formed it in 1967 and the tin remains all Al Bergler. The Logghe II chassis is complete with all its original suspension components that include Air Lift air bags, coil-over shocks, tube axle, and a 9-inch rear end. Wheels remain the original magnesiums, and believe it or not, the fronts still mount the original tires.

The engine in the car today is a 1968 Holman-Moody 427 SOHC mounting a pair of ultra-rare (less than 100 made) factory aluminum cylinder heads. Topping the SOHC is a Littlefield 6-71 blower fed by a Hilborn four-port injector. The heart of the overhead cammer is the Crane Nitro 600 camshafts. The estimated 1,200 horses pass through a prepped C-6 transmission.

Kevin called upon Rollie and Dickie Lindblad of Northridge, Massachusetts, to restore the chassis and tin work. Rollie and Dickie have a great reputation; they have built cars for Jungle Jim, Lew Arrington, Fred Goeske, and others. Ed Duval restored the body and sprayed the stunning pearl yellow and white fade paint. Bob Malila did a bang-up job hand-painting the lettering and graphics, which match the original work.

The Schartman Cougar retains the majority of its original parts including the magnesium wheels and original front tires. Steering components are all original as is the chrome plating. (Photo Courtesy Ted Pappacena)

Jungle Jim Liberman's Twin Novas

In 1968 Jungle Jim was the first to field a two-car team with this pair of Chevy II Novas. With Clare Sanders driving the Kanuika car, the team went on to win the inaugural NHRA Funny Car Eliminator that took place at the 1969 Winternationals. Clare had plenty of Funny Car experience having previously driven the popular Lime Fire *Barracuda. (Photo by Doug Huegli, Courtesy worldofspeed.org)*

Russell James Liberman, "Jungle Jim" to you and me, was born in the East, adopted by the West, and loved by all. To simply say he was a drag racer would be an understatement. He was a showman of the first degree and never failed to entertain. He rarely ran NHRA national events; he focused instead on the high adrenaline world of match racing. Jim's life came to an end just shy of his 32nd birthday and many say that the sport has never been the same.

Jungle Jim first gained fame in 1965 campaigning an injected, Experimental Stock Chevy II on the West Coast. The nitro-injected 427-powered Chevy caught the attention of Lew Arrington who soon hired Jim to wheel his blown nitro-fed *Brutus* Pontiac. Driving for Lew, Jim quickly learned that, one, match racing was where the action was and, two, to cash in on the action he needed a car of his own. So in 1966, Jim built himself an altered-wheelbase Chevy II.

He hooked up with Clare Sanders in the *Lime Fire* Barracuda and Don Williamson in the *Hairy Canary* Plymouth and headed east to match race. Jim and company were filling the tracks, entertaining the fans with thousand-foot burnouts and wheelstands that would put some exhibition cars to shame. By 1968, Jim was ready for a full assault on the masses: He fielded not one but two nearly identical Chevy II AA/Funny Cars.

Like all early flip-top funnies, Jungle Jim's Novas appeared stock on the outside but hid a state-of-the-art chassis and components. Both cars featured the best equipment available including Ron Pellegrini's Fiberglass Limited bodies over the Logghe Stage 1 chassis. Al Bergler completed the tinwork while the final paint was sprayed on by Norm "Bogie" Bogill.

A Chevy man through and through, Jim relied on big-block Chevys of 427 inches to power both cars. Both engines were equipped with Hilborn injection and 6-71 blowers feeding on nitro in doses of 55 to 70 percent. Chrysler's proven Torqueflite 3-speed transmissions transmitted the power to an early-Oldsmobile rear end carrying 4.10 gears.

Jim's first choice to drive the second car was Clare Sanders. He ended up taking the wheel of the Steve Kanuika Speed Shops–sponsored Nova while Jim drove the Goodies Speed Shop car. Clare had grown up in Washington but quickly moved to the drag racing hot bed of California. Said Clare in a previous interview, "We just wanted to go fast and win races. Drag racing was our life: 100 percent." Well, in 1969 it certainly became his life.

While Jim focused his attention racing in the Midwest with the Goodies Nova, Clare crisscrossed the United States with mechanic Larry Petrich campaigning the Kanuika Speed Shops car. Jim debuted his Goodies Nova at ATCO in New Jersey where, true to form, he

Batten your hatches as Jungle Jim's Nova rolls in like a storm. Many competitors fell to Jim's Novas, both of which were very competitive. The Jungle Nova is sitting pretty on its Ansen wheels. The Jungle name came about while Jim was still driving the Lew Arrington Brutus *Pontiac. (Photo By Doug Huegli, Courtesy worldofspeed.org)*

64   Drag Racing's Quarter-Mile Warriors: Then & Now

wowed the crowds with a record-setting run of 7.61 at 193 mph. Although Jim wasn't always the quickest, he always entertained and his two-car attack quickly became a favorite with the fans.

Both cars were hauled to the 1969 NHRA Winternationals where Clare's car qualified in the middle of the pack with a respectful 8.03 at 191 mph. All the hot shoes were on hand with Tom "The Mongoose" McEwen taking the low qualifying position with a 7.796. Jim failed to qualify the Goodies Nova but was there with Pete Williams pulling wrenches for Clare.

The final eliminator boiled down to Clare facing off against the Hemi-powered Barracuda of Ray Alley. Clare, a seasoned veteran by this point, made the win look easy, with a 7.88 to Ray's lagging 8.11 time. Recalls Clare, "The day after, the phone started ringing and Jim booked both cars solid with appearances." Clare achieved an 86-percent match-race win-average and his best time turned in the Nova was a 7.53 ET with a top speed recorded being 200.44 mph.

Clare's Nova became the subject of an interesting article in the February 1969 issue of *Super Stock & Drag Illustrated* magazine, "What Does It Really Cost to Build a Funny Car." With most of the car's components laid out for a centerfold photo shoot, the total cost was $24,331.65. Seems relatively cheap but remember, this is 1969 dollars. In 2013, that equated to $157,360. Hmmm, still relatively cheap.

Toward the end of 1969, Clare's Nova was sold to racer Gene Altizer. Says Gene, "I paid $5,000 for the car, $2,500 went to Jim and $2,500 went to Logghe to pay off the car." Gene himself raced the car through 1971 before

A long way from his modified production Studebaker Lark, Jim's Nova was good for 7.50 times in early 1969. Typical match-race money back in the day for a Jungle Jim Funny Car was $2,000. (Photo by Doug Huegli, Courtesy worldofspeed.org)

selling it to Nick Boninfante who campaigned the Nova as *Bushwacker*.

Both Jungle Jim cars eventually became part of the Ralph Whitworth "America's Car Collection" that went under the RM Auction hammer at the Petersen Automotive Museum in September 2009. Scott Davis and Ron Huegli completed the restoration of the "Jungle Jim car" with help from Brett Davis and Dave Loney. Guy Mitchell built the fresh 427 while Leo Giroski did the transmission. Body and paint were handled by Brian Beldin, Fred Davis, and Mark House while Mitch Kim and Bill Kirkpatrick did the lettering and striping. Ron Huegli also restored the "Jungle Clare" car with help from Zig's Street Rods and Parker's Race Shoppe. Both cars are now on display at the World of Speed in Wilsonville, Oregon.

Jungle Jim's Goodie-sponsored Nova was a much-feared opponent on the match-race circuit and won close to 90 percent of its races. If alive today, Jim would be humbled by the restoration, which was carried out by Scott Davis, Ron Huegli, and others. (Photo By Doug Huegli, Courtesy worldofspeed.org)

Chapter Two: Funny Cars and Not So Funny Cars

Chi-Town Hustler Charger

The Chi-Town *team raced a lot of 8-16 car shows and was very prolific. In December 1969 they took the show on the road and won the first Funny Car Nationals that was held at Lions, defeating all the big names of the day. There was nothing quicker in 1969–1970. Says Pat Minick, "It was drag racing's heyday. We lived through it and didn't even know it." (Photo Courtesy James Handy)*

Hustle. Look it up in the dictionary and you'll come up with something along the lines of "to move or act energetically and swiftly." Hailing from Chicago, the *Chi-Town Hustler* Funny Car had no problem moving swiftly. Relying on an Austin Coil–built 426 Hemi, Pat Minick wheeled the car to its first 6-second clocking at his first race in Cincinnati, Ohio.

Pat was a seasoned driver; he raced his own car before hooking up with John Farkonas in the early 1960s. The pair campaigned a couple of Super Stock Dodges including one for renowned Mr. Norm before Pat decided to take a few years off. There were families to support and even though the pair had all but dominated action around Illinois, there was little money to be made.

With the birth of the Funny Car, the pair once again came together and brought in Austin Coil to build the engines and pull wrenches. The first *Chi-Town Hustler* was a Hemi-powered Barracuda that the guys built in the two-car garage behind the home of John's mom. John was an engineer by trade; he designed and did most of the chassis layup himself. Recalls Pat with a chuckle, "We screwed up enough ourselves and didn't need someone else to do it." In all seriousness, the chassis was right from the get-go and required few adjustments. The Barracuda compiled an 80-percent win record before the team moved on to the Charger you see here. Trying to compete with one car while building another necessitated that a lot of the work on the Charger had to be farmed out.

Fiberglass Limited used a showroom '69 Charger 500 to mold the new shell, which was further sliced and diced to bring it down to size. The engine location dictated the length of the hood and where the cockpit was located. To lower the car even more, the driver was positioned to the left rather than over the top of the driveline, which was more common.

As the guys focused their attention on UDRA and AHRA races, they weren't too concerned with the NHRA rule regarding body dimensions and ran what they felt was best. John put the slide rule to work and came up with an ideal rake of 18 degrees. This measure prevented top-end lift that seemed to hamper other cars. Austin Coil put together the cast-iron 426, which, when compared to what we have today, was fairly stock. Aftermarket pieces included the blower, intake, cam, pistons, and rods.

Although the guys had a reputation of "lunching" plenty of engines, Pat states otherwise, "The perception

Chi-Town Hustler *ran 100 times per year, sometimes twice per week and set records at most tracks where it raced. The car was the first in the 6s and hit 6.80s at Cincinnati, Ohio, and Gary, Indiana. The 6-second times were rarely announced as no one else was running them. (Photo Courtesy Geoff Stunkard)*

Lee Austin did most of the tinwork on the Chi-Town car. It had no specific home track but it frequented Union Grove, Cordova, and Martin on a regular basis. The guys usually stuck within a 400-mile radius of Chicago, which allowed them to occasionally run multiple events on any given weekend. (Photo Courtesy Geoff Stunkard)

Austin Coil joined the Chi-Town team in 1966 and according to Pat, brought brains and money. The car had 22 sponsors, more than most, and the guys prided themselves on never having to buy anything for the car. Aftermarket internals on the cast-iron hemi included ForgedTrue, Mickey Thompson, and Engle. (Photo Courtesy Geoff Stunkard)

was that we blew up a lot but what we would do was take the preventive measure of tearing down between rounds. We were probably the first to do this." Another first the *Chi-Town Hustler* can lay claim to is the long, smoky Funny Car burnout. Pat perfected the smoke show during a "match race" against a Top Fuel car. "It was done more to amuse the fans. After seeing the Top Fuel car light them up, I tried it with the Funny Car and it became a real crowd pleaser. All of a sudden every track owner wanted the Funny Cars to be doing them." Although the fans loved it, Austin initially hated it. People were no longer interested in elapsed times and top speeds; they all wanted to see the big burnouts. Of course a side benefit of the half-track burnout was improved traction, which led to quicker quarter-mile times.

Initially backing the cast-iron hemi was a Torqueflite. As times changed, the Torqueflite went the way of the Dodo bird and was replaced by a 2-speed. It was a tough decision, as it seemed no matter where the car went, it set the low qualifying time. The chassis initially consisted of coil-over shocks on all four corners, which later gave way to rear struts and steel straps up front. The rear suspension was a Dana 60, which by 1971 was solid mounted.

The guys prided themselves on a 90-percent win record that the Charger had compiled but by 1971, the troops were catching up and it was time to replace the Charger. The car was sold as a roller to Montreal late in 1971 after Pat's dad complained about it sitting in his backyard and killing his grass. The car disappeared into Canada and didn't rear its head until sometime around 2000 when it showed up in Toronto.

Pat purchased the car, which was rough but pretty complete. The chassis was complete and although the hood had been cut open for an injected hemi, it still retained its original paint. Pat started the restoration before selling the car to current owner Greg Wosley, who completed it. All of the parts for the restoration of the hemi came courtesy of Chrysler and were assembled by Greg and company.

The *Chi-Town Hustler* Charger could easily be judged the most popular Funny Car of the 1960s. Few were as quick and even fewer were as entertaining. The restoration is spot on and was completed with original and period-correct parts. (Photo Courtesy Geoff Stunkard)

Ramchargers 1972

This is where it all began for the Ramchargers. Even though The High & Mighty *looks quite unorthodox, the car was scienced out and worked to record-setting times. This '49 Plymouth was powered by a 354 hemi featuring 392 heads and drag racing's first tunnel ram manifold. This photo was shot in 1960 but* The High & Mighty *had made its debut at the 1959 NHRA Nationals. The car was parted out years ago and has since been recreated by the original Ramchargers group. (Photo Courtesy Dave Davis)*

One could say that modern-day Chrysler performance started with a group of Chrysler engineering students, the Ramchargers. Born in the late 1950s, the Ramchargers consisted of a group of enthusiastic students who decided to take it upon themselves to shake the manufacturer's stodgy reputation by building a drag car. Without direct factory involvement, they debuted their first venture, a 1949 Plymouth, at the 1959 NHRA Nationals. Although lacking visual appeal, the ugly duckling did prove successful thanks (in large part) to the methodical, scientific approach taken by the team members during its build.

A number of successful Ramchargers cars followed: everything from stock-bodied cars to Funny Cars and Rails to Pro Stock. Dean Nicopolis campaigned the last Ramchargers car, a 1970 SS/DA Hemi 'Cuda, through 1986. Over its long career, the 'Cuda racked up 37 class wins. Even though the Ramchargers legend lives on, only two of the original cars are known to survive: Dean's restored car, which sold at Barrett-Jackson in 2007, and the last Ramchargers car built, the 1972 Demon Funny Car featured here. Lost but definitely not forgotten, the Demon was campaigned into 1974 before the crew packed it in because of escalating costs.

Like most Ramchargers cars, the Demon was a standout. With Clare Sanders handling the wheel, the Demon became the first Funny to crack

The Ramchargers were regulars at Detroit and always a crowd favorite. Their Funny Car was the first to crack the 230-mph mark, a feat they accomplished in 1972.

230 mph. In 1971, Clare took over the controls from Leroy Goldstein, who had found the car a handful. Clare notes that initially the car was a little tricky to drive, "Crew Chief Phil Goulet was not one to ever be 'down on power' (way too much horsepower is just about right) so the car, even on slick tracks, required a lot of driving. I would often see tire smoke still curling into the cockpit as I approached the finish line." At times Clare may have suggested that Phil "dial down the combination just a little" if it wasn't the best of tracks. "Use your right foot; that's what we're paying you for," Phil would answer gruffly, through the flash of his knowing smile.

The torsion-bar front end was out of sorts initially but once the "demons" were exorcised, Clare found the car tracked as straight as an arrow. The car carried the front wheels until you hit high gear then settled down into its groove. Powering the Demon was a Hank the Crank stroked Hemi displacing 488 inches. Producing 1,800 horses, the Hemi ran on 85-percent nitro and featured Brock Pistons swinging from Ramchargers aluminum rods, 6.0:1 compression, and an Enderle injection sitting atop a magnesium 6-71 Blower. A flat-tappet cam of Ramchargers design actuated the valves, which expelled the spent gases through a pair of Cyclone zoomies. The original block had been "ventilated" so an exact replacement block was secured from AA/FC racer Della Woods.

Ed Schaider, an original crewmember on the car,

Jim and Julie Matuszak's Funny Car is one of two Ramchargers cars remaining today and was the last Ramchargers Funny Car built. Features include P&S steering and spindles and American spoke mags rims mounting Goodyear tires. (Photo Courtesy Tom Fedrigo)

had purchased a Ramchargers 488-ci nitro engine to race in a front-engine dragster. Ed happened to have the engine; it was just collecting dust in his garage. He generously parted with many of his original Ramchargers pieces, most of which had been run in the Demon in the early 1970s.

The list of original items that are in the current restored engine include the fuel pump, oil pump, dual oil filter housing, oil pan, pistons, red anodized rods, magnesium injector, Danekas blower (reworked GM-671), Mallory Magneto (still set on 60-degrees lead), special baffled valve covers, and zoomie headers. Behind the hemi is a Hays triple-disc slider clutch and 2-speed Lenco. The magnesium rear-end housing holds 4.88 gears and Summers axles. Bringing the car to a halt from its 6.30 runs were Hurst Airheart brakes and twin Simpson chutes. All this rests on a Logghe 4130 chrome-moly tube chassis with a 115-inch wheelbase.

At the end of the 1973 season, Clare left the team and Dick Roseberg took over behind the wheel. Unfamiliar with the car's idiosyncrasies, Dick crashed the car during an early outing. This brought an end to the Ramchargers involvement in Funny Car. It was just as well because for the past year or two, the Funny Car had been a money-losing venture. Sponsors wanted them to race national events but the money was in match racing. The car had no major sponsor so it had to earn money and it just became impossible.

The car was sold to Stan Rosen who repainted the car and campaigned it as *Ego Trip*. The post–*Ego Trip* history is unclear and its whereabouts were unknown until the day it turned up on an online auction site in 2010. John Denski, who watched the auction but missed out, later bought the car from the winning bidder. John ran the car briefly with a supercharged Keith Black alcohol Hemi before selling it to Mopar collector Steve Atwell. Current owner Jim and Julie Matuszak purchased the car from Atwell.

Once it was determined that it was indeed the real Ramchargers car, the hunt for original parts began. Jim contacted Clare Sanders and former crewmembers Ed Schaider and Dorne Rigby looking for original parts. Al Bergler, Dorne Rigby, and Dan Van Auken carried out the restoration, with further help from Dan Cook Racing. Jason Enos sprayed the fresh paint and the lettering was completed by J. A. Mitchells.

With cackle flames fed by a 96-percent nitro load, Jim and Julie's last Ramchargers Funny Car is a real crowd pleaser and leaves them longing for more.

Although the original block was "ventilated" long ago, the majority of parts found on the stretched-out Hemi are original to the car. Its best ET was a 6.39; the best MPH was 230.17. (Photo Courtesy Tom Fedrigo)

There are no wheelie bars on the Ramchargers Funny Car as Crew Chief Phil Goulet didn't believe in them. Goodyear slicks sit on 16 x 13 ET spun-aluminum rims. Rear gears are 4.56. (Photo Courtesy Tom Fedrigo)

CHAPTER THREE

The inaugural Pro Stock race at the 1970 NHRA Winternationals boiled down to the 430-inch Camaro of Bill Jenkins and the Hemi 'Cuda of Sox & Martin. Jenkins' aging Camaro trailered the 'Cuda with a 9.99 time. Sox turned in an off-pace 10.12. (Photo Courtesy Les Welch)

ROCKIN' PRO STOCKS

The "run what ya brung" (and hope you brought enough) heads-up match racing of the early 1960s is where you'll find the roots of the Pro Stock category. The pedal-to-the-metal all-out racing was in direct contrast to class racing, which by the mid-1960s was limited by handicap starts and break-out rules. By late 1968, a group of Super Stock racers headed by Bill Jenkins, Don Nicholson, Dick Landy, and Sox & Martin approached the NHRA seeking a professional heads-up category.

Buddy Martin was the spokesperson for the group and presented rules that were similar to the Experimental Stock rules run at the recent Super Stock Nationals. Engines had to be of the same manufacture as the body and limited to a maximum of 427 ci. No blowers or injectors were permitted but any carburetor, manifold, or camshaft was acceptable. Hood scoops and lightweight body panels were also permitted and all cars, regardless of engine, had to carry the same minimum weight of 2,800 pounds. Even though the NHRA initially balked at the idea, the category finally became a reality in 1970. The rules were similar to those initially proposed: 430-ci maximum, 2,850-pound vehicle weight minimum.

The inaugural race was held at the season-opening Winternationals and saw Bill "Grumpy" Jenkins' Camaro turn a 9.99 to defeat the 10.12 turned by the Sox & Martin Hemi 'Cuda. You couldn't count Sox & Martin out; they went on to dominate the category during the latter half of 1970 through 1971. To break the Hemi Mopar monopoly, the NHRA introduced weight breaks, which heavily favored small-block-powered tube-chassis compacts. At the time, many felt that this was the demise of the category as it deviated from the original heads-up concept.

THE PEDAL-TO-THE-METAL ALL-OUT RACING WAS IN DIRECT CONTRAST TO CLASS RACING.

Al Joniec's Match-Race Mustang

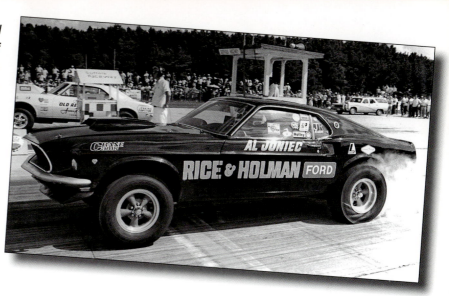

Al Joniec and his heads-up Mustang come hard off the line at Suffolk against the 427 Camaro of Dave Strickler. Al's overhead-cam Mustang was good for low-10-second times and served as his first Pro Stocker.

Al Joniec, a proud member of Ford's Drag Race Team in the late-1960s, preferred heads-up match racing rather than the restrictions of class racing. He has plenty of fond memories running heads-up against Grumpy Jenkins. He relishes having more than once blown the doors off Grumpy with his big-block Mustang.

Al's SS/E Cobra Jet Mustang was unbeatable in 1968. Nevertheless, looking to build a fresh car for heads-up competition, Al dropped $4,200 at sponsor Rice-Holman on this 1969 Boss 429 Mustang. Before purchasing the car, Al measured the engine bay to ensure that it was big enough for the SOHC 427 he planned to install. Once he was sure the mill would fit, the car was driven to Al's speed shop where he and mechanic Bud Rubino went to work converting the car for drag race action.

The new match racer doubled as Al's first Pro Stocker in 1970 and epitomizes how many of the initial Pro cars were built at the inception of the category. Before debuting his class-specific SOHC Maverick, Al and the Mustang made an anything-but-memorable appearance at the 1970 NHRA Gatornationals where he qualified 16th in a 16-car field with an ET of 10.36. By the time the Summernationals rolled around, the SOHC Maverick was good to go. The original Boss 429 was dropped back into the Mustang and the car was sold.

Years later when the Mustang was discovered in Marcus Hook, Pennsylvania, its current owner had no idea that the car had once belonged to Al. It had a 351 Cleveland with a C-6 automatic transmission. However, it was obvious by looking at the VIN and modified shock towers that it was a factory BOSS 429 car. The car was eagerly purchased but was missing a title that dashed any hopes of ever putting it on the street. It wasn't until the second owner, Lou Guglielmo, was located that the missing title appeared. Lou had kept the title after the person he had sold the car to failed to pay him in full. In trade

Lou Guglielmo, the second owner of the Mustang, did an exceptional job building and tuning the Boss 429, turning 9.39 times in B/Gas and C/Altered.

After collecting dust for 20 years, the Mustang was ready for a new lease on life. The 'Stang retains the original magnesium rims. Although she looks pretty rough here, the car was solid and fairly complete.

Chapter Three: Rockin' Pro Stocks

Al ran the car with an SOHC 427. The current owner chose to restore the car with a correct Boss 429. The rest of the car is as meticulous as the engine bay.

The interior of the Mustang appears relatively stock, just as the original Pro Stock rules mandated. Al replaced the factory bucket seats with a single fiberglass unit. A vertical gate shifter with reverse-lockout controls gear changes, while a four-point cage adds a measure of safety.

for the car, Lou was to receive a new Ford F250 truck and $1,000 but the money never materialized.

With the title in hand, the current owner was now free to title the car and return it to the street. Lou now informed the new owner that he had purchased the car from Al Joniec a number of years before. Of course that changed everything and the goal now was to restore the car to the way it was when Al raced it. One exception was made during the restoration: The correct BOSS 429 engine was installed.

Restored, the Mustang made its debut in 2006 at the York U.S.-30 Reunion. Al, seeing the car for the first time in 35 years, was a little overwhelmed. "The car never looked that good," he commented. He later said that he could not believe that his cars were still cherished and admired after all these years. Al's winning ways have made the cars impossible to forget.

The Joniec rear suspension was simple yet functional. Springs were reversed and additional clamps were added to stiffen them up. The ladder-bar front-mounting plates double as support for the four-point roll bar.

The restored Mustang looks ready for action. Brandywine Coach Works in West Chester, Pennsylvania, sprayed the paint, while Dan Danzenbaker applied the lettering. Many refer to this car as the "Mr. Speed Car." If you look closely at the rear quarter panel you will notice the "Mr. Speed Inc." logo in reference to Al's speed shop.

Don Nicholson's 1970 Maverick

Remember when model boxes looked this cool? Jo-Han made some of the best drag car kits and many of us started with this one. Along with his second Maverick, Don enjoyed seeing a number of his cars in scale.

Dyno Don may not have had the most career wins in any specific category but he could lay claim to winning in more categories than any other driver. From Stockers in the early 1960s to the first flip-up Funny Car to Pro Stock, Dyno was a threat regardless of his race category. After spending the early 1960s behind the wheel of a few Chevys, Don became a contracted driver for Mercury. In 1964 he ran a Factory Experimental Comet wagon and later a blown, fuel-burning sedan.

In 1966, he campaigned the first flip-up Funny Car, propelling his *Eliminator 1* to the first 7-second Funny Car elapsed time. Eventually he had the Comet turning consistent 7.30s. It was his fear of injury that made Don jump ship at the end of 1968, leaving his Experimental Stock Funny Car Cougar for a door car in 1969. Purchasing Jerry Harvey's old Factory Experimental Mustang, Don ran the car in heads-up Super Stock and Modified Production, and banged-off consistent 10-second times. Running A/MP at the 1969 NHRA Springnationals, he captured Street Eliminator, defeating the B/SR of Ralph Smiderle with a record time of 10.49 at 120.96.

Don's career was full of firsts. In 1964 he had recorded the first 10-second stock sedan run with his Mercury, which also won 90 percent of its matches. In 1977, he recorded the first Pro Stock 7-second run when he accomplished the feat during a match race against Grumpy Jenkins. Don turned in a 7.97 ET in his Mustang II.

When the NHRA debuted the Pro Stock category at the 1970 Winternationals, Don was ready with an SOHC 427-powered Maverick. M&S Race Cars was the go-to shop for Dyno Don and seven days of whirlwind activities were spent building the body-in-white car. Crew Chief Earl Wade assembled the 427, which featured such goodies as a fabricated intake, Hemi rods, and a Crane Cam. As nice as the car was, the rush build showed in the car's on-track performance.

Dyno Don earned his winning reputation in the early 1960s with a handful of Chevys. In 1963, he was the recipient of one of the only 57 Z-11 Impalas produced. When Chevy pulled out of racing, Don jumped to Mercury in 1964 and continued with his winning ways. (Photo Courtesy Robert Genat)

Dyno Don's first Maverick was built in seven days and debuted at the inaugural NHRA Pro Stock meet in 1970. Qualifying high in the 32-car field, the new car fell early in eliminations. (Photo Courtesy James Handy)

Don's second Maverick was also built by M&S Race Cars and took a little longer than seven days. Hired driver Ken Dondero recalled that the two cars were like night and day. This Maverick is a true survivor and retains all the original pieces; it still carries the original paint and stickers. (Photo Courtesy Geoff Stunkard)

Like any race car, the interior relied on the bare minimum to get things done. The sponsor, Mr. Gasket, supplied the vertical gate shifter with reverse lock to control the Doug Nash 4-speed. Ken Dondero recalls that the tach saw 8,500 rpm regularly. (Photo Courtesy Geoff Stunkard)

The early Pro Stock rear suspensions were primitive yet functional. Don's Maverick carries a Dana 60-series rear end with adjustable ladder bars. (Photo Courtesy Geoff Stunkard)

Earl Wade was responsible for making the SOHC 427 perform. And perform it did, cranking out 9.40 times. At one point, the Maverick seemed nearly unbeatable during match races, going 45 rounds through August 1971 without a loss. (Photo Courtesy Geoff Stunkard)

The Maverick was always in the thick of things and even won an AHRA Super Stock race but because of inconsistencies due to breakage and just plain poor luck, the big wins proved to be elusive. As team driver Ken Dondero recalls, "If M&S built the first car, I don't think they would admit to it. The second Maverick debuted at the Springnationals in 1971 and was much nicer."

Relying on a freshened SOHC 427, Don eventually had the new car knocking out 9.40 times. He played runner-up to the dominant 'Cuda of Sox & Martin at the NHRA Springnationals and grabbed all the marbles at the following Summernationals. Proving it was no fluke, he won two AHRA Grand-American races and defeated Grumpy Jenkins at the Super Stock Nationals.

By late 1971, the NHRA had agreed to weight breaks for the small-inch compacts, allowing the Pintos, Vegas, and Gremlins to compete against the big-block-powered cars. It seemed that the Maverick had become obsolete by season's end; it made its final national event appearance at the 1972 NHRA Winternationals. The Maverick was sold to Robert Rashid in Michigan, then to Rick Hamilton, and finally to Doug Kenny in Florida. Somehow the car remained intact all those years and is a prime, unmolested example of what Pro Stock used to be.

An A&A fiberglass scoop fed fresh air to a pair of Holley 4500 carburetors. Don modified the scoop in search of additional horsepower. Limited by rules to a 7-inch height, many drivers modified their scoops in similar fashion. (Photo Courtesy Geoff Stunkard)

Don's starting point for the Maverick was a Ford-supplied acid-dipped body in white. The trunk lid and front-end panels are fiberglass. Today, the car remains unmolested and is the most original early Pro Stocker in existence. (Photo Courtesy Geoff Stunkard)

Red Light Bandit 1970 Challenger

Bill prepares to "let it all hang out" during a Bakersfield meet. The Challenger was later updated to incorporate a 1972–73 grille, taillights, and a revised paint scheme. (Photo Courtesy James Handy)

Bill Bagshaw's "Red Light Bandit" nickname came courtesy of his lightening-quick reflexes behind the wheel of an early Corvette. His abilities caught the attention of Chrysler reps and in 1968, he was handed the keys to a factory-supported Super Stock Hemi Dart. In 1970, Bagshaw and his Dart joined the heads-up ranks of the newly formed NHRA Pro Stock category. Although campaigning a three-year-old car, he still managed to make it in the tough 16-car field, holding down the number-8 position and surviving until the third round before falling to Dick Landy's new twin-plug-Hemi Challenger. Payback came at season's end when Bill squeezed out Dick to earn the Division 7 Pro Stock points crown.

Bill made do with his Hemi Dart through the summer of 1970 before Mother Mopar supplied him with the Challenger pictured here. The acid-dipped body in white was quickly prepped and a donor car purchased for its trim pieces. What would be considered pure insanity today is the fact that the donor car was a Hemi-powered R/T Challenger. A Southern California dealer had ordered the Challenger and had planned to drag race the car to help promote sales. The dealer went out of business and the Challenger was among the assets. Bill and his car builder, Ron Butler, stripped the car and disposed of the remains.

Ron, a New Zealand–born fabricator, had recently parted ways with Shelby American after production of the Shelby Mustang ceased in 1970. He went into business for himself and leased a building that proved to be much larger than necessary. The two first met when Bill signed a lease on the other half of the building. As the two men came to know each other, Bill quickly recognized just how talented Ron was and proposed that they build his Dodge drag car together.

Bill and current owner John Gastman pose with the stripped Bandit. *Note the liberal use of a hole saw throughout. An optioned-out stock Hemi Challenger could weigh well over 3,700 pounds. This one could weigh as little as 2,700 pounds. (Photo Courtesy Geoff Stunkard)*

Bandit *is primed and nearly ready for paint. When the car was discovered, the hood was missing; it featured a unique scoop reportedly fabricated from leftover Shelby stuff. Bill recalled that running the IR (individual runner) intake, the Six Pack E-body scoop left no room for the carbs. Shortly after Indy, Ron rigged up the new, taller scoop and the car immediately picked up 2 mph. During the restoration, Bucky fabricated a new scoop using old photographs and then Cole built an air box to seal the carbs to the hood. (Photo Courtesy Geoff Stunkard)*

Construction of the new *Red Light Bandit* commenced in spring 1970 with plans to have the car ready for an Indy debut on Labor Day. Ron and Bill went to work using all of the tricks to get the car down to its minimum allowable weight of 2,700 pounds. Chrysler provided a lightweight K-member that relocated the front wheels a little farther forward. To ensure the stock wheelbase was maintained (as per class rules), the rear end housing was moved forward an equal amount.

The Butler-designed chrome-moly roll cage extends from the front suspension mounts and all the way to the rear of the car. Back when three-point "safety hoops" were still in fashion, *Red Light Bandit* had to be one of the safest and stiffest cars in the class. Joe Allread was brought in to build the Hemi, which featured a Racer Brown camshaft, twin Holley 4500 carburetors on a Weiand Hi-Ram intake, and rare aluminum heads. Backing the Hemi is a Lakewood explosion-proof bellhousing bolting up a Hurst slick-shifted 4-speed.

Debuting the car on schedule at the NHRA Nationals, Bill qualified with a 10.12 and advanced to the third round before falling to Ed Hedrick in Bill Stiles' Duster. The debut had to be considered a success, having turned 9.90 times and garnishing the meet's Best Engineered Award. Bill kept the Challenger for several seasons; he continuously updated it for performance gains as category rules permitted.

The original Fenton rims support the refurbished Bandit *and measure 3.5 x 15 front and 8.5 x 15 rear. Approximately 700 hours went into building the car in 1970. I assume a similar number of hours were spent on the immaculate restoration. (Photo Courtesy Geoff Stunkard)*

In 1974, Ron put together a second car for Bill: a tube-chassis Dart Sport, which, despite the unfavorable weight breaks, was fairly competitive. Bill chose to retire in 1976 after crashing the Dart twice in two years.

The current owner of the Challenger, John Gastman, purchased the car from an eccentric southern gentleman in 1994. John traveled south with a large sum of money to purchase a pair of 1993 Vipers from him; he reportedly had to move them as he was in the midst of a divorce. The gentleman insisted on a cash sale and drove John into the country where the cars were located. Along the way, this fellow filled John's head with wild stories of cross-border vigilante activities that he was "supposedly" involved in. John isn't a man who scares easily but he was a little nervous and relieved when they finally made it to gentleman's country home. Looking the cars over, John decided to buy both Vipers, a white Superbird showing 28,000 miles and the remains of an old Challenger Pro Stocker tucked away in the corner. It was obvious that the Challenger needed a lot of work but John thought it would make a fun project. He had no idea of the car's drag race background but through extensive research, he

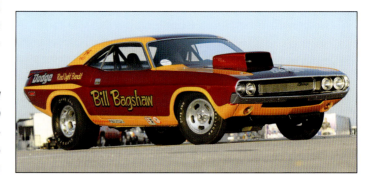

The legendary Hemi dominated Pro Stock in the early days and propelled the *Bandit* to mid-9-second times. Bill Bagshaw, who was consulted throughout the restoration, built the Hemi, which produced 679 horses at 7,800 rpm. (Photo courtesy of Geoff Stunkard)

The restored interior features nothing but the bare necessities. Fiberglass seats, fiberglass dash, Stewart Warner gauges, and a Hurst to control the slick-shift A-833 transmission are original to the *Bandit*. (Photo Courtesy Geoff Stunkard)

discovered that the Challenger was the remains of Bill Bagshaw's *Red Light Bandit*.

According to a Geoff Stunkard *Mopar Muscle Guide* article, the car was handed over to Bucky Hess for a complete restoration. Bucky contacted Bill who told him of a few telltale signs that would show whether it was the real deal or not. Bill mentioned that all his hemi engines were painted red, which Bucky confirmed by scraping off a bit of hemi orange from the engine. Bill also suggested he look at the head exhaust port surface for the marking "Mullen & Co." (Bob Mullens had once worked as a Chrysler engineer). The markings were there. This proved it was the same hemi engine that had been in the car when Bill sold it.

To help along the restoration, Bill went through his treasure trove of parts and found a bunch of pieces he had either removed before selling the car or spare parts left over from the build. As the restoration proceeded, as many of the original parts that could be refurbished were reused. Bucky, his son Travis, and Cole McCallister redid the rear suspension, switching from a ladder-link to the factory leaf-spring layout of 1970. The roll cage was also restored, removing bars that had been added at a later date.

A fresh set of fiberglass fenders from VFN was purchased to replace the worn-out originals. Old photos were used to measure the change in the wheel well location due to the custom K-frame. Even though the car was rough when discovered, it retained a number of hard-to-find original race pieces. Among other things, the car still retains its original radiator, distributor with dual cable drive and rev limiter, the original driveline, along with the A833 transmission and Dana rear end with its 5:13 gears.

After getting exact paint chips from Bill, Travis "TUKI" Hess was turned loose with House of Kolor paints, spraying the car with Brandywine Candy and Sunrise Pearl. The gold-leaf lettering was expertly applied by Nelson Grimes.

The completed Challenger made its second Indy debut, this time in 2012, and was placed on display. Throughout the weekend, throngs of admirers continuously surrounded the car. Bill Bagshaw arrived on Thursday to see the car and, needless to say, was taken aback by how great it looked. *Red Light Bandit* was key to the evolution of the category and its always immaculate appearance and entertaining wheels-up launches are dearly missed in today's Pro Stock.

Bill Bagshaw is all smiles after seeing his restored Challenger for the first time at Indy in 2012. The *Bandit* had made its initial debut at Indy 42 years before. (Photo Courtesy Geoff Stunkard)

Sandy Elliot/Barrie Poole 1971 Comet

John, Sandy, and Barrie pose proudly with their three cars and a sampling of the awards earned for all their efforts. Sandy was voted to the Car Craft magazine all-star team in 1971, earning Super Stock Crew Chief of the Year. The team is probably best remembered for their pair of dominating, striped Mustangs that they used to terrorize Super Stock in the late-1960s.

Through the years, Canada has produced its fair share of celebrated drag racing personalities. In Top Fuel, Gary Beck blistered the tarmac through the 1970s while 240 Gordie Bonin tore things up in Funny Car. In the door slammer ranks, the Sandy Elliot Race Team of Chatham, Ontario, is unquestionably one of the most recognized names. Between 1966 and 1972, the team came to be known as the Border Bandits because of their ability to cross into the U.S. and capture national event victories before sneaking home. The team consisted of Barrie Poole and John Elliot and in total, they competed in 17 NHRA national events, made class finals 16 times, and captured category wins three times while playing runner-up at two more.

Based out of Sandy Elliot's Mercury dealership, the team emerged in 1966 with a 390-powered D/SA Comet Cyclone. A slightly heavier convertible was chosen rather than a hardtop to avoid the factory wars in C/Stock where 45 cars competed for class at the NHRA Nationals. Liking his chances of success, Barrie took the car to Indy where he eventually bowed out in class semi-finals. Locally he fared much better with the Comet, garnishing 34 trophies and a class record.

A 427-powered SS/C Comet wagon followed in 1967 while in 1968, Sandy's young son, John, joined the team. John took the wheel of a Poole-prepped, single 4-barrel 427-equipped Comet sedan and earned A/S honors at the 1968 NHRA Winternationals with an ET of 12.72. Along with the win came the distinction of being the first Canadian to take stock class at an NHRA national event.

The cars we're most familiar with are the 428 Cobra Jet Mustangs. Barrie debuted a fastback at the NHRA Springnationals where he grabbed SS/EA honors. He recalled, "We had the quickest car in class that year with an 11.77." Referring to the Cobra Jet engine, Barrie adds, "We broke a few engines as the Cobra Jets were a little frail. They didn't have very good rod bolts but once we got better bolts and bearings, they lived better. We broke a lot of parts early on but thankfully, Ford of Canada was generous with its parts, although not so much with the money."

A class record came that summer while attending a points meet in Indiana. "I kept thrashing down there that Sunday wanting to get the record. Fellow racer Dick Arons says to me, 'Keep running and you'll get it,' and sure enough I did, turning in an 11.87," remembers Barrie. The Border Bandit legend was born the next day when the team won the eliminator, which didn't make many people happy.

A factory-equipped Cobra Jet–powered Mustang coupe joined the foray in 1969 and so did the memorial black-and-white bumblebee stripes. As Barrie relays it, "The idea for the rear stripes actually started with a meeting over in Detroit. Don Green of Car Craft was with the Rat Pack boys [Wally Booth and Dick Arons] and he was commenting on how they need to do something to make their cars stand out. I brought the idea home and discussed it with Sandy. We spoke to a commercial artist in London, Ontario, who presented some ideas." Added Sandy, "It was probably the most important thing we did when we were racing because it gained us a lot of publicity. The fact we had two cars doubled the impact."

In this snapshot, Barrie Poole looks on as the Comet receives the race team's well-earned stripes. The Poole-built 429 was fed by a pair of modified Holley 660 center-squirt carbs. Barrie fabricated the long runner intake that features an Edelbrock Chevy TR2X plenum.

Coming hard off the line at St. Thomas, the team's home track, the Pro Stock Comet was slow in the making and by the end of the 1971 season, was considered obsolete. Today the Comet resides in Windsor, Ontario.

Barrie kick-started the 1970 season by grabbing all the marbles in Super Stock at the NHRA Winternationals, turning in an ET of 11.26. This was another first for the team as no other Canadian had ever won an NHRA national event. Barrie returned to Pomona the following season and won the whole thing all over again.

Eager to wet their feet in the new-for-1970 Pro Stock category, the boys received a test mule Maverick from Ford and, pulling a lowly 1971 Comet from Sandy's lot, began to build themselves a Pro Stock Comet. The car initially ran with a 429 wedge but a Boss 429 later filled the engine bay. The car never really made much of an impact since the build process was slow and in the early days of Pro Stock, things evolved quickly. Backing the Poole 429 was a choice of either a Nash-prepped Toploader or a Chrysler slick-shift box. A Dana rear from a '69 Super Bee was stuffed with Henry axles and 5.38 gears. SCCA Trans-Am Mustang rear springs and Lakewood track bars helped plant the Firestones.

Pro Stock rules of the day permitted any tire that would fit the stock wheel well. These wheel wells weren't stock; they'd been stretched to allow for additional tire width. During the car's restoration, current owner Ivan Landry also noted the frame rails were "smashed in" to clear the Firestone sidewalls. To make room for the 429, Barrie removed the shock towers, cut a few inches off the top, reversed them, and tucked them under the fenders. The towers were then braced to the frame with round tubing. Drum brakes and 6-cylinder springs rounded out the suspension. Fiberglass panels replaced the front clip while the liberal use of a hole saw throughout the car dropped additional weight.

Changes were coming fast and furious in the early days of Pro Stock, and the lack of a tube chassis pretty much made the car obsolete by the end of 1971. Says Barrie, "We always had the support of other racers and even manufacturers. We ran a Chrysler transmission in the Comet and Chrysler gave us parts to fix it." With a chuckle, Barrie adds, "I think part of it was that they knew I wasn't going to beat them."

Considering that the car languished for 10 years out in the elements, it was in remarkably good condition. The current owner reports the car showed no signs of rust. (Photo Courtesy Ivan Landry)

Restoration of the Comet was completed in the owner's home garage. Welcome helping hands came courtesy of Mike Landry, Mike DuFour, and Bill LaFramboise. (Photo Courtesy Ivan Landry)

Barrie relied upon a home-brewed 429 wedge to keep his Comet in competition. Although hard to see here, the shock towers have been reversed to make room for both the wedge and Boss engine. Owner Ivan Landry relied upon Barrie to ensure the restoration was authentic. (Photo Courtesy Ivan Landry)

The car shows well and frequents events in the Detroit and Windsor areas. Stories are plentiful from onlookers of the days when the Border Bandits pillaged U.S. tracks of its hardware. (Photo Courtesy Ivan Landry)

The Comet was finally sold in 1974 minus the engine and languished in Windsor, Ontario, for a number of years. The second owner installed a 427 and took the car to cruise nights (with illegal tags) but did little else with the car. Now painted black, the Comet was sold again to an owner who did nothing with the car but let it sit in his driveway for 10 years.

Ivan came along in 2000 and rescued the Comet; he spent a year and a half restoring it. The car was modified little over the years and retains the majority of the parts Barrie had installed long ago. Regarding the Sandy Elliott Race Team, John dropped out of racing at the end of 1971 and wasn't involved in the team's final effort, a Pro Stock Pinto that Barrie drove in 1972. During the winter of 1972–1973, Barrie broke his back in a horrific snowmobile accident that brought a premature end to his drag racing days. The Pinto, which showed so much promise, was sold to the team of Gapp & Roush.

Today, Barrie works out of his home garage, building killer Fords for local racers. He has healed well enough from his accident and he now keeps a 460-powered heads-up Thunderbird ready to race. In the late 1970s, John Elliot briefly ran a Poole-powered early Mustang but when the brakes failed him at St. Thomas Raceway, leaving him bumped and bruised, he figured it was time to retire.

Ivan Landry did the Sandy Elliot Race Team proud. The 1969 Corvair Monza red paint matches the original; it was applied by CR Auto Body. (Photo Courtesy Ivan Landry)

Dutch Irrgang's 1972 Vega Wagon

The Jungle Vega wagon in action at the New England Dragway. Dutch raced the wagon into 1974 before growing tired of the sport and retiring. Today, he and his wife own an RV parts and accessories business and travel the West Coast. (Photo Courtesy Marlin Huss)

In 1972, Funny Car ace "Jungle Jim" Liberman expanded his horizons by partnering with Dutch Irrgang and throwing sponsorship behind Dutch's Pro Stock Vega wagon. Starting with a theft recovery vehicle, the pair immediately went to work in Jim's two-car garage; they relied heavily on parts from Jim's previous Funny Cars. Probably the most unique part of the wagon is the early Funny Car–style rear suspension.

Starting with a '64 Olds rear housing that had been used in an early *Jungle Jim* Nova, Jim, with the help of local Top Fuel racer Fred Forkner installed Logghe Funny Car coil-over shocks along with Logghe ladder bars and wheelie bars. To stabilize and equalize suspension loading, a Watt's linkage was fabricated. Filling the rear was Strange axles and 5.57 gears mounted in a magnesium center section. Up front, a Pinto gave up its steering rack, Roger Lamb supplied the spindles, and Hurst Airheart supplied the disc brakes on all four corners. Jim fabricated many of the parts himself including the pedals, motor plates, and various mounting brackets.

Previously, Dutch noted that the car was all steel except for the hood and when it was completed, the wagon weighed less than Jenkins' Vega. When Dutch was ready, he called upon Joe Siti to perform the bodywork and lay the candy blue paint and offsetting flames. Jim was so impressed with how well the car turned out, he had Siti duplicate the paint scheme on his '72 Camaro Funny Car. Rounding out the body was silver- and gold-leaf lettering applied by Jim the Painter.

Powering the wagon, then as now, is a 331, which was initially built by K&G Speed Associates. Internals include a Howards camshaft featuring 0.570 lift, Manley pistons supported by 6-inch rods, reworked Chevy angled plug

Construction of the Vega took place in Jungle Jim Liberman's two-car home garage. Leftover parts from Jim's previous Funny Cars were used throughout the construction. Unlike the carbon fiber billboards you see today in Pro Stock, Dutch purchased his Vega as a theft recovery vehicle. Excluding paint, all work was done at home. (Photo Courtesy Marlin Huss Collection)

The wagon was booked to run against the Sox & Martin 'Cuda in a match race at Aquasco on March 12, 1972, but the race was canceled because the wagon was unfinished. As the promoters had no photo of the car, they used their imagination as to how they thought it might appear. (Photo Courtesy Marlin Huss Collection)

Chapter Three: Rockin' Pro Stocks 81

Dutch qualified for at least two NHRA national events in 1972: the Summernationals and Indy. He gained enough Division 1 points during 1972 to qualify for the World Finals held in Amarillo, Texas. The best times recorded were 9.51 at 152 mph. (Photo Courtesy Marlin Huss Collection)

Jim Bollinger became the third owner of the panel, purchasing the car in 1977. He did quite well, winning track championships at York, Cecil County, and Maple Grove. (Photo Courtesy Marlin Huss)

heads, and a pair of Holleys atop an Edelbrock tunnel ram intake. Horsepower is estimated to be in the 550 range. Dutch, having spent two years as Grumpy Jenkins' transmission specialist, prepared his own BorgWarner Super T-10 4-speed.

The wagon made its debut at Englishtown early in 1972 and immediately drew the ire of tech. They refused to let Dutch run the car as they felt the Funny Car–style rear suspension must be illegal. They didn't know what to make of it, as they had never seen anything like it under a Pro Stocker. Using Jenkins' Vega as a comparison, Dutch noted, "They let him run with Corvair spindles on his Vega and they are not stock to a Vega so what's the difference?" The tech crew finally relented and the rear suspension was never again an issue.

The short-wheelbase car could be a handful but Dutch reported that it launched and ran straight.

However, there was that one incident before the NHRA World Finals when he did take out a Christmas tree.

For the 1973 season, the car featured new fiberglass panels and a new paint job. Dutch went to work for Manley briefly and had the car repainted in the company's candy red and blue colors. "CIRCUS" laid the paint, which included a mural on the rear hatch that depicted a coast-to-coast theme. Dutch left Jungle Jim's team on good terms in 1973 and has said that right before Jim died they had been talking about starting a company together to build Funny Car bodies.

Tired of drag racing and the growing hassle of running the car, Dutch sold everything in 1975. For $6,000, the new owner, George Rupert, got the car and a truckload of parts, which included a half-dozen engines measuring anywhere from 316 to 331 ci. The new owner installed a small-block turbo 400 combination and went bracket racing for a couple years.

The Vega passed through another set of hands before George Shupp purchased it. George had big plans to

By the late 1990s, the Vega wagon was looking a little worse for wear. Although mostly complete, the car obviously required a ground-up restoration. Vega wagons were never a popular Pro Stock choice and it's believed no more than a handful was built. (Photo Courtesy Marlin Huss)

The Vega had a rough life and showed it by the time Marlin came along. Key pieces remained of the original build including the fiberglass dashboard and cage when the car was purchased. Just like the original build, the majority of the car's restoration took place in a home garage. (Photo Courtesy Marlin Huss)

Dutch was skilled at fiberglass fabrication and, during a spell in the early 1970s, he worked at RPM, which made composite parts for industry. Dutch laid up the glass hood, rear hatch, bumpers, and dash for the Vega. (Photo Courtesy Michael Mihalko)

restore the car to its *Jungle Jim* livery but got no further than dismantling the car. What's the old saying about the best-laid plans? The car sat in a warehouse for the next decade, disassembled, as George had fallen on hard times.

Current owner Marlin Huss got word that the wagon was for sale and came to the rescue. Picking up the story, Marlin says, "I knew the Vega well; I saw it run Super Pro and Super Gas. It was one of my favorite cars because it was a station wagon and I knew it was the former *Jungle Jim* Pro Stock car. I had heard that the car was for sale but word was spreading and I knew that if I wanted to own it, I'd better act fast. Within a week, I contacted Shupp and made arrangements to see the car. We went down to the warehouse in Reading, Pennsylvania, to see the car and wow, was I disappointed. The body and bare chassis were sitting on the floor with parts scattered about. As the initial shock started to wear off, I took a closer look at the car and the parts and gradually things began to look a little better.

"The original fiberglass front end had been trashed long ago because it was weak and broken up from 15 years of weekly bracket racing, but a lot of the original parts had survived. The Super Trick wheels were still with the car; the original fiberglass hatch, hood, dash, and rear bumper were there. All of the original Funny Car suspension parts were there along with the Lindblad front coil-over shocks and a T-10 transmission stamped IRRGANG. All the original front and rear Hurst Airheart brakes, Jack Arnew custom A-arms, Moon gas pedal, cut-down Vega gas tank, steering wheel, and the Pinto rack were all there.

Currently, a single 4-barrel and Edelbrock single-plane intake sits atop the 331. The current owner says, "The car is no longer raced and the tunnel ram and twin Holleys proved to be a hassle when it was time to move the car from show to show." (Photo Courtesy Michael Mihalko)

"What I really liked was that nobody had ever updated the car to a Funny Car–style roll cage and the complete chassis was still intact. We worked out a deal on the spot and within a week I went back to get the car. I took my brother and a friend along and we literally picked the car up and loaded it onto my trailer."

Marlin started on the restoration almost immediately, relying on the help of Ken Johns, who fabricated the necessary flooring, firewall, and inner panels. Ken was also there to fabricate replacement suspension pieces to match the worn or missing original parts. Once Ken finished working his magic, the car was hauled to Jeff Ludwig at Ludwig's Custom Auto in Schoeneck, Pennsylvania, to have the body restored.

The first thing they did was to sand the car to find any of the original blue paint to use for color matching. Once that was found, the car went to the media blaster where it was given a "twice" over. The wagon spent close to a year at Ludwig's ensuring both body and paint turned out spectacularly.

Once it was back in Marlin's garage, he and Ken Johns disassembled the car again to install the new aluminum paneling, drivetrain, brakes, and suspension. Dick Gerwer finished the interior with new carpet and roll-bar padding. Jim the Painter was back, 30 years later, to repeat the lettering. Marlin adds, "Jim still had the original stencils and used them to paint the Jungle Jim logo on the doors in real gold leaf, the Briggs Chevrolet logo in silver leaf, the Castrol logo in another gold leaf, and the Revell and K&G Speed Associates logos in another. When done, Jim autographed the stencil and framed it before presenting it to me."

The *Jungle Jim* restoration was completed in 2002, 30 years after it was first built; it made its debut at Darwin Dolls Musclecar Madness show in York, Pennsylvania. Too nice to abuse on the dragstrip, the old Pro Stocker has been relegated to a life on the show circuit.

Chapter Three: Rockin' Pro Stocks 83

Bob Glidden's 1973 Pinto

At the 1974 NHRA Springnationals, Bob earned his second national event win by defeating the independent Duster of Roy Hill. Bob parlayed this win along with wins at the U.S. Nationals and World Finals to grab his first Championship. It seemed that he was a natural after taking his first Pro Stock ride in Bob Frensley's Maverick in 1970. (Photo Courtesy Tom Nagy)

Indiana's Bob Glidden has won everything NHRA Pro Stock has to offer at least once. He started out behind the wheel of a 406-powered '62 Ford. He continued to perfect his driving skills behind the wheel of a number of Stock and Super Stock Fords before stepping into the professional ranks. In his 25 years as owner/driver, Bob and his Pro Stock Fords won 85 national events and 10 championships. At one point Bob went 50 consecutive rounds without a loss, and qualified number-one at 23 consecutive races. These are absolutely phenomenal numbers in anyone's book.

In 1972, Bob quit his day job as a mechanic at Ed Martin Ford and purchased a Pro Stock Pinto from the team of Gapp & Roush. Along with the car came the trailer and spare parts: everything needed to hit the track running. The Gapp & Roush Pinto was one of five commissioned by Ford and built by Tom Smith at Wolverine Chassis in Michigan. In a sign of better things to come, Bob and his new Pinto came close to putting the reigning champ, Grumpy Jenkins, on the trailer at the season-ending NHRA Supernationals. It was Bob's first Pro Stock race and he and his new ride turned a quicker time than the Grump but lost the race on the line to a hole shot.

In 1973, Bob propelled the 351-based 377-powered Pinto to a NHRA U.S. Nationals win over Wayne Gapp and in the process, reset the class record with a 9.03 at 152.54. In his first full season behind the wheel of a Pro Stocker, Bob finished third in the point standings and easily won the Division 3 Pro Stock crown. His wife and acting crew chief, Etta, recalled, "Because we only had one engine, we ran divisional meets only in 1973." That is, of course, until Indy, where they defeated the similarly equipped Pinto of Gapp & Roush.

Coming off Pro Stock Rookie of The Year honors in 1973, Bob was ready to do battle in 1974 with a freshly built Norm Paddack Pinto. Bob captured the Springnationals, U.S. Nationals, and finally the World Finals with the new car. The points race had been a battle all season between Wayne Gapp, Bob, Grumpy, and Wally Booth; by late in the season, the team of Gapp & Roush seemed to be the odds-on favorite. However, Bob and his Pinto were quickly gaining ground. During a mid-season Division 3 points meet, Bob earned an additional 400 points by resetting the class record to an 8.83 at 154.90 mph. At the U.S. Nationals he dropped the record again with an 8.81. Beating Wayne at the same race brought him within striking distance. It took a win at the World Finals to earn Bob the championship.

With a change of NHRA weight breaks in 1975, Bob sold the Pinto and replaced it with a more favorable long-wheelbase 1970 Mustang. Clyde Brandon was the

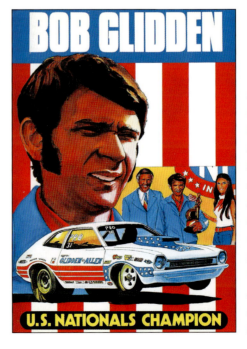

Bob's 1974 press kit touted his previous U.S. Nationals win. Being from Gary, Indiana, this was one for the memory banks as it was his first national event win and it was in his own backyard. Widely known John Jadauga was responsible for the kit's artwork.

84 Drag Racing's Quarter-Mile Warriors: Then & Now

The Pinto interior shows a resemblance to stock with its fiberglass dashboard and twin 'glass seats. A Moroso tach and Stewart Warner gauges kept tabs on the Cleveland while an eight-point cage and five-point harness kept Bob safe. The transmission is a Nash, which at some point in the car's history replaced the Lenco. (Photo Courtesy Scott Hoerr)

The Pinto was purchased at auction and went through a thorough restoration. This was the only car that Bob ever sold with the engine intact. Even though the car's complete history is unknown, the engine remained the same. (Photo Courtesy Scott Hoerr)

Restoration of the Pinto revealed original underpinnings. The trunk held the battery, fuel cell, and weight bars. Rear coil-over shocks can be seen here along with twin fuel pumps, padded wheel tubs, and parachute mount. (Photo Courtesy Scott Hoerr)

The Norm Paddack 2 x 3 chassis mounts a Pinto rack-and-pinion and Hurst Airhearts braking. The lower A-arm is pressed steel whereas the tubular upper arm is believed to be a replacement for the pressed-steel arm Bob initially ran. Note the large-diameter number-1 header tube routes through the upper arm. (Photo Courtesy Scott Hoerr)

The 351 that was sold with Bob's Pinto measures 377 inches. Back when the car was hitting its stride, Clevelands of various inches were trialed (366, 343, etc.). At times, Bob worked 16-hour days searching for additional horsepower; he found plenty in the extensively modified intake and Cleveland heads. Jimmy Barton was responsible for building the restored engine. (Photo Courtesy Scott Hoerr)

lucky recipient of the Pinto and went on to campaign it with moderate success in C/Gas. But the long-wheelbase Mustang wasn't working out for Bob and even though he took the Winternationals with it, by mid-season he had hit a wall (figuratively speaking) and the wins stopped coming.

Enter the Pinto once again. Bob borrowed the car from Clyde and went on to take the Fallnationals and earn his second World Championship, taking the World Finals against Larry Lombardo in the *Grumpy's Toy* Chevy Monza. In December 1975, Bob took the Pinto on one last road trip, all the way to Puerto Rico, before handing the keys back to Brandon & Tunage. Bob debuted a new Don Hardy Pinto at the 1976 NHRA Winternationals and defeated archrival Wayne Gapp. Bob had little luck with the car in NHRA competition but he did earn the IHRA Pro Stock crown.

After leaving the hands of Brandon & Tunage, the history of the two-time World Championship–winning Pinto is unclear. The Pinto was a no sale during a 2011 auction after bidding was halted at $210,000. Since then, the car has passed into the hands of Don Wallace and has gone through a thorough restoration. Today it is one of a handful of preserved Bob Glidden cars.

Wally Booth's AMC Brigade

When AMC couldn't land Dyno Don to head their Pro Stock program, Wally Booth was persuaded to do so. Wally was joined by fellow racer Dick Maskin and Penske carryover Rich Lamont. Wally raced two different Gremlins between 1971 and 1973. The first Gremlin met an early demise when it was lost in a towing accident on its way to its new owner. Backing Wally's destroked 360 in the Gremlins were a BorgWarner Super T-10 transmission and Dana 60 rear end carrying 5.57 gears. Leaf springs, ladder bars, and air shocks helped get the power to the ground.

Wally Booth had built himself quite the reputation drag racing Chevys as far back as the early 1960s. His *Rat Pack* '68 Camaro, rebodied as a 1969 model, was one of the few bright lights in the Chrysler-dominated first years of Pro Stock. He had high hopes for a '72 Camaro that he was just working the bugs out of when AMC came calling. The manufacturer had recently hired Bob Swaim from Ford to head their performance program and wanted to compete in the popular Pro Stock category. Bob had initially set his sights on signing up Dyno Don Nicholson and the rumors were flying at the 1971 season-ending Supernationals that it was a done deal. Well, they say "Never count your chickens . . ." When Ford got wind of AMC's offer, they upped the ante, which AMC failed to match. It was a casual lunch meeting between Bob and drag racer Dick Maskin that led to Wally taking the place of Nicholson.

Wally was considered the number-two Chevy guy in the nation behind Bill Jenkins at the time and with Dick doing the promoting, Bob took up his suggestion to reach out to Wally. Wally took a gamble accepting the AMC deal, giving up his fairly successful Chevy combination for a nonexistent Pro Stock program that he had to develop. The aftermarket offered little help for him and partner Dick Arons. Because of the lack of demand for AMC parts, few manufacturers invested their time or money. Wally would be building the program from scratch and relying on only a few manufacturers including Edelbrock, General Kinetics, and JE to help out.

Between 1972 and 1979, Wally ran a pair of Gremlins and one Hornet. His first Gremlin was based upon a body in white, which he further gutted before having the remains acid dipped. Aluminum floorboards replaced the factory metal and covered a heavily modified chassis. The rear unibody rails were moved inboard before 2 x 3 boxed rails were added that tied the front and rear together. A 10-point chrome-moly roll cage was added to further stiffen the 96-inch-wheelbase chassis and add a healthy measure of safety. A Pinto steering rack was incorporated up front, while a leaf-spring-mounted Dana rear end carried the rear load.

By the time 1970 rolled around, drivers had realized that top-end speed and stability could be increased by getting the car low to the ground. To get the Gremlin out of the air and drop weight, Wally incorporated a Pinto rack-and-pinion steering setup. This Gremlin was sold to someone in Florida in 1973 where it continued to run Pro Stock for the following couple of seasons. It spent time as a Pro Gas car in the 1980s before being parked and slowly parted out. Thankfully it was rescued before it was completely stripped. (Photo Courtesy Greg Rourke)

Wally's 96-inch-wheelbase Gremlin weighs 2,300 pounds and looks good riding on its Cragar aluminum rims. Wally left his mark on Pro Stock: He won five national events, played runner-up at two more, and also won a couple Division 3 points championships. He kept busy match racing through the mid-1970s and maintained a 70-percent win rate. (Photo Courtesy Greg Rourke)

The Hornet was Wally's last ride and in 1976, came within rounds of winning the world championship. In 1978 the Hornet received a face-lift and became an AMX. In 1979, its final guise saw it appearing as a Concord. (Photo Courtesy Todd Wingerter)

AMC provided the 360 block and cylinder heads that had been developed during the early stages of the Penske Trans-Am program. Wally spoke highly of the AMC engine and at one time compared it to the small-block Chevy. To power the Gremlin, he and Arons settled on 354 ci by destroking the 360 and boring the block .080 over. JE pistons were incorporated; they squeezed out a reported 13.25:1 compression. Fueling the cylinders were a pair of Holley 6214 carburetors perched atop a heavily modified Edelbrock UR-18 manifold. The initial Gremlin cranked out 9.50 times and captured a couple WCS points meets, which brought respectability to the upstart AMC.

With a second, more refined Gremlin ready to go, Wally sold the initial car to Jesse Childree and Max Smith of Florida. While in transit, the truck hauling the Gremlin was involved in an accident and the car was lost in the ensuing fire. The pair waited patiently for Wally to make good on the deal.

Running the second Gremlin (Pro Stock's first panel car that was built with the help of Detroit's *Car Craft*), Wally quickly tuned into the fact that Dick Maskin's more-aerodynamic Hornet was more than .1 quicker and a couple MPH faster. Wally wasted little time and immediately started on his own Hornet. By late spring 1973 the Gremlin was headed south to Childree and Smith. The Gremlin was raced into the 1990s and remained in Florida until the current owner brought it home to Kenosha, Wisconsin. The years of dragstrip use hadn't been kind to the car and the restoration was extensive.

Wally debuted his sleek, new, Tom Smith Hornet at the 1973 NHRA Springnationals and noted an immediate improvement. It took a while, but Wally worked the bugs out of the combination and with the help of revised weight breaks in 1974, he gave AMC their first NHRA national event victory. Wally defeated Jack Roush in the Gapp & Roush Mustang II with an 8.95 at 152.80 to Jack's 9.01 at 152.02. As Wally had stated previously, that win probably saved the AMC drag race program.

Bob Swaim had been moved to another department and the dollars allotted to the race program were going to be shifted elsewhere. With the future looking bright, Wally and Dick Arons marched on with further development, searching for that additional 5 or 10 hp that made a difference in early Pro Stock. The pair focused their attention on the flow characteristics of the dogleg cylinder heads.

A little imagination goes a long way and the partners started by sawing four heads in half, horizontally. The saw cuts were at different heights for each pair of heads so that when the top portion of one head was mated with the bottom portion of another, the new combination came out slightly taller. This allowed the guys to raise the port floors, which helped improve flow by creating a smooth radius turn. Plugging the new design onto the flow bench showed flow characteristics improved almost 25 percent. On the dyno, the heads were good for an additional 40 horses whereas on the track, the Hornet picked up .2.

Wally had a very quiet 1975. Although he set the low qualifying time at Indy, he had little to show for his efforts. With another adjustment in weight breaks in 1976, which benefited both the small-block Chevys and small-inch AMCs, some of the shine was taken off of the Cleveland Fords. Ford started the year with a win at the Winternationals; by spring, Wally had it all together and captured the Springnationals. He backed it up with wins at Indy, the Fallnationals, and finally the World Finals where, in the all-AMC final, he put away Dave Kanners with a hole-shot 8.78.

The NHRA reported that Wally came within six rounds of winning the world championship. He played runner-up at the Cajun Nationals in 1977 but by then, the AMC sponsorship deal was done. Wally hung on for a couple more seasons, supporting his drag racing out of his own pocket, before hanging up the helmet in 1979.

The Hornet relied on a bored and destroked 360 that measured 340 inches. Aftermarket goods included Holley, Edelbrock, General Kinetics, and Manley. The transmission was a Lenco, while a multi-link Dana mounted Cragar rims and Firestone tires.

After years of neglect down south, the lone surviving Gremlin of Wally Booth today calls Kenosha home. The car has been painstakingly restored by Donny Schmitz using period-correct parts, including twin Holley carbs and a modified Edelbrock tunnel ram on an equally modified 390 block. (Photo Courtesy Scott Litzau)

Sox & Martin 1973 Duster

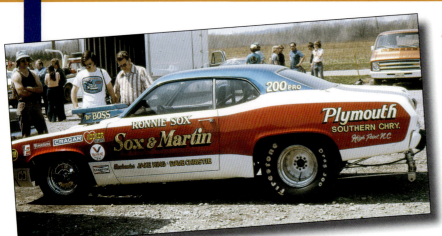

In Chrysler's eyes, NHRA Pro Stock had become so imbalanced by 1974 that the manufacturer chose to boycott the pro category. They ordered their contracted teams out and into the Super Stock and modified ranks. Between 1973 and 1979, Chrysler's once-dominant Hemi won just three NHRA Pro Stock national events, compared to the five won by the "still green to the sport" AMC. (Photo Courtesy Todd Wingerter)

My, how quickly the face of Pro Stock changed within just a few years. What started as the bare-essential rules, 430-ci maximum and 7 lbs/ci for everyone, had deteriorated into multiple weight breaks by 1972. By the time the 1973 season rolled around, the once-dominant team of Sox & Martin couldn't buy a national event victory. The weight breaks, which heavily favored Ford's short-wheelbase Cleveland-powered cars, left little hope for the big-block and hemi guys. Chrysler had no short-wheelbase domestically produced car to compete with and had yet to develop its small-block program. They gave it their best shot with the hemi in the subcompact Duster or Dart Sport.

Ronnie Sox and Buddy Martin fielded their final factory-backed effort in 1974, campaigning the Duster seen here. The same season, Chrysler canceled its Pro Stock program. It was easy to deduce that with the additional weight placed on the hemi cars, there was no way they stood a chance of winning.

Sox & Martin were in the market for a new car after losing their earlier Duster in an on-track accident. At a St. Petersburg, Florida, race the Duster sustained major damage after the brakes locked on the top end

Erik Lindberg was called upon to restore the paper-thin body. Like the original, expandable foam was used to help strengthen the body. In its day, the body flexed at speed despite being steel. Wheels on the Duster are period-correct Cragar Super Tricks. (Photo Courtesy Geoff Stunkard)

Ronnie did his best driving with a 4-speed Hurst and switching to a Lenco only seemed to slow him down. The all-business Duster is one trick piece and makes use of magnesium floorboards, fiberglass seats, and dash. Note the fabricated lightweight clutch and brake pedals. (Photo Courtesy Geoff Stunkard)

causing the car to slide into a light pole. Ronnie walked away from the crash but the Duster sustained extensive damage. The news was no better in the other lane as the opponent, Larry Lombardo, crashed Jenkins' championship-winning Vega.

Ronnie and Buddy had to look no further than Don Grotheer for their new ride. Don had recently lost his factory backing and was looking to part with his Duster. Don's car was one of the sweetest things going at the time; it featured a Don Hardy tube chassis and many magnesium parts. As was typical of the time, the body was acid dipped and featured such subtle changes as a slightly altered wheelbase. Additional weight savings was found in fiberglass fenders, hood, and trunk lid as well as narrowed glass bumpers.

Although the car showed promise with solid 8-second match-race times, the weight breaks made it uncompetitive in legal competition. Powering the Duster was a stock-inch hemi that produced approximately 750 horses. It relied on all the proven parts of the day including a Weiand tunnel ram mounting a pair of 4500 Holleys, Mallory dual ignition, Milodon wet sump oiling, and aluminum cylinder heads. To further reduce vehicle weight, the block itself lost an additional 40 pounds by drilling and grinding. No one could throw a stick like Ronnie and in place of the trendy Lenco went an A833 4-speed, at least temporarily. Under pressure from Chrysler, the team was later forced to install a Lenco and in Ronnie's own words, "The car slowed down." Power was transmitted to a four-link rear suspension and Dana

Although the engine is not original, the twin-plug hemi is all Sox & Martin. Twin Holleys sit atop a highly modified Weiand intake. The engine setback meets the rules of the day. (Photo Courtesy Geoff Stunkard)

A Don Hardy chassis supports a four-link suspension and coil-over shocks. It's a basic setup by today's standards but it got the job done. The fabricated rear features a Ramchargers magnesium center section. (Photo Courtesy Geoff Stunkard)

rear end that featured a Ramchargers magnesium center section and 5.57 gears.

With the Sox & Martin partnership ending in 1974, the Duster went up for sale and found a buyer in Anthony Christopher. Anthony spent a number of years racing the Duster around his home state of Ohio before selling it. The history of former owners is spotty, but it was parked for some time before Dean Klein purchased it in the mid-2000s. The car was in remarkable condition and, except for the original engine and transmission, it retained all the trick parts. Even though it is not the original engine, it is a hemi built by the Sox & Martin team. Dean spent approximately eight months restoring the car and relied on Heath Hite to restore the paint. Today the car is a welcome part of Kathy and Greg Mosley's collection.

Sox & Martin pretty much owned NHRA Pro Stock through 1971 with nine wins and two runner-up finishes. They parted with their Duster and briefly campaigned a match-race Hemi Colt before splitting as a team. Heath Hite completed the restoration at the direction of then-owner Dean Klein. (Photo Courtesy Geoff Stunkard)

Dick Landy's 1973 Dart Sport

It's 1975 and Dick is captured at Ohio's National Trails for the 11th running of NHRA Springnationals. He qualified 14th overall with a higher-than-average 9.17 but he fell in the first round to Larry Huff. (Photo Courtesy Todd Wingerter)

Before the inaugural NHRA Pro Stock meet at the Winternationals in 1970, Dick Landy and his line of Dodges were a dominating force in Super Stock and Modified Eliminator. When he showed at the winter meet with a Hemi Challenger, you knew he had to have been one of the odds-on favorites to win it all. However, he proved to be a little too eager against the eventual winner, Bill Jenkins; Dick fell to a red light in the third round.

Things got no better for Dick and the Mopar contingency as the 1970s unfolded. With the NHRA hammering them with additional weight at every turn, he focused the majority of his attention on running AHRA events. The Dart Sport (shown here) is one of three (possibly four) cars built in 1973 by Dick in conjunction with chassis builder Kent Fuller. Recipients of the other two cars were Larry Huff, who received a second Dart Sport, and Irv Beringhaus, who received a Plymouth Duster.

All three Darts started out as bodies in white and each paid a visit to Aerochem for an acid bath as a way of eliminating unwanted weight. To remove additional pounds, fiberglass panels replaced the front clip, bumpers, and trunk lid, while Lexan replaced most glass. The 108-inch-wheelbase Kent Fuller chassis features rack-and-pinion steering, which was a Pro Stock staple by 1973.

Larry ran his Landy/Fuller Dart into the spring of 1976 before the car was purchased by Dick. Larry drove the car to the AHRA Pro Stock Championship in 1974. Here he is seen during the summer of 1975, heating the hides before a trip down Ohio's famed Dragway 42. (Photo Courtesy Todd Wingerter)

Originally built in 1973, the Landy Dart was restored in 2002 and features paint by Randy Mueller. Sometime in 1975, Dick updated to the new-style grille. All body panels and Cragar Super Trick rims are original to the car. (Photo Courtesy Geoff Stunkard)

Dick's hemis were always some of the quickest in the nation and the one powering his Dart was no exception. To help bang off track-record-setting 8.50 times were proven parts from Holley, Weiand, Crane, and Hooker. Fuel came courtesy of a pair of Carter pumps while Dick's own dry sump system oiled the hemi. The remainder of the driveline consisted of a Weber clutch, Lenco 4-speed planetary transmission, bulletproof Dana rear end supported by Koni shocks, and multilink suspension. Larry Huff initially campaigned the car pictured here; it helped earn him the 1974 AHRA Pro Stock Championship. Larry put the car up for sale late in 1976 and it was purchased by Dick after he crashed his own car.

Dick raced the Dart into 1978 when he took a hiatus from drag racing to focus his attention on Dick Landy Industries and building engines for others. His final Pro Stock effort came in 1980 when he campaigned a small-block-powered Omni. The Dart was sold to Dave Giese minus the engine and the Landy paint scheme. Dave dropped in a wedge engine and ran the Dart as a Pro Gasser for a couple of seasons before retiring.

Unlike many of these old drag cars, this one had not been heavily modified or cut up over the years. When purchased by Dean Klein in 2002, there was no major reconstruction required. Dean hired Erik Lindberg to head up the restoration and called on Dick himself for technical assistance. Dick also supplied the hemi, an engine that features period-correct twin Holley 6214 Dominator carburetors on a modified Weiand intake manifold,

Dick made use of both the single- and twin-plug heads in 1976 and supplied the single-plug engine for the restored car. The twin-plug head is something he perfected for the good folks at Chrysler. Note the trimmed (and filled) cowl, which was necessary to clear the Weiand intake manifold. (Photo Courtesy Geoff Stunkard)

This interior is all business and features fiberglass seats and dashboard. Original Stewart Warner gauges monitor the hemi, while Lenco levers helped move Dick through the four gears in a hurry. (Photo Courtesy Geoff Stunkard)

The rear view of the Dart highlights the Dana 60, wheelie bars, and twin electric fuel pumps. The Dart needed only a little bit of freshening when it was discovered. Dean received permission from Dick to paint the car its original colors. (Photo Courtesy Geoff Stunkard)

single-plug aluminum heads, and a set of Hooker's finest. Randy Mueller applied the paint and relied on photos for correctness; Dick supplied the original paint codes. The proverbial icing on the cake was the lettering that was applied by Brian Truesdell. The restoration of the Dart Sport was completed in 2003 and today the car is in the hands of Marco DeCesaris.

Ronnie Sox's Hemi Colt

Match-racing Pro Stockers were all the rage in the mid-1970s and the Hemi Colt driven by Ronnie Sox was in the thick of the action. This is a scene that was repeated weekly: Ronnie doing battle with Grumpy Jenkins at Pittsburgh. (Photo Courtesy Bill Truby)

The fact that the Hemi Colt was outlawed from competing in NHRA Pro Stock because of its short wheelbase and its import status didn't really matter. NHRA Pro Stock wasn't the only game in town. The Colts competed strongly in IHRA, AHRA, and UDRA competition as well as in NHRA's own Altered and resurrected Factory Experimental categories. By the middle of 1974, a number of Colts had been constructed with outfits including Mr. Norms, Gary Dyer, The Rod Shop, and the Mutt Brothers getting in on the action.

The Mutt Brothers turned to Don Hardy to build their Colt chassis and the team of Sox & Martin to supply them hemi engines measuring 366 and 428 inches. Randy Dorton tuned the Colt and the team competed with the car in NHRA A and B/Altered along with IHRA Pro Stock. With the split of Sox & Martin, Ronnie was hired to drive the Colt; 8.40 ETs became the norm. Although these short-wheelbase Colts had a reputation for being ill-handling, Ronnie had no real issues with the Hardy-built car. He put this down partly to the fact the car had a finely tuned chassis that featured a wheelbase a couple inches longer than the standard Colt's 95.3 inches.

With team leader Eugene Coard walking away from Pro Stock because of the weight-break issue, both their Pro Stock Duster and the Hemi Colt went up for sale. Ronnie continued to run the Colt as late as 1976 before Dave Heitz bought it. Dave partnered with Joe Siglar to run the car in A/FX. With Joe at the wheel and Dave pulling wrenches, the car ran a quick 8.32 in 1977.

As speeds of the Colts increased, so did their poor reputation. The high-profile death of Don Carlton in 1977 behind the wheel of a Colt, in combination with

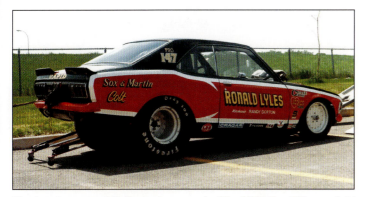

The hemi-powered Colt was borne out of the NHRA's stifling weight breaks placed upon Chrysler's legal Hemi Pro Stockers. Even though it was illegal to run in NHRA Pro Stock because of its short wheelbase and import status, the Colt found a home in the alternate sanctioning bodies and match racing. Ronnie Lyles built his in 1974 and was a dominating force in the NHRA Altered classes, match races, and UDRA action. (Photo Courtesy Dan Williams)

This Hemi Colt has quite the history, passing through the hands of the Mutt Brothers, Ronnie Sox, Bill Stepp, and Dave Heitz. It has run Pro Stock, Altered, and Factory Experimental, posting record times in the 8.30s. (Photo Courtesy Geoff Stunkard)

changing NHRA rules, spelled the beginning of the end of the cars' popularity. Dave said good-bye to his car, sold it in the early 1980s, and briefly retired from drag racing to tend to his transmission business.

As the old saying goes, once the drag racing bug is in your system, it never leaves. Dave was no exception. He sought out the owner of the Colt and bought the car back. He upgraded the chassis, certified it to run 8-second times, and ran the car well into the 1990s as a Nostalgia Pro Stocker. Dave had no problem putting the car well into the 8.60 range.

It seems that few drag cars were as exciting as a Hemi Colt but Dave managed to find one in the Pro Mod '58 Plymouth dubbed *Christine*. The Colt was sold again and passed through a number of owners before Clark Rand purchased it in 2005. Clark had AAA Restorations go through the car and paint it the old Ronnie Sox colors. Today, Greg and Kathy Mosley own the car and should the occasion ever arise, the Hemi is still raring to go and ready to pump out 8-second times.

The Colt is no mantelpiece as its current hemi and drivetrain make it capable of running 8-second times. Twin Holleys sit atop a fabricated intake manifold and aluminum heads. (Photo Courtesy Geoff Stunkard)

The Ronnie Sox Colt was last raced in the 1990s when it clocked 8.60 times running with the National Nostalgia Pro Stock Association. The Hemi Colts were the most feared drag cars of their time and to drive one took some mighty big cajones. (Photo Courtesy Geoff Stunkard)

Chapter Three: Rockin' Pro Stocks

Grumpy's Toy X 1972 Vega

Bill "Grumpy" Jenkins revolutionized Pro Stock in 1972 when he debuted his small-block-powered Vega, *Grumpy's Toy IX*. It brought an immediate end to Chrysler's domination and for the next 10 years, set the tone in Pro Stock. Seen here is *Grumpy's Toy X*, Bill's second Vega, which debuted at the 1973 NHRA Gatornationals. He pushed the rules to the limit with his new car, which started out as a gutted acid-dipped body in white. Super crewmember Ed Quay welded up the yards of chrome-moly tubing while Bill went to work building the potent 331-inch engine.

Driver Larry Lombardo looks on as Grumpy makes necessary adjustments to the twin Holley 660-cfm center-squirt carburetors. The Edelbrock TR-1Y manifold has been heavily reworked. The plenum was reduced in size by approximately 50 percent while the runners' length and volume were also modified. Grumpy's Vegas were the only Pro Stock Chevys to win an NHRA national event in the Ford-dominated years of 1973, 1974, and 1975. (Photo Courtesy Michael Mihalko)

Grumpy campaigned the Vega into 1975 with team driver Ken Dondero making use of the car in AHRA competition. Using both the Vega and Grumpy's later Monza, Ken won the AHRA Championship with 8.50 clockings. Grumpy sold the Vega to Jack Trost who ran it for a of couple years in modified eliminator. Paul Thimms Jr. became the next owner and successfully bracket-raced the car. It was a dreary early morning in 2011 when this photo was shot. This was the day that Paul parted with the car; he sold it to current owner Mark Pappas. Paul had hoped to restore the car someday but was realistic enough to know it was out of his realm. Getting to know Mark, Paul quickly realized that the car was going to the right person. (Photo Courtesy Mark Pappas)

Although the Vega originated with a 1973 fascia, its final configuration was with a 1974 front clip. Mark chose to restore the car this way. The restored 331 is probably the last small-block Chevy Grumpy worked on. Sadly, Grumpy didn't survive to see the restoration completed. (Photo Courtesy Mark Pappas)

Westside Motor Coach performed the restoration. The Vega was repainted its original Chevy Ermine White and Ford Poppy Red. A Lenco transmission was installed behind the Jenkins-built 331. To date, four of the seventeen Grumpy's Toys cars have been restored. (Photo Courtesy Greg Rourke)

Grumpy's Toy XI 1974 Vega

Grumpy Jenkins collected his last national event win as a driver at the 1975 NHRA Springnationals. He drove the Vega to an 8.98 at 152.28 to defeat Roy Hill's Duster, which turned in a 9.16 at 149. Grumpy's Toy XI was the only Chevy to win any NHRA national events in 1974. The quickest class legal time turned in by the Vega in 1974 was an 8.74 at 154 mph. (Photo Courtesy Tom Schiltz)

Bill "Grumpy" Jenkins was a true drag racing legend whose reputation for winning long preceded *Grumpy's Toy XI*. He first gained fame in the early 1960s building winning Mopars, Junior Stockers, and the *Old Reliable* Chevys for Dave Strickler. Between 1961 and 1963, the *Old Reliables, I* through *IV*, dominated categories from Stock through Factory Experimental.

In 1965, Bill climbed behind the wheel of a Super Stock Plymouth and took Top Stock at the NHRA Winternationals. The following season saw the debut of the first of 17 *Grumpy's Toys* Chevys. Bill took on the big-blocks and Hemis with a 327-ci Chevy II and would have owned A/S with its low-11-second times if it weren't for the one street Hemi of Jere Stahl. Bill took on the Super Stock ranks through the late 1960s with a number of Camaros before graduating to Pro Stock in 1970. He won the inaugural Pro Stock race, downing the still-fresh Sox & Martin Hemi 'Cuda with his three-year-old Camaro.

Bill's status as the man who couldn't be beaten grew with an NHRA Pro Stock World Championship win in 1972. That season, his revolutionary, 331-ci-powered Vega won six of seven NHRA National events entered.

How popular was the one they called Grumpy? In 1973, *TIME* magazine carried an article enlightening the outside world on the nation's highest-paid sports figure. *TIME* gave a brief history on the man they referred to as "Grumpy the Drag King" and took the time to break down his earnings based upon his trips down the race track. They calculated that Bill was pulling in $5,650 per minute.

Grumpy's Toy XI, a 1974 Vega, was by far the most innovative Pro Stocker to date. What made this car unique among Pro Stockers of the day was its full-tube chassis, the McPherson strut, rack-and-pinion front suspension, and dry sump oiling system. These innovations remain staples in the Pro Stock category to this day.

Unlike the Grump's previous two Vegas, *Grumpy's Toy XI* was a true full-tube-chassis car. Bent by SRD Race Cars to Bill's own specifications, the new chassis extended through the fabricated firewall, eliminating the last of the stock Vega underpinnings. The folks at Jenkins Competition designed the front suspension in conjunction with Dick Whitman at SRD and Roger Lamb of Lamb Components.

Skipping through a magazine one evening, Bill's employee Ed Quay spotted an advertisement for a car

The nearly complete skeleton of Grumpy's Toy XI *is laid up on the chassis jig at SRD. The completed chassis weighed a shade more than 100 pounds. Note the high-strut mount that required additional hood clearance. The strut was modified on later* Toys, *allowing for a lower profile.*

The acid-dipped body is in place so final fit and finish can be carried out. The wheel tubs were fabricated from lightweight aluminum and the 4130 chrome-moly tubing was Tig- or Heliarc-welded.

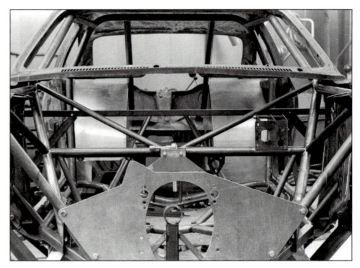

A head-on shot of the nearly complete chassis reveals the fabricated motor plate, underdash cross bracing, and wheel tubs. Motor plates were fabricated for both small- and big-block engines, even though a big-block was never installed.

that incorporated the suspension design and thought it was exactly what they needed to free up room in the new car. "We always had problems in the previous Vegas with the A-arm front suspension, trying to gain enough room for the headers to exit the head without a quick turn."

Roger Lamb said, "Bill invited me to come east as they had an idea for a strut suspension. The idea was to get the car down out of the air and open up the engine compartment." Roger laid up the plans on paper and, once given the dimensions (top mount, center line, etc.), went to work. The fabricated uprights were bolted to a set of Lamb-designed struts, which were loosely based upon Datsun 240Z units but at approximately one-third of the weight.

The strut dictated the general layout; for geometry purposes, the spindle was at the strut centerline and the upper strut mount was high. The struts bolted to the upper chassis tube that doubled as the engine plate mount. The struts were so high that the hood required notching for clearance. Finishing the suspension was your basic Pinto rack, fabricated tubular lower control arms, and 1/8-inch steel cables incorporated to limit suspension travel. The new chassis and strut suspension cut approximately 150 pounds off the new car over the previous Vega.

To compensate for driver weight the 680-hp 331 Lenco transmission and rear end were offset 1 inch to the passenger's side of the car. The Lenco transmission carried a 2.95 first gear, while shortly into the season the initial 12-bolt rear end gave way to a Dana unit that

Jimmy Smith at Street Customs in Mooresville, North Carolina, shot the GM Ermine White and the 1950–1960 Ford Poppy Red to match the original colors. Jim the Painter did the stripes and lettering, just as he had in 1974. (Photo Courtesy Scott Hoerr)

Restoration of the Grumpy's Toy interior is nearing completion showing the protected tinwork installed and the Lenco levers poking through the tunnel. Accel ignition components are mounted inside to keep them away from the heat of the engine bay. (Photo Courtesy Scott Hoerr)

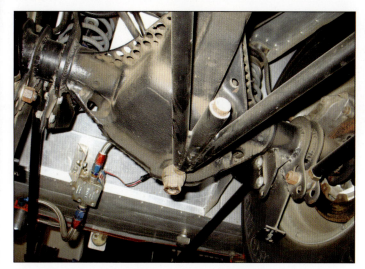

The drilled Dana housed gearing up to 6:176.17 and was supported by a Jenkins-designed three-link suspension. Springs are Chevy Corvair units, the shocks are Koni, and the rear disc brakes are Hurst Airheart. (Photo Courtesy Scott Hoerr)

The heart of *Grumpy's Toy XI* was the 680-horse 331. A pair of heavily modified Holley Dominator carbs is fed through an equally trick Edelbrock TR-1X manifold. Compression was in the neighborhood of 15:1. Having a back door to General Motors, Bill was able to have the cores to the 292 Turbo cylinder heads modified to his liking. (Photo Courtesy Scott Hoerr)

measured 40 inches across and usually housed 6.17 gears. Supporting the rear was Bill's own design three-link rear suspension with its 48 possible positioning points.

The body in white was shipped to Aerochem and given a dip in their acid bath to remove excessive weight. Expandable foam was then used in strategic locations to give added support to the lightened body. Fiberglass bumpers, hood, and rear hatch were hung before Jack Trost laid on the Ermine White paint. Jim the Painter was given the chore of laying on the lettering.

Bill debuted the Vega in March 1974 at ATCO Raceway during a match race against the Cleveland-equipped Pinto of Gapp & Roush. He defeated Wayne Gapp three straight times, turning a best of 8.86 at 152 mph. With Chrysler's ongoing boycott of NHRA Pro Stock due to what they felt were unfair weight breaks of 7 lbs/ci, the category became very much a Chevy versus Ford versus AMC battle. The superior Cleveland-headed Fords, which were the odds-on favorite at any given event, ran the same 6.65 lbs/ci as the small-block Chevrolet.

For the third year running, Bill and his super crew won the NHRA Summernationals. With Larry Lombardo behind the wheel, the Vega defeated Scott Shafiroff, Bob Glidden, and Dave Kanners in his AMC Hornet X before meeting the Gapp & Roush's new four-door Maverick in the final round. In what must have been one of the most satisfying races of his career, Larry strapped a hole-shot lead on Wayne, which he just couldn't make up. The Vega tripped the lights with a 9.11 at 150 to Wayne's quicker but losing 9.02 at 151.77.

Top Fuel racer Don Garlits organized the Third Annual National Challenge drag race in 1974 and Bill, having won the previous two, attended with hopes of making it a three-peat. The Professional Racers Organization held that year's race at the New York Speedway the weekend before the NHRA Nationals. Although the $15,000 win money, which now included contingencies, was down from the previous year's payout, it was still close to double what the NHRA was paying for a professional category win at the Nationals.

In a blow-by-blow dissection of the event, *Super Stock & Drag Illustrated* reported that the race went down as one of the worst in history due to its poor organization,

Joe Tryson was Bill's engine assembler and right-hand man for close to 35 years. He was called upon to rebuild the 331. Here Joe lends a hand during the first firing of the car. (Photo Courtesy Scott Hoerr)

Chapter Three: Rockin' Pro Stocks 97

an inadequate field of cars, poor weather, and a lack of attendance. The Pro Stock field, which generally ran 32 cars, had to make do with the 23 that showed up for the event. All Pro Stockers ran at the same 6.75 lbs/ci and even though one would think that this would favor Chrysler's Hemi cars, things played out differently. Bill qualified his Vega .10 second quicker than the fastest Hemi.

On Bill's march to another final-round appearance, he put away the Ronnie Sox, Don Carlton, and Gapp & Roush. In the final go, he showed the Hemis once and for all that his small-block Vega could meet them head-on by defeating Mike Fons' *Motown Missile* 'Cuda.

In winning the event, Bill banged-off times of 8.81, 8.81, 8.79, 8.78, and 8.80 at speeds in excess of 155 mph.

Looking to overcome the advantage of the Cleveland-powered Fords, Bill built himself a new Pro Stocker in mid-1975 based upon the aerodynamically superior Chevy Monza. The last race for the well-worn Vega was the 1975 NHRA Summernationals where team driver Larry Lombardo fell to Wayne Gapp in the final round. Bill sold the Vega to Harold McCready immediately after the race. Harold removed the *Grumpy's Toy* stickers and ran the car for the next few seasons, "horsing around" with a 302.

Glen Sharp then bought the Vega, performed a restoration, and sold the *Grumpy's Toy* in 2007 for a cool $525,000. The Vega was torn down once again and gone through thoroughly by Scott Hoerr for current owner Don Wallace.

Grumpy's Toy XI has its place in drag racing history. It played a key role in the evolution of Pro Stock, having introduced many key components that are still in use. Today, the restored Vega has proven to be too valuable to race. It now only makes special appearances. (Photo Courtesy Scott Hoerr)

The Mopar Missile That Wasn't

Have no doubt: This would have been the fourth Pro Stock Missile *car had Chrysler not pulled the plug on its Pro Stock program. The car went way beyond the Pro Stockers of the day and featured extensive use of magnesium and titanium. It's hard not to look at the car and think what might have been. (Photo Courtesy Arnie Klann)*

What you're looking at here folks is the Pro Stocker that never was. This '74 Duster, the "wire car" as it has come to be known, is the last of Chrysler's test cars in their once-bright early-1970s Pro Stock program. The same group who brought us the *Mopar Missile* cars engineered this car; no doubt this would have been the next *Missile*.

The *Motown Missile* group first came to prominence in 1970 with a tricked-out Hemi-powered Challenger. The group's main objective in building the car was to research, develop, and test parts that would benefit Chrysler's contracted teams. In 1972 a 'Cuda replaced the Challenger; both were powered by a Ted Spehar–built, twin-plug Hemi. Things were progressing quickly in the early days of Pro Stock and even though the car featured such innovations as rack-and-pinion steering, a motor plate (rather than motor mounts), dry sump oiling, and a trick rear suspension with adjustable links, the car was considered obsolete before it hit the track.

Engineer Dick Oldfield recalled that the original idea was to build a tube-chassis car but they had been told by the NHRA that if they showed up at the season-opening

The interior remains just as it was in 1974. Most of the interior paneling is magnesium. The dashboard and seats are fiberglass. Note that the clutch is cable operated. Also visible in this photo is the hood scoop with its experimental side inlets. Not visible is the extensive bodywork that included moving the doors ahead 2 inches and lengthening the quarter panel. (Photo Courtesy Arnie Klann)

As you can see in this suspension shot, featherweight was the name of the game. Many of the suspension components came courtesy of Trick Titanium. The liberally drilled magnesium engine plate on the left tied the chassis together. At this time the Duster houses a healthy 377 engine originally pegged for Bob Glidden's Pro Stock Arrow. Who wouldn't love to see the car make a quarter-mile pass just as its original builders intended? (Photo Courtesy Arnie Klann)

Winternationals with such a car, they would be tossed. To the *Missile* crew's surprise, Grumpy Jenkins and his Vega, with its yards of chassis tubing, were welcomed.

In 1973, the *Missile* team fielded a Duster that featured a Ron Butler tube chassis and newly developed D-5 heads on a destroked hemi that measured 396 inches. The fewer cubic inches allowed the car to carry less weight under NHRA rules. The Duster was constantly evolving and proved to be the most successful of the *Missile* cars. It was the first Pro Stocker to make use of a data recorder that was instrumental in helping driver Don Carlton overcome a sea of Fords to capture the 1973 NHRA Springnationals and the IHRA Pro Stock crown.

The wins were of little consolation since the Hemis continued to get hammered. It seems every time they made headway in NHRA competition, they were saddled with additional weight. Late in 1973, Chrysler pulled out all the stops, headed back to square one, and developed a small-block-powered Duster.

The wire car featured here derives its name from the fact that the chassis all but ended at the rear suspension and the rear body panels relied on steel cables to hold them in place. The car was a featherweight and made extensive use of titanium and magnesium parts and panels. Ready to race with a small-block and Lenco transmission, the Duster reportedly weighs a measly 1,867 pounds.

The car was unique when compared to Pro Stockers of the day, featuring what Dick Oldfield referred to as a monocoque-style chassis. The frame rails are formed using chrome-moly sheet steel and then boxed. According to current owner Arnie Klann, Dick Oldfield had informed him that when it was ready to race, "The car should have run in the low-8s. In the 'yellow car,' (a second Duster used during development) 8.80 times were recorded." Arnie feels that the car could have broken into the high-7s on an ideal track under perfect weather conditions. These are phenomenal numbers when you consider match-race Pro Stockers of the day were hovering around the 8.40 range.

Rounding out the wire car was a third member that was as unique as the rest of the car; it was fabricated using a Ramchargers magnesium center section along with titanium axle tubes and brake rotors. The car was nearing completion at the end of 1974 and would have debuted in 1975 as the next *Mopar Missile* had Chrysler not pulled the plug. The racing program ended and so did the manufacturer's dream of once again owning Pro Stock.

The wire car ended up in Don Carlton's hands in North Carolina, and there she sat. Jeff Johnson was the next owner until Arnie Klann came along and purchased it in 1998. Arnie devoured all the published information he could find on the wire car and spoke extensively with the original builders: Tom Hoover, John Pappas, Dick Oldfield, and others. Keeping the lines of communication open during the restoration proved to be an invaluable asset.

The adjustable four-link rear suspension is one of the few things on the Duster that was standard Pro Stock gear in the mid-1970s. Adjustable coil-over shocks help support the rear end, which was fabricated using a Ramchargers magnesium center section and titanium axle tubes. (Photo Courtesy Arnie Klann)

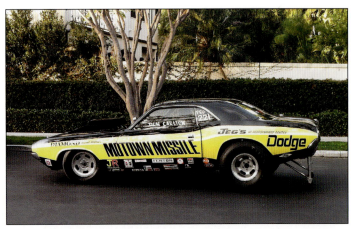

The first of three Missile car debuted in 1971. It was an innovative car that initially made use of a ClutchFlite automatic transmission. The unique Pro Stock transmission relied on a 2.45 first gear and a heavy flywheel to launch like a standard-transmission car. Don Carlton took over the driving chores from Dick Oldfield late in 1971 and convinced the guys to replace the ClutchFlite with a 4-speed. The Motown Missile name was changed in 1972 due to possible infringement with Motown Records. (Photo Courtesy Arnie Klann)

Gary Hansen Race Cars did the initial teardown and was responsible for reworking many of the original pieces. The guys at 401k Car Club were called upon to massage the body back into shape and apply the paint. Today, the Missile that "never was" houses a 377-inch small-block that was once pegged for Bob Glidden's Pro Stock *Arrow*. Superior Automotive went through the engine while Dick Oldfield and Arnie rebuilt the drivetrain.

At this time, the car still needs pieces to complete the dry sump oiling. These parts need to be fabricated because the original parts created specifically for this car have long since disappeared. Too valuable to race now, the guys gave "the little mouse that could" a pull on the dyno and recorded an easy 900 horses.

Led by engineer Dan Knapp, the Duster was built to become the 1975 version of the Mopar Missile car. Owner Arnie Klann spearheaded the restoration, which provides a glimpse as to how the car would have appeared. In the mid-1970s the NHRA measured the wheelbase from the center of the wheel to the edge of the doorframe. The body had been moved back on the chassis and the quarter panel extended at its leading edge. This maintained the appearance of a stock-location wheelbase. (Photo Courtesy Arnie Klann)

CHAPTER FOUR

THE WILD BUNCH

The rule that the shortest distance between two points is a straight line never seemed to occur to the Competition and Street Eliminator set. The categories, which included Gassers, Altered, and Roadsters, shared similar characteristics and their on-track antics never failed to entertain. These categories predate organized drag racing and were direct descendants of the 1940s salt flats runs. Unlike the early Gassers and street roadsters, which required things such as headlights and fenders, the altereds were free of such pretension. As per the early 1960s NHRA rulebooks, these altereds could be "explicitly" modified and designed for drag racing. As each of these categories evolved, combinations of a short wheelbase, high center of gravity, and gobs of power in the upper-class cars made a straight-line run an exception rather than the rule. This may be in part why cars such as Willys and the Street Roadsters were becoming scarce by the late 1960s. By the mid-1970s the NHRA felt it necessary to eliminate them altogether in its move to streamline its categories.

ALTEREDS COULD BE EXPLICITLY MODIFIED AND DESIGNED FOR DRAG RACING

Above: This Altered is a push-start car and has no battery on board. The paint was applied by Roger Burchak in 1971 and looks just as good today. (Photo Courtesy Chadly Johnson)

Stone, Woods & Cook Willys

In a 2008 informal NHRA online poll, the Willys of Stone, Woods & Cook was voted fans' favorite race car of all time. *Swindler II* in the near lane later became *Swindler B*. In 1965, both cars were painted an almost identical candy blue. The restoration of the near Willys to *Swindler II* status was chosen to not detract from *Swindler A*. Many people are not aware of the fact that Stone, Woods & Cook toyed with a lightweight '33 Willys in 1963 before building *Swindler A*. *(Photo Courtesy Dave Davis)*

"Pebble, Pulp, and Chief Defeat Big June Two Out of Three at the Beach" screamed the Engle camshaft advertisement. Big June was none other than Big John Mazmanian, archrival of Stone, Woods & Cook. It was the early 1960s and the height of the Gasser Wars. Stoking the fires were those villainous camshaft manufacturers: Howards, Engle, and Isky. They openly exchanged jabs, fueling track rivalries that lasted through a good part of the decade. At the end of the day, who were the big winners? The fans, of course.

The drag racing team of Fred Stone and Timothy Woods came together in the late 1950s. Tim, an Alabama transplant, had settled in Southern California and started his own successful construction company. He hired Fred as an acting manager and they shared a passion for the sport. Their first venture was *Swindler*, a blown Studebaker driven by K. S. Pittman. The car was a terror at such Southern California tracks as Santa Ana but met an early demise in a towing accident.

The Studebaker was replaced by an equally potent 1941 Willys powered by a blown Olds and dubbed *Swindler II*. Before the 1961 Nationals, driver K. S. Pittman and Crew Chief John Edwards split to campaign their own Willys and were replaced by Doug "Cookie" Cook. Cookie, who had built himself a reputation with his record-holding B/G '37 Chevy, must have felt lady luck had deserted him because the Nationals was a trip best forgotten. The team lost three engines during qualifying and was unable to compete. On top of that, K. S. and John took C/GS honors with their Willys. The final blow to the weekend was another towing accident that heavily damaged the Willys.

The guys fought back in 1962 with a new 467 Olds-powered Willys and took A/GS class at the season-opening Winternationals. They bombed the class record early in the year with a 10.25 at 140.84 mph, returned to the Nationals in September, and copped class. A Nationals win was always big news and garnered plenty of ink but the real money was being made on any given weekend where the match races between A/GS rivalries were filling the stands.

Drawing the majority of headlines were the teams of Stone, Woods & Cook and John Mazmanian. The rivals met regularly, facing off in the best of two-out-of-three matches. In a match anticipated by many, the pair faced off for class honors at the 1964 Winternationals with

Swindler II held the B/GS record through 1961 with a 10.99 at 128.57. Doug "Cookie" Cook took over the driving chores from K. S. Pitman the same year and, at the same time, replaced John Edwards as the top wrench. Note the use of windshield wipers. Not seen in the photo are the dual exhaust tailpipes. Both were class requirements until 1962. The 425 Olds-powered car was wrecked on its return home from Indy in 1961. (Photo Courtesy Richard McInstry)

As many parts as possible were salvaged from the wrecked Willys and installed on the new car, which debuted at the 1962 NHRA Winternationals. Cookie took class at the meet running a 467 Olds. Weight breaks for a A/Gas Supercharged car in 1962 was a minimum 5 lbs/ci. This was raised to 6 lbs/ci in 1963. As good looking as it was fast, *Swindler II* won class at the big Mickey Thompson car show held at the Los Angeles Sports Arena prior to the 1963 Winternationals. (Photo Courtesy Richard McInstry)

Black Widow, as she was informally referred to, debuted in April 1964. The Willys used a punched-out hemi and plenty of lightweight parts to ensure the team remained King of The Gassers. Many considered 1964 to be the height of the Gasser Wars. During that time Stone, Woods & Cook needed two cars as they were running matches up to eight times per month. (Photo Courtesy Richard McInstry)

Mazmanian's driver "Bones" Balogh losing a close one to Cookie on a hole shot. The war between the two came to a head after Fred placed an advertisement challenging Big John to a put-up or shut-up showdown.

Early in 1964, Big John replaced his small-block Chevy with 467 inches of blown Chrysler. At the March Meet at Bakersfield, driver Bones dropped many jaws after cranking out a 9.77 with the new combination. With John willing and able to meet Fred's challenge, the two rivals agreed upon an early-May showdown at the fabled Lions Drag Strip. The pre-race hype ensured an eager crowd and the Gassers did not disappoint.

Bones took the first round with a 9.91 with Cookie hot on his heals with a 9.96. The second round went to Cookie after Bones jumped the light and caught a red. So it came down to the final round. Do you think anyone was sitting for this one? Fans battled for a better viewpoint as the cars inched to the line. This was what it was all about. The Gasser Wars couldn't get any better than this!

The pair of screaming Willys left the line at the hint of green, side-by-side they battled for every inch and in less than 10 seconds, it was all over. The finish line passed under Cookie's wheels .06 second before Bones, tripping the lights to the tune of 9.93 seconds at 141.06 mph. Bragging rights meant everything and the team of Stone, Woods & Cook had earned them.

If Stone, Woods & Cook were to remain King of the Gassers and meet the increasing match-race demands, a new Willys had to be built. In April 1964 the team debuted *Swindler A,* a lightweight '41 Willys powered by a poked and stroked Hemi. *Dark Horse,* as it was unofficially dubbed, featured plenty of fiberglass and was reported to be 1,000 pounds lighter than the original Willys. It left its mark on the record books and went down as the first Gasser to top 150 mph.

The *Swindler II* Willys was rechristened *Swindler B* and both Willys received new candy blue paint jobs for 1965. When category rules were revised Ohio George introduced the sleek new Mustang to the Gasser Wars.

Stone, Woods & Cook knew what their next car had to be. The *Swindler B* shell was traded to Cal Automotive

In 1965, both Willys were painted a dark candy blue. Telling the two apart was fairly easy: Swindler A *featured gold lettering while* Swindler B *featured white lettering. Although hardly noticeable in this 1966 photo, a gold stripe runs the length of the car. You can clearly see the lower body has been shaved as a means of dropping weight. Tim Woods considered drag racing a family venture and this is reflected in the fact his son, Leonard Woods Jr's name adorns the car. The team of Stone, Woods & Cook broke many barriers, one being the first competitive interracial team in drag racing.*

Chapter Four: The Wild Bunch

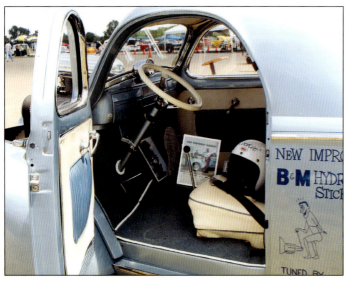

The Ed Martinez upholstery is all-original and, in typical 1960s fashion, carries over into the trunk. The bucket seats were pirated from a 1958 Thunderbird. Safety in the day came courtesy of a lap belt and roll bar. (Photo Courtesy Dave Davis)

In 1962, Gene Adams, Hilborn, Jocko, Mickey Thompson, and (of course) Engle helped the 425 inches of Olds produce in excess of 600 horses. Backing the potent mill is a B&M Hydro Stick and an early-Olds rear end supported by quarter-elliptic springs. In 1964, a hemi replaced the Olds. (Photo Courtesy Dave Davis)

in 1966 for a truck full of fiberglass Mustang parts. *Swindler A* was wrecked the same year and a replacement was built to fulfill bookings and driven by Cookie's brother, Ray. *Swindler A* was retired in 1967 and passed on to Cookie's teenage son, Mike, who restored the car in the 1970s.

Cal Automotive made use of *Swindler B*, installing a small-block Chevy, and racing the Willys for a couple seasons around Southern California. It spent some time chained up behind the shop before being sold to engine builder Paul Gommi. Paul was in the midst of building a Hemi for a customer and purchased the Willys on the customer's behalf. When Paul's customer backed out of the deal, the Willys (minus engine) was sold to Holman-Moody employee Cotton Colthrap.

Cotton hauled the car east to Charlotte, North Carolina, where he raced it through 1969 with a Chevy motor. Looking to sell the car, Cotton placed an ad in *Drag News*, which was answered by Ron Ladley in Philadelphia. Ron collected Willys and had dreams of restoring the car to the way she looked in 1941. Thankfully he never got around to it. Other projects took priority and in 1972, he placed an ad that stated simply, "Willys car and parts for sale."

Joe Troilo answered the ad and could barely contain himself when he realized the car in question was *Swindler B*. The car retained its original Cal Automotive glass front clip, chassis, quarter-elliptic–supported '57 Olds rear end, Martinez interior, track bars, and more. The only things missing were the Olds engine and Hydro transmission. With no demand at the time for these early Gassers, Joe converted the Willys to a small-block Chevy–powered street cruiser. He coated the car in a light blue and attended many rodding events through the mid-1970s. The Willys was a hit and turned more than a few heads as those familiar with the car were amazed to see the once-dominant Gasser cruising main street.

With a growing family taking priority, Joe was forced to place the Willys on the block and in 1976, Mike Wales became the new owner. Mike had his fun with the car but in 2003, he was ready to begin the restoration. All the original Stone, Woods & Cook parts were tracked down and with Joe's helping hand, the once-familiar Willys began to look as she did in 1962.

The original chassis, which had been swapped out years before, went back under the car along with a Willys front axle. Out back, the coil-spring rear suspension, which had been installed in 1966, was replaced with the earlier quarter-elliptic setup and Olds rear end. Rounding out the rear were the original traction bars that were traced to someone in New Jersey.

Coming across a 394 Olds engine was easy enough and the new engine was bored and stroked to 425 inches and fashioned with period-correct parts. A B&M Hydro transmission backed the Olds in 1962 but over time, these transmissions have become difficult to find. However, the Gasser gods had it covered and a chance discussion led a friend of a friend to a friend who happened to have a new, unused B&M Hydro just waiting for the right car to come along.

Before paint, the body was stripped and minor repairs made. The rear pan below the deck lid needed extensive work, as over the years it had been beat up pretty badly. Stone, Woods & Cook melted lead into the area to add

Ruben sprayed the original paint while Ed "Big Daddy" Roth performed the lettering. Larry Hook had the honor of duplicating Big Daddy's fine work. Slicks are M&H while wheels are Halibrands. All the bright work is original to the Willys. (Photo Courtesy Dave Davis)

Mike Cook took over ownership of *Swindler A* when it was retired and restored the car in the 1970s. Doug Cook initially drove both Willys. In 1966, his brother Ray took over the controls of *Swindler A*. (Photo Courtesy Dave Davis)

weight. When the time came to lighten the car again, they beat the area with a hammer to break the lead down to scoop it out. Many helping hands went into the restoration of *Swindler II* including Larry Hook, who laid the stripes and lettered over the period-correct blue applied by Joe.

The restoration was completed in 2006 and in 2007, Mike was honored to accept the Preservation Award at the Detroit Autorama. Today, you can catch both of the restored Stone, Woods & Cook Willys at most Hot Rod Reunions, if you can make it through the throng of people that usually surrounds them.

The team of Stone, Woods & Cook went on to further success with their *Dark Horse II* Mustang but when a crash nearly cost Cookie his life in 1967, he chose to hang up the helmet. Stone and Woods continued on before retiring in the early 1970s, comfortable in knowing they had left a lasting legacy.

Jolly Dolly C/Gas 1939 Chevy

Running a 283 stroked to 307, the D/Gas Jolly Dolly was good for low-11-second times in the late 1960s. The Chevy ran as good as it looked, setting records and winning awards for appearance and safety. (Photo Courtesy Charlie Gauthier)

Gasser! The word conjures up images of a rambunctious highboy, dancing across its lane (or its opponent's lane) as the wild-eyed driver battles to maintain control. It took mighty big cojones to drive one of these and the men who did became almost as legendary as the cars themselves. Guys such as Ohio George, the Kohler Brothers, and Stone, Woods & Cook traveled the nation becoming household names while guys such as Maryland's Bob Bernardon, tended to stay in their own region and trailer those "big-name guys" who dared to set foot on their turf.

In March 1957, Bob bought this 1939 Chevy coupe, a car that he raced for the next 16 years. Always a fan favorite, Bob's Chevy went on to become one of the most successful Gassers of the era. Initial power for *Jolly Dolly* came by way of a punched-out 265 Chevy displacing 276 inches. The little mouse was strong enough to earn Bob

Chapter Four: The Wild Bunch 105

As a means of restoring the car to its mid-1960s C/Gas status, a healthy small-block was installed. Pistons, rods, and crank were original right out of storage; they're from the Crankshaft Company. Crane controls the valves while fuel was fed through Hilborn injectors. Bob constantly changed cams and ignition systems. In use here is a rare aluminum Roto-Faze dual-point distributor. (Photo Courtesy Dave Davis)

The pleated interior dates to 1956 and remains in show condition to this day. The Hurst shifter controls the Muncie 4-speed and pokes through an aluminum floor. Gauges are by Sun and Stewart Warner. (Photo Courtesy Dave Davis)

the Gas title at the 1957 Automobile Timing Association of America (ATAA) World Series of Drag Racing held at Quad Cities Dragway in Cordova, Illinois.

To remain competitive, *Jolly Dolly* continuously evolved. In 1958, cubic inches were increased to 301. In 1959, an early set of Hilborn injectors was installed and the Chevy rear gave way to a Halibrand quick change. The continual upgrades resulted in *Jolly Dolly* lowering the NHRA C/Gas ET record in 1959 to 13.35 and again in 1960 to 13.17.

As the 1960s unfolded, Gassers were getting faster and *Jolly Dolly* was no exception. Cubic-inch displacement was once again increased, this time to 333 inches, which ran either twin 4-barrels or Hilborn injectors. At the same time, Bob took advantage of the category rules and set the engine back the allowed 10 percent of the wheelbase.

The move necessitated a new firewall that Bob fabricated himself from aluminum. The rules dictated that the wheelbase had to remain stock, but nothing said you couldn't replace the bulky OEM suspension. In place of the Chevy knee-action sprung suspension went a lighter Willys straight axle supported by custom springs.

Bringing the Chevy to a halt were Airheart discs brakes on all four corners. Bob continued with the overhaul, replacing the Chevy's third member with a 31-spline Olds rear housing. At the same time, multi-leaf elliptic springs were replaced with coils, airbags, and a Watt's linkage. To aid traction, Bob fabricated long traction arms.

How did *Jolly Dolly* react to her new underpinnings? Fantastic! The car immediately set the Eastern Drag News C/Gas ET record with a 12.05. And lowered it once again in 1965 with an 11.93. The same year, Bob and *Jolly Dolly* were divisional champions in the NASCAR Drag Racing Division and held the C/Gas NASCAR National Record at 11.69.

By 1968, Bob was adding or removing ballast from *Jolly Dolly* so that he could run both C/Gas and D/Gas. Another record came the same year, this time in D/Gas with an 11.29. Bob went looking for more speed in 1969 and added a Van-Charger 6-71 blown 431-inch big-block Chevy. Briefly competing in BB/GS, the combination managed a 9.64 at 150. The NHRA eventually abolished the Gassers and Bob went on to bracket race the old Chevy with an injected big-block. *Jolly Dolly* was mothballed in the mid-1970s and stayed in hibernation for the next 20 years.

During its drag racing days, *Jolly Dolly* was a tough one to beat and on the show circuit, it proved equally competitive. At the annual Washington, D.C., Rod & Custom Show put on by the Ram Rods car club, one of the most prestigious honors given was the P. A. Sturtevant Company award for Engineering Achievement. This award was handed out annually to the Best Engineered race car. *Jolly Dolly* won the award three times in a row during the mid-1960s.

In 1993, Charlie Gauthier became the new owner of the Chevy and with significant help from Bob, the pair restored *Jolly Dolly* to its 1960s racing form. At Bob's insistence, the engine of choice was an injected big-block Chevy, similar to the one that Bob had used during the car's bracket-racing days.

The front axle is Willys, while Bob fabricated the steering. The Chevy rides on its original American rims, while the tires are Firestone and M&H. The fenders are the original Kellison fiberglass parts. (Photo Courtesy Dave Davis)

Excluding a repaint in the mid-1990s (1956 Chevrolet Sherwood Green) by Musclecar Unlimited, the Chevy is all original and a fine example of a mid-1960s Gasser. *Jolly Dolly* is seen here at the 2011 NHRA Gatornationals where it was guest of honor. (Photo Courtesy Dave Davis)

Says Charlie, "Bob owned the car all those years and tossed out nothing. Every part of the car is either original or period correct." The restoration was completed in 1995 and the guys did some nostalgia drag racing with the car through 2002. The same year, Bob was inducted into the East Coast Drag Times Hall of Fame and the old Chevy was once again retired. Says Charlie, "The car became a piece of drag racing history and needed to be preserved." Rightly so, Charlie.

Moody-Jones C/Gas 1937 Chevy

The scourge of C/GS in the early 1960s, the Moody-Jones '37 Chevy dominated no matter where it ran. With Sam Jones behind the wheel, the Chevy took class at Indy three years running starting in 1963. (Photo Courtesy Richard McKinstry)

Dale Moody and Sam Jones partnered in 1958 and success came fairly quickly. Using Sam's $75 '37 Chevy as a springboard, the pair, with the help of Sam's brother Mack, built the car into a C/GS winner. Powered by a blown small-block Chevy, the guys built a reputation around the small tracks of Illinois before venturing out into the big league.

In 1961 they took the Chevy to the World Series of Drag Racing held in Cordova, Illinois, and won with an 11.88 at 120 mph. The guys followed with a trip to Indy in 1962 and even though the Chevy was "humming," the guys felt their trip was fruitless. The "Big Go" served up the country's best and they questioned whether they would be competitive.

As it turned out, not only was the Chevy competitive, it ran away from the pack. They took class then waded their way through stiff competition to win the Street Eliminator category. In the process the guys set the MPH record at 115.08. Later that month they dropped the ET record to 12.05. Powering the Chevy was a new-for-1962 327 engine

Chapter Four: The Wild Bunch 107

The all-business interior features a pair of early Mustang bucket seats, AutoMeter gauges, an ancient Sunen Tach, and the mandatory Hurst shifter. (Photo Courtesy Madonna Jones)

Circa 1963, a young Jeff Jones looks on while Dad makes a few adjustments to the '37 at home in the drive. Today father and son operate the very successful Jones Engineering. (Photo Courtesy Madonna Jones)

backed by a B&M Hydro. You just knew that 327 had to be making some real power to haul the 4,250-pound Chevy down the track at those speeds.

The 1963 season brought more of the same success as Dale and Sam went undefeated in class the whole season. They returned to Cordova in 1963 for the World Championship and won it all again. A trip to Indy gave them a class win and another record of 11.70 at 117.80 mph. They came up short in the Junior Eliminator final, falling to the B/SR, 1927 T of Weiler & Reider. Another C/GS class win at Indy in 1964 made the team a three-time winner, a feat rarely accomplished by anyone. Dale earned a trip to the world finals in Tulsa but surprisingly, fell early in the competition. Shortly after, Dale briefly retired from racing. The Chevy spent the next few years taking up residence in the garage until Dale got around to selling it.

The early 1970s saw Moody-Jones back at the track, teaming up with Wally Dougherty to campaign a Modified Production 1969 Firebird. The car saw some success locally before being sold. Moody and Jones parted ways; Dale turned his attention to tractor pulls while Sam went on to start Jones Engineering. With his son Jeff at his side, the pair has seen great success in building midget and sprint car engines along with cylinder head development.

In 2004, Sam was able to purchase his old '37 Chevy from a local resident and after a complete restoration, he now shows the Chevy regularly. In 2005, Sam was honored with a selection by the NHRA to appear at the 50th anniversary of the Nationals as part of the golden-fifty participants. The Chevy had come full circle; and was once again a hit with the Indy crowd.

THEN

It's the fall of 1962 and left to right, Dale Moody, Mack Jones, and Sam Jones pose proudly with some of their dragstrip awards. Note the early Moon discs covering the stock wheels. Custom rims had yet to make the scene. (Photo Courtesy Madonna Jones)

NOW

More than 50 years later, the same group poses proudly with the restored Chevy. Halibrand rims had long since replaced the discs. The Chevy was the first C/Gasser to hit an 11-second quarter-mile time. (Photo Courtesy Madonna Jones)

Gene Moody's D/Gas 1955 Chevy

Gene Moody, seen here at the 1963 NHRA Nationals, ran primarily in D/Gas. He bombed the record to an 11.90 at 115.38 during an outing at Cecil County, forcing himself to add weight and run E/Gas. (Photo Courtesy Madonna Jones)

Few door cars have seen more trips down the track than the '55 Chevy. From lower-class stockers through 6-second Pro Mods, the '55 Chevy has been modified every way imaginable to fit every category possible. During the heyday of the Gasser Wars, the '55 ruled the lower Gas classes. Gene ran this D/Gas competitor and like his brother Dale, it won more than it lost. Hailing from Bloomfield, Indiana, Gene took the Chevy to class wins at the NHRA Nationals in 1963, 1964, 1966, and 1967. In 1965, he headed to Tulsa and drove around plenty of stiff competition to win the Street Eliminator World Championship. Having won the Inaugural World Finals, Gene and the car were invited to travel to Hawaii that fall on an NHRA Tour and match race Ferd Napfel in his *Storming Bull* '55 Chevy. Ferd had won the Street Eliminator title at the Nationals that year and gave Gene a run for his money during the match race.

Power for Gene's '55 came courtesy of a 283 punched out to 292 and featured the best parts of the day. Hilborn injectors with Algon nozzles and fuel pump filled the cylinders, which housed JE 12.5:1 pistons. Mickey Thompson rods gave support, while an Isky 550 camshaft actuated the valves. Initially, Gene relied on his homemade headers to expel the spent gases but winning the World Championship in 1965 got him a free set of Doug's to bolt on. The engine was set back by 10 percent of the wheelbase, as allowed by the Gasser rules, which helped aid traction. Rounding out the drivetrain was a BorgWarner T-10 transmission rowed by a Hurst shifter and a floating rear end from a mid-1960s Chevy 3/4-ton pickup. The truck also gave up its trailing arms, which Gene modified to use as ladder bars.

Filling the third member was a tall 6.33 gear. As was customary on these Chevy Gassers, the front frame rails were cut off behind the front crossmember and replaced by channel stock that supported a transverse-leaf spring and model 60 Ford oval-tube axle. The Ford radius arms were incorporated; the stub axles and steering arms were modified to connect to the stock Chevy steering box. Ground support came from Firestone slicks mounted on 10 x 15 slotted mags; up front, American Racing LeMans 5 x 15 magnesium rims gave support. The body is real

The record-setting small-block Chevy is an overbored 283 displacing 292 inches. Gene apparently didn't bore to the maximum of 301 inches because he felt the cylinders became too thin. The fuel injection was a combination of a Hilborn-style manifold fitted with Algon injectors and nozzles. Gene, with help from Sam Gelner, designed this very tunable system. The original injector holes were plugged since the Algon injectors were mounted differently so they pointed directly at the valve, not at the top like a Hilborn, which sprayed at a 90-degree angle. When the current owner purchased the car, the original engine and transmission were long gone. The hunt continues for original parts. (Photo Courtesy Peter Broadribb)

The austere interior features a Hurst shifter to row the 4-speed with Stewart Warner gauges and a Sun Tachometer to monitor the engine. A three-point roll bar and lap belts were the extent of safety features in the lower Gas classes during the early 1960s. Gene installed the lightweight VW buckets at the time of the original build. (Photo Courtesy Peter Broadribb)

Seitz Auto Body in Kingman, Arizona, did a beautiful job of matching the original PPG Saddle Tan paint, which Gene and friends laid on back in the early 1960s. Gene raced the Chevy at many tracks throughout Division 1 and also competed in the NHRA Traveler's Division. In 1965, he was a member of the *Hot Rod* magazine Top 10 racers. (Photo Courtesy Peter Broadribb)

steel and was originally painted a Chevy saddle tan by Lloyd Thompson with help from Gene and a few buddies.

The current bodywork was completed by the late Tom Morris who unfortunately used PPG Saddle Tan, which is a different shade than the original. The car was then repainted in a DuPont color by Seitz Auto Body, of Kingman, Arizona. Current owner, Peter Broadribb, remembers that, "The painters 'loved' me because there are two decals from Indy on the dash and I made them clearcoat the decals, then reverse mask them so they were not lost."

What became of the old girl after Gene stopped racing it in 1967 is unclear. One story has it that the car was sold and the engine pulled and placed in a race boat. The other story is that a couple guys purchased the car and raced it until they blew the engine, and so retired the car. Gene lost track of the car in 1972 when it was stored in a man's basement. When the man moved, he took the car with him.

Fast-forward many years to the ghost town of Calico, California, where a couple guys see an old 1955 sitting beside a building and one of them decides to buy it from the old man. The car passed through a few more hands before ending up in Peter Broadribb's hometown of Kingman, Arizona. Before he could finalize a deal to purchase the Chevy, it was traded to another man who thought he had just picked up one of Joe Hrudka's old cars. When he realized it wasn't the car he thought it was, he sold it to Pete.

Peter recalls, "I bought it in September 2001. When I proudly trailered it home, my wife said, 'You paid money for that P.O.S.?' So, throughout its restoration it was affectionately known as the 'P.O.S.' Within a few days of purchase, I took it to the CHRR at Bakersfield and got four minutes of airtime on a TV show called *Inside Drag Racing* as Most Significant Find."

Outside of body, paint, and upholstery, Peter did most of the restoration himself, taking the car down to its bare frame and reassembling it in his home garage. He's quick to give credit to Dave Hales, who provided a wealth of information during the early going of the restoration; Bob Thompson, who gave up a long Saturday to do the lettering; and late friend Chris Worsell, who helped out during assembly. Peter says, "The best part of owning this car is the looks on people's faces when they see it and the memories it brings back."

Peter takes pride in the restoration of the Chevy and shows it when he can. He is British and you can be sure they never enjoyed Gassers like this one across the pond. (Photo Courtesy Dave Davis)

Jersey Jimmy's Altered

Charlie's early 1950s Crosley Super Sport gave him his first shot at the NHRA Nationals in 1961. The Crosley body gave way to its current fiberglass Bantam shell in 1962. Charlie has few photos of the Crosley; his first wife never liked it and referred to it as the ugly yellow rat. (Photo Courtesy Charlie Seabrook)

As proof that not all Altereds were blown nitro-induced fire breathers, here is Charlie Seabrook's 6-cylinder Bantam. Those located on the East Coast may be familiar with Charlie and company's Seabrook Foods but only a few may recall the Crosley Charlie had originally built and raced in 1960. Powered by a bored and stroked 302-inch GMC six, the E/A Crosley proved to be grossly overweight for class and was shut down more times than not. In 1962, Charlie ditched the Crosley shell and in its place went a Cal Automotive fiberglass Bantam body. The switch saved Charlie more than 300 pounds of dead weight and immediately put him in the winner's circle.

Now running D/A, the Bantam dominated at his home track of ATCO, putting together a phenomenal string of victories. As Charlie recalls, "I went through a streak of 165 wins with only five losses." A regular at the NHRA Nationals throughout the 1960s, Charlie took class honors in 1962, 1963, 1965, 1966, and 1969.

Always unorthodox, Charlie started his drag racing career behind the wheel of a Studebaker coupe before switching gears and running a blown Packard-powered Henry J. He frequented Vineland in New Jersey with the Henry J before moving on to the Crosley, which he found in a junkyard.

Charlie loved to experiment and was always tinkering with the car. He enjoyed making changes and going to the track to see if they worked or not. By 1965, he had the Bantam churning out 11.14 at 119.68. Initially Frank McGurk supplied the camshaft and cast pistons for the GMC, which helped squeeze out 13.5:1 compression. Charlie fabricated the headers and intake himself. The three Rochester 2-barrel carbs were from a 389 Pontiac and fed the fuel through the rubber-hose intake runners. Charlie found that playing with different-length hose helped with the fine-tuning.

The Bantam served him for 27 years and had everything from a twin supercharged straight-8 Buick to a twin overhead-cam Jaguar between the frame rails. Charlie remembers, "I won Indy one year with a GMC 292. It ran strong, right on the record, and turned 9,000 rpm but I couldn't keep the crank in it for more than 10 runs. I tried a forged crank from Canada but that only lasted 20

For those too young to remember old automotive terminology, the Jimmy name on the side of the Bantam refers to the GMC 6-cylinder powering the Altered. Charlie initially ran a 302 with a 1/8-inch bore increase backed by a Chrysler ClutchFlite and a 4:56 Chevy rear. Front tires are 3 x 12 while the rear slicks are 9 x 15 on American mags. The wheelbase is 96 inches. (Photo Courtesy Charlie Seabrook)

Charlie was pretty handy with a wrench and loved to experiment. He fabricated many of his own parts including headers and ram tube intakes. He was pretty handy with a lathe as well and turned his own cranks. (Photo Courtesy Charlie Seabrook)

Riding high on the Crosby frame, the little Bantam featured an owner-fabricated front and rear suspension. In this late 1960s photo the straight-8 Buick features three 2-barrel carbs. The Bantam saw six different brands of engine over its career. (Photo Courtesy Charlie Seabrook)

runs. The straight-8 Buick was heavy and the first time out, I broke the ClutchFlite's output shaft."

As the car continued to evolve over the years, Charlie finally settled on an Aston Martin engine. S&W Race Cars was hired to build a new, 108-inch-wheelbase chrome-moly chassis to handle the newfound power. Clockings of 9.0s at 140-plus became common for the 1,125-pound car thanks in part to the camshaft design specifically for Charlie by Harvey Crane. The roller cam features .470 lift at 0.050 and 276 duration.

Other "motivational equipment" included Howards rods, 11.4:1 compression, Weber 48DCOE carbs, 2.10 intake valves, 1-7/8 exhaust, and a Vertex Magneto. A Lenco 3-speed transmission featuring a 2.62 first gear transmitted the power to a 4.30 magnesium rear end.

Business and insurance costs finally led to Charlie retiring the car in 1989. "I had the car out maybe four times the last year. The bank that financed our repurchase of Seabrook Foods was charging me $500 every time I took the car out." *Jersey Jimmy* made a number of appearances at Darwin Doll's York Reunion and today rests peacefully in Charlie's garage.

Today, the Bantam appears just as it did when Charlie retired it in 1989. The front tires are 2 x 25 while the rears are 14.25. The car ran NHRA E/A in its final days and its class weight break was 4.5 lbs/ci. (Photo Courtesy Charlie Seabrook)

Lil Screamer II 1934 Ford

The Lil Screamer *debuted in 1963. With its wheels up and nerf bar dragging wheelies, it quickly became one of the most popular B/Altereds in the nation. Seen here at the 1966 NHRA Springnationals, Ditmars propelled the car to class win.*

In 1955 Jack Ditmars took in the drags at Lawrenceville Airport in Illinois and witnessed the sport's first 150-mph run. The *Bustle Bomb* of Lloyd & Scott cranked out a 151.07 and that was all it took to get Jack hooked. Graduating from high school in 1956, Jack raced a D/Gas 1949 Ford that he built with money earned from a part-time job in a body shop. By his own admittance, the '49 Ford wasn't much; it proved to be too heavy for class but it was a start. He built the first *Lil Screamer,* a '34 Ford Altered, a couple of years later and raced from 1960 into 1961. The car was showing promise racing at tracks in Illinois, Indiana, and Wisconsin until a garage fire destroyed it, forcing Jack back to square one.

Quick to get back onto the horse, Jack hooked up with lifetime friend Herb Moller and immediately got to work on *Lil Screamer II*. The car was ready to race in 1963 and immediately became a crowd favorite. Jack, now working full time as a body and paint man, laid on the eye-popping mother-of-pearl and candy blue himself.

Moreover, this B/Altered had the brawn to back up its beauty. On the track, with the Ford's wheelie bar dragging, all-wheels-in-the-air launches left the crowds in awe. Initially powered by a 283 punched out to 301 inches, Jack swapped in a bored-and-stroked 327 and hit times in the high 9s. With a shot of 30-percent nitromethane, low 9s at 150 were common. A BorgWarner 4-speed initially backed up the screaming small-block before Jack installed one of B&M's new ClutchFlite transmissions. Out back, a Chrysler 8.75 rear end carried 4.88 gears. The chassis consisted of model A rails that Jack boxed for added strength. Due to damage caused by tremendous wheelies, the fragile chassis forward of the roll cage was replaced in 1966 by a boxed 2 x 3.

As the current owner Mike Sleeth reports, "The front half of the frame was later widened by the third owner to make room for a big-block Chevy. When restored, the choice was made to front-half the model A rails, again, and remove the wider box tubing added by the previous owner. Today, 90 percent of the original Ditmars chassis remains. As with the original build, the engine was set back 25 percent and the body slid back 20 inches. These changes were allowed under the rules of the day." Although most of today's drag cars feature chassis and suspensions of similar likeness, the 1950s and 1960s were still a time of free thinking and experimentation. This car incorporates many unique design features including an adjustable wheelbase.

Mike adds, "The 33-inch-long ladder bar's front rod ends are mounted in a horizontal series of holes on frame brackets near *Lil Screamer*'s fulcrum point. Frame-mounted C-type brackets for the transverse torsion bars, retained by two bolts per side, allow the rear axle and suspension assembly to slide fore or aft on the frame rails in tuning for traction at various tracks. The wheelbase can be adjusted from 96 to 102 inches in 1-inch increments in less than five minutes. The two-piece splined driveshaft is adjustable in length as well. The ladder bars are one-third of the 99-inch wheelbase length and two-thirds of the car's total weight [2,325 pounds] is on the rear tires while static."

To aid traction on any given track surface, ride height for the tube front axle and rear suspension was also adjustable. Mike continued, "Ditmars fabricated a pair of rear torsion bars based on two Model A driveshafts so he could dial in this car's static height. By using torsion bars to suspend the rear end, Ditmars was also able to adjust weight bias on the rear tires, which is important for straight wheels-up launches. *Lil Screamer* employs a rear sway bar and sits lower than most cars of the day for good stability and handling." To further aid weight transfer

Chapter Four: The Wild Bunch 113

It was as beautiful as it was fast, and Jack's Screamer never failed to draw attention, whether it was on the track or on the show circuit. Another class win came at the Nationals in 1964. Herb Moller helped to build Lil Screamer and remained Jack's lifelong friend.

and to keep the drivetrain in alignment, the height of the engine and transmission was also adjustable.

Lil Screamer's track record was quite impressive. Alongside local success, Mike added the following class wins to his scorecard:

- World Series of Drag Racing 1963, 1964, 1965
- AHRA Summer Nationals 1963, 1964, 1965, 1966
- AHRA Winter Nationals 1965, 1967
- NHRA Nationals 1964, 1965, 1967
- NHRA Springnationals 1966
- NHRA Winternationals 1967

Old magazine images were studied to determine the mounting points of the front axle and radius rods. Once mounting points were locked in, Mike Bridgeman Tig-welded it all permanently in place. Seen here, the motor plate is in the process of being fabricated and trick, but a simple front-end flip mechanism is in place. (Photo Courtesy Mike Sleeth)

Although all of the key parts remained intact, Lil Screamer required an extensive restoration after years of abuse. The frame rails had been widened at one point to accommodate a big-block Chevy. Here the body is temporarily mounted to determine the location of mounts, crossmember, and engine location in the new chassis. (Photo Courtesy Mike Sleeth)

The 1965 NHRA Nationals win was quite impressive; Jack had to drive the '34 around 46 class entries that included numerous factory-backed cars.

Jack sold Lil Screamer in 1967 to make way for an equally impressive AA/FA Opel. He raced the Opel into 1973 before retiring from racing. Lil Screamer passed through a few hands before Mike purchased it in 1979. He had visions of turning the Ford into a blown street rod before discovering the car's history. Lil Screamer has since been restored to its 1963 race status.

Lil Screamer has come a long way since 1979 when it was just about ready for the junkyard. The story has it that some Chrysler engineers recognized how hard this altered-wheelbase car hooked up on the tires available at the time. The son of one of those engineers says that by taking pictures of Lil Screamer's adjustable wheelbase, suspension, and wheelie bars they were able to determine the formula for what made this car work. Apparently, they then applied this formula to their own 1965 altered-wheelbase cars. The restored Lil Screamer was chosen as one of the 50 most influential drag cars of all time and made its debut in 2004 at the 50th anniversary of the NHRA Indy Nationals. (Photo Courtesy Mike Sleeth)

Dave Hales' S&S Race Team 1937 Willys

What's not to love about this 1965 photo of Dave's Willys? Shot at Vargo Dragway in Pennsylvania, it epitomizes mid-1960s drag racing: bolt-on tow bar bracket, drilled axle, and deep steelie rims out back. Front rims are American Racing magnesium LeMans. (Photo Courtesy Ken Gunning)

Dave Hales bought this 1937 Willys in November 1962 and by June of the following season, the Willys was Chevy-powered and terrorizing the dragstrip as part of the S&S Race Team. Running out of Falls Church, Virginia, Dave was one of the original members of the team, which was assembled by Chuck Stolze, owner of the S&S Parts Company. Chuck had started S&S by selling speed equipment out of his Falls Church home but brisk sales quickly forced the opening of the first of two stores. To further promote the business, Chuck signed up a number of local racers: Gene Altizer (signed first), Malcolm Durham, Fred Bear, K. S. Pittman, Charlie Hill, Porky Zartman, and Dave Hales.

At the 1963 NHRA Nationals, the S&S team was a standout in the Gasser classes, taking A/Gas, C/Gas, with Dave himself playing runner-up in D/Gas. Between 1961 and 1972, when S&S finally closed its doors, the team campaigned a dozen different cars. During the 1960s, team members appeared in a total of 28 class and eliminator finals with 23 wins.

Today, Dave's Willys is the only surviving original S&S Race Team car and it has been restored to its 1965 condition. As then, the Willys now uses a 1957 Chevy 283 block bored 0.125 giving 301 ci. Original go-fast goodies include ForgedTrue pistons, a Summer Brothers gear drive, Crane cam, Vertex Magneto, and rare set of early-1960s Jocko-prepped cylinder heads. Backing the potent small-block is a BorgWarner T-10 4-speed transmission. Initially Dave ran the big Pontiac/Olds rear with 6.14 gears but switched to a Halibrand quick-change in 1964, using steep 6.28, 6.42, or 6.58 gear sets. When it was time to restore the ultra-rare rear housing, refurbished or quality used parts were hunted down in four different states. The best quarter-mile times recorded by the Willys were the following.

- 1963–1964 D/Gas, 12.21 at 110 mph
- 1965–1967 C/Gas, 11.50 at 116 mph
- 1967 D/Gas, 11.40 at 119 mph

The Willys held an astounding record throughout these years. Starting with 1963, Dave was runner-up in class at the NHRA Nationals. In 1964, he was the Eastern Drag News record holder, in 1965 the UDRA Eastern Meet Class Champion, and an NHRA record holder in both 1965 and 1967.

After selling the Willys late in 1967, it passed through six or seven different owners before resurfacing at a Carlisle, Pennsylvania, swap meet in the late 1990s. A little worse for wear, the Willys was purchased by someone in Michigan who did little with the car before Dave pried it from his hands in 2000. It was surprising to Dave that the Willys retained so many of its original parts. "The complete firewall, floorboards, roll bar, and even the original Eddie Swartz upholstery is there."

Dave spent $25 wisely back in 1962 by purchasing the rough-looking Willys. The car didn't run but that mattered little to Dave. He bought the car to replace his wrecked D/Gas '55 Chevy. (Photo Courtesy Dave Hales)

Dave sold the Willys in late 1967 to Chuck Speacht who repainted the car blue and then a gold/bronze color. It stayed that color until he sold it in late 1969 or early 1970. Chuck tried his luck in C/Gas and D/Gas, depending on engine size and weight and what association rules he was running under. (Photo Courtesy Dave Hales)

The restoration of the Willys is nearing completion in Dave's home garage. Les Pomeroy, the same person who painted the car in 1963, applied the poppy-red paint. The lettering to come would be all hand-painted. No vinyl stickers on this car. (Photo Courtesy Dave Hales)

Dave did a fine job representing the S&S Parts Company with his hauling Willys. S&S was a speed shop with two locations. The main store was in Falls Church, Virginia. The other was in Winchester, Virginia. The S&S stood for owners Chuck Stolze and his wife, Micki. (Photo Courtesy Dave Hales)

Restoration on the Willys started shortly after Dave bought the car and every effort was made not to over-restore it. Everything that was original to the car was used no matter how rough it looked. The driveline components are as close to original as possible. The original Hill/Zartman fiberglass front end, doors, and seats remain on the car. The rest of the body and frame are original to the Willys. Many years' worth of accumulated paint was removed from the shell before Les Pomeroy blasted on the Matador red. Les happens to be the same person who painted the car in 1963. The finishing touch was the hand-painted lettering.

The original firewall, floorboards, fiberglass seats, roll bar, and all the interior upholstery is original to the car dating to the early 1960s. (Photo Courtesy Dave Hales)

In 1965 the Willys moved up one class to C/Gas by removing some ballast and by 1966 a 301-ci engine was in the mix (again adding more ballast to stay in C/Gas). Engines of 268, 283, or 301 inches filled the engine bay at one time. You would never know it but this is a recent photo of the restored 301 engine. (Photo Courtesy Dave Hales)

The restored Willys spent some time at the NHRA museum and today can usually be found at any number of East Coast Gasser reunions. In 2003, the S&S Race Team was inducted into the East Coast Drag Times Hall of Fame. (Photo Courtesy Dave Hales)

Dave's Willys is a spot-on time machine back to the days when S&S ruled the Gas classes. You wonder what's missing from drag racing today? The inviting camaraderie shared by guys like Dave is one example. (Photo Courtesy Dave Davis)

Hugh Tucker's AA/SR Chevy

By 1966, Hugh's glass Chevy owned the Street Roadster category. The blown Olds had given way to a Hemi that propelled the highboy to 9.70 times. Although the fenders and headlights seem out of place, category rules at the time made them a requirement. Hugh's aluminum-coated protective gear is by Deist. (Photo Courtesy Hugh Tucker Collection)

Part of the popularity of 1960s drag racing is the diversification of cars. Today's drag racing seems to have no place for a car as unique as Hugh Tucker's '28 Chevy Street Roadster but 40 to 50 years ago, these cars were a common site on America's dragstrips. Between 1961 and 1967, Hugh's Chevy ran a number of categories, going from Little Eliminator in 1962 to Junior Eliminator in 1963 to Street Eliminator in 1965 and finally Super Eliminator in 1966. The evolution of the NHRA didn't really matter much to Hugh because it seemed that no matter who or where he ran, he just kept right on winning.

Hugh started gathering a hodgepodge of parts to build his roadster in the late 1950s. He rescued the body from a salvage yard in Ojai, California, while the '34 Ford rails and 2-speed Columbia rear end came courtesy of a friend. This friend was getting married and decided to sell his five-window. Hugh only needed the chassis from the Ford since the salvage yard owner wouldn't sell him the one under his Chevy.

Once the Ford was stripped of needed parts, the remains were scrapped. Hugh's own '49 Ford gave up the 402-inch Olds engine, which came by way of a bored and stroked 303. It was a healthy engine and featured six Stromberg carburetors and an Engle camshaft. A LaSalle transmission, which was considered bulletproof in its day, backed the engine. In a marathon three-day thrash, Hugh and a few buddies brought all the pieces together. With high hopes, they hauled the roadster to Indy for the 1961 NHRA Nationals . . . and were soundly beaten. Hugh recalls, "Our Strombergs didn't stand a chance against the supercharged cars in class."

It was then that Hugh decided to get serious about his drag racing. He briefly partnered with Dave Stolls

Chapter Four: The Wild Bunch 117

The blown Olds measured 402 inches and initially ran six Stromberg carbs. Bolting on a 6-71 Blower (it sounds so easy on paper), courtesy of Dave Stolls, propelled Hugh's Chevy to a 155-mph clocking in 1965. Even though his Hemi ET'd better, hitting 9.25, it never matched the Olds MPH mark. (Photo Courtesy Hugh Tucker Collection)

*There are thousands of these rustic old garages scattered about the country and who knows what treasures may be lurking within? In the case of this dilapidated old building, nestled inside were the remains of Hugh Tucker's **Street Roadster**. Hugh's son went in search of the car and in 1997, a lead led him here. (Photo Courtesy Hugh Tucker Collection)*

who offered the 6-71 blown Olds engine that had been powering his speedboat. At the same time, Dave contributed a B&M Hydro transmission. Prior to the 1962 NHRA Winternationals, Hugh swapped out the 4.40 Columbia rear end for an Olds supported by quarter-elliptic springs and a ladder-bar suspension.

At the Winternationals, the roadster was hitting 130 in the mid-10-second range. He defeated defending champs Cassiday & Sons to win the first of three eliminator titles. He followed up with a class win at Indy but not before having to hunt down a blacksmith in town to build him a set of radius rods. Hugh had built his own rods out of aluminum and every time he hit the brakes, the front end wanted to twist. Eventually this twisting motion crumpled his lightweight rods. The blacksmith that Hugh found bent up a new set out of black iron. Class finalist Conway and Woodhouse screamed foul,

"They can't be safe!" but officials saw nothing wrong with the new rods and let the final race proceed. Even though the Olds was hitting respectable times, it still wasn't as quick as the Willys Hugh had to face in eliminations.

Heading to Fresno for some testing and tuning, the blown Olds was trailered by a blown Chevy roadster. Upset by the loss, Dave immediately wanted to build a new engine but instead, Hugh chose to stick with the Olds and decided it was time to buy Dave out of the short-lived partnership.

He started tuning the Olds himself, and in short order, he was hitting the 9s at 144. Once again he returned to the Winternationals in 1963 and took Junior

When the garage door was finally pried open, this is what greeted Hugh Jr. It seems the then-current owner had thoughts of transforming the car into a street rod. The body was crudely channeled and the Chevy silver paint had given way to a poorly executed orange featuring unorthodox pinstriping. Thankfully the majority of original parts remained. (Photo Courtesy Hugh Tucker Collection)

Hugh's roadster miraculously survived the years of inactivity with the majority of original parts intact. The aluminum Triumph front fenders are original to the car along with the front axle, spindles, Halibrand 15 x 4.5 rims, and Pirelli tires. Headers are fabricated and original along with the aluminum rear traction arms installed before the 1961 Winternationals. The rear fuel tank is an aluminum army surplus tank installed by Hugh in 1964. (Photo Courtesy Hugh Tucker Collection)

Once the body was installed on the restored chassis, the modification to the body was made apparent by the extended rear chute tray. The frame was not equally shortened. Looking closely, you can see that the wheelie bars were fabricated using shortened leaf springs. (Photo Courtesy Hugh Tucker Collection)

Eliminator, defeating Bob Culbert's Mercury-powered A/A with a 10.30 at 138.24 mph. Hugh joined the growing match-race crowd and was one of the first to tow east, making stops in Maine and Massachusetts before heading to Indy. Hugh again won class and made it all the way to the Middle Eliminator final where he was to face the Willys of Ohio George.

George was having issues getting his Willys to fire and instead of the usual bye run, which was given to the opponent, starter Bob Daniels instead had Hugh shut off and wait for George. In no time, the Willys fired but now Hugh couldn't get his Olds to start. So what did Daniels do? He sent George off on a bye for the eliminator win. Hugh was in shock. He had no idea what just happened, and neither did Don Garlits, who was standing nearby and watched the whole fiasco unfold. Don screamed "bloody murder" to officials on Hugh's behalf but the complaints fell on deaf ears. When it was all over, Hugh went home feeling short-changed.

By the end of 1963, Hugh could feel the competition gnawing at his heels and decided to put the roadster on a crash diet. He had been running the car at 2,800 pounds, 400 over minimum, so he called upon Cal Automotive who formed a one-off fiberglass shell to replace the original steel and wood. While the body was being laid up, the wheelbase was shortened to the allowable 103 inches by moving the differential forward. The same amount was removed from the glass body behind the door; it really wasn't noticeable at first glance. His trip to the Winternationals in the new year saw the lighter car crank out a 9.70 at 149.70.

Hugh and Street Roadster were invited to the NHRA Winternationals in 2010 as part of the 50th anniversary celebrations. Here Hugh and his son prepare to fire the Hemi for the cackle part of the event. As then, a Torqueflite now backs the Hemi. A 9-inch Ford replaced the Olds rear as parts were then, and are today, much easier to come by. (Photo Courtesy Hugh Tucker Collection)

It was an interesting year for Hugh. He took the wheel of Mazmanian's Willys through July and August, beating Bones Balough at Bakersfield and then drove the car at Indy where he lost class to Stone, Woods & Cook.

Hugh considers 1965 an off year, having missed the class eliminator call at the Winternationals and being disqualified at the Hot Rod Meet. The one upside of 1965 was the fact that he had cranked out 155 at Long Beach with the blown Olds and Hydra-Matic combination. Hugh was doing a fair amount of testing and development work for B&M during this time and actually helped to get the ClutchFlite transmission into production.

Before the 1966 Winternationals, he installed a B&M Torqueflite behind a hemi and defeated the C/Gas Willys of Walt Marrs for his third Winternationals eliminator win. Hugh was the first person to accomplish the Winternationals three-peat and the only one to have ever done it using the same car. He followed the win by taking class at Indy where he cranked out a best of 9.25. However, it seemed he just couldn't buy an Indy eliminator title.

Hugh retired from drag racing after winning the Hot Rod Meet in 1967, stating that a growing family deserved his devoted attention. He parted with the roadster in 1970 or 1971, selling it to a man in Washington. The car was raced for a number of years with a small-block

Chapter Four: The Wild Bunch 119

Chevy and by the time it was discovered in 1997, still in the Northwest, it was painted a "hideous orange" and was cut up pretty badly. The owner was in the process of channeling the body and turning it into a street car. Thankfully many of the key parts remained with the car including the front and rear suspension, frame, and body. Even the old Ferguson tractor headlights were still intact.

The old saying goes, "Many hands make light work" and the number of helping hands with this "resurrection" were innumerable. Hugh mentions people including John Peters of *Freight Train* fame who helped with machine work; Jeff Harbert, who donated a number of parts for the 392; Tony Nancy, who stitched the interior in 1964 and came out of retirement to do it again; and painter Phil McCurdy, who matched the 1957 Chevrolet Inca Silver paint. The car was completed early in 2004 and, appropriately, made its debut at the NHRA Museum in February.

In all its beauty, you could say that Hugh's Chevy never looked so good. No expense was spared during the car's "resurrection," which was carried out by father and son. Ventura Motors was a Chevy-Olds dealer that sponsored Hugh from 1963 through 1965. (Photo Courtesy Hugh Tucker Collection)

Mr. C Competition Roadster

Gary set out to build himself a roadster to do battle in both B/Competition Roadster and A/Fuel Modified Roadster, and boy did he build a winner! Initially powered by an Algon injected 352, he won nearly every Saturday night at his home track of Lions. Reath Automotive helped out a lot. Gary was a big proponent of drag racing, letting the neighborhood kids help with the car. The roadster's original paint and lettering was applied by Steve Harris. (Photo Courtesy Forrest Bond)

Skipping through the 1964 NHRA rulebook, it's apparent that the Competition category was pretty liberal. Here's a tidbit straight from the book itself: "The Competition Section is designed for cars with production bodies that have been fully modified. Body, engines, drivetrains, chassis, etc. may be altered, modified or relocated . . ."

As you can see, it was pretty much anything goes. To Fountain Valley, California, resident Gary Cochran, it made for one attractive category. He turned a serious eye to drag racing in 1963 and with the helping hands of Chuck and Laroy Barnes, Gary built a '23 T highboy, which hit an 8.90 ETs while powered by an injected 352. In 1965, the engine found its way into a fresh Bellflower Auto Center three-point chassis, which was, for the most part, enclosed in a new Tex Collins Cal Automotive fiberglass '23 T. The chassis consisted of .049-inch wall and 1.5- and 1.25-inch Tig-welded chrome-moly. Weighing this body and chassis separately today, current owner Robert Casado discovered that the bare thin-wall chassis actually weighs 4 pounds less than the fiberglass body.

Gary initially relied on his injected 352 before stepping things up in 1965, bolting in a 427 top-oiler. Making the 427 Ford come alive to the tune of low-8-second times were a GMC 6-71 blower topped with Enderle showerhead injection. A Vertex magneto mounted in an offset Mickey Thompson magnesium magneto front cover helped ignite the 30- to 60-percent nitro Gary fed through the engine. During the car's restoration, the

The lightweight Bellflower chassis was rescued from its Palmdale desert resting place in 2011. The previous owner said it probably would have been scrapped if they hadn't bought it. You have to wonder how many of these old chassis have met such a fate. (Photo Courtesy Robert Casado)

After piecing together all the parts of the puzzle that he had purchased, Robert was able to determine his starting point. The roadster retains the majority of its original steering components. It has the original formed rear seat and motor plate, which at one time had been drilled for a small-block Chevy. For unknown reasons, the cowl had been sawed in two and needed to be repaired. The wheelbase is 126 inches. (Photo Courtesy Robert Casado)

showerhead and magnesium cover proved to be the most difficult parts to find. These early Ford parts just aren't as plentiful as Chevy or Mopar stuff and when the parts are found, they usually cost a lot more.

Robert, however, seems to have a knack for finding the right people, those who were eager to help the project along, which was something his bank account appreciated. Behind the 427 mounts an in-out box that transfers the power to an early 1950s Oldsmobile rear end carrying 3.08 gears. *Mr. C* rolls on Borrani 16-inch spoke wheels up front, which mount Avon Speed Master tires. Yes, they are the original tires. As are the axle, drag link, spindles, and hubs.

Then as now, the glass body is sprayed 1965 Chevy Marina Blue. Gary chose this color as it matched the color on his tow car, a Chevy Caprice wagon. Gary raced *Mr. C* into 1967 before selling it to someone long forgotten. The car's history after that is unknown, although at one point it may have raced as a Junior Fueler with a small-block Chevy.

In 2011, then-owner Robert Casado was looking to build a replica of a Tony Nancy car when the father of a friend pointed him to an online auction listing a fiberglass T body. It wasn't exactly what he was looking for, but it did pique his interest. When the auction ended as a no sell, Robert contacted the seller. After exchanging information and viewing photos, he made a deal to purchase the body for the list price. To Roberts's surprise, the seller also had the original chassis.

By the time Robert was ready to drag the car home, he had the body, chassis, front suspension, form-fitted aluminum seat, upholstery, and an early-Olds rear end. Robert was eager to discover who once raced the car and by pure chance, he found out just weeks later.

Robert's friend Steve Poe made a trip to Advance Gas in Huntington Beach to pick up some welding supplies and struck up a conversation with owner Frank Beels. Steve mentioned that he was helping to build an old competition roadster, which aroused Frank's interest. Steve described the car and Frank became more and more sure that it was the old *Mr. C*. How did he know? Easy. He was the old crew chief on the car. An inspection of the body and chassis proved him to be correct; it was the original *Mr. C*. Now that they knew the origins of the car, the restoration and the hunt for original parts could begin.

Parts were sourced at swap meets from coast to coast and online. The rear Halibrand four-slot rims were another auction find. It seems a fellow in the Midwest had been using them as a coffee table on his porch. A friend of Robert's happened to have an unmolested 427 side-oiler for sale, which Robert had built by Mike Kuhl.

Even though the hunt goes on for original M/T rocker covers, the restoration is considered complete. Mr. C experienced its first push-start in more than 40 years at the 2013 CHRR. (Photo Courtesy Robert Casado)

The block was bored and stroked and to help feed the 85-percent nitro, new, larger showerhead nozzles were installed. Estimated horsepower is now in the 1,800 to 2,000 range, approximately double what the old 427 pumped out back in the car's heyday.

Even though the car doesn't meet today's safety standards, the healthy dose of nitro and added horsepower make for one mean-sounding flame-throwing cackle car. Completed in mid-2013, Mr. C made its debut at the AAA national headquarters in Orange County, California, and in Gary's eyes, the car never looked or sounded so good.

The current engine in Mr. C is a cross-bolt 427 featuring a 4.232 stroke and a .030-over bore that features a GMC 6-71 blower and an Enderle showerhead injector. The front engine cover is an ultrarare Mickey Thompson magnesium part that features an offset for the Vertex Magneto and an extension to mount the fuel pump. Mike Kuhl of Kuhl & Olson built the engine. They won top fuel at the last drag race at Lions in 1972. (Photo Courtesy Robert Casado)

Is there any doubting Gary when he says this was his favorite car? He was nearly brought to tears upon seeing the car for the first time in more than 40 years. The bang-on restoration was performed by owners Robert Casado, Steve Poe, his dad Ron Poe, Fred Seay, George Scarpenti, and others. (Photo Courtesy Robert Casado)

The Grove Boys 1940 Willys

In a sea of Gassers, The Grove Boys Willys was always a standout. Its candy mist blue paint covered steel and fiberglass panels and is contrasted nicely by blue-tinted windows. Seen here in 1967 at the Championship drags at Cordova, Jim wheeled the car to its first of three A/G championship wins. Jim, Jerry, and cousin J.R. raced the Willys between 1960 and 1969. Jim drove initially before JR came onboard. (Photo Courtesy Pete Gemar)

Fort Dodge, Iowa, residents Jerry and Jim Grove joined the Gasser ranks in 1960. The boys purchased a $50 Willys from a little old lady in 1956 and spent the next few years building themselves a competitive A/Gasser. Initially, a 394 Oldsmobile powered the all-steel car but in 1966, it had given way to a 427 Chevy. While the car was out of commission, the boys took the opportunity to put it on a crash diet; they replaced the front end, doors, and trunk lid with lightweight fiberglass parts. When it was time for paint, the color of choice was a star mist, candy apple blue, which was applied by cousin, Roger "J.R." Groves. With J.R. joining the team in 1966, the Grove brothers' Willys was aptly rechristened *The Grove Boys*.

The Groves traveled the country with the Willys and frequented tracks including Cordova, Cedar Falls, Sioux

The stock bore and stroke was built by Morely Performance in Fenton, Montana. The 14-inch stacks sitting atop the 427 were fabricated by Gary Blasey, duplicating the originals. Innards include parts by TRW, Manley, and Comp Cams. (Photo Courtesy Dave Davis)

Between 1960 and 1969, The Grove Boys Willys left many lasting memories at its home track of Cordova. One of those who remembered the car well was current owner Ron Normann who spent three years resurrecting the legend. (Photo Courtesy Chadly Johnson)

City, and Des Moines where they were regular winners. Their first national event win came in 1964 when they took class at the AHRA nationals. They headed to Indy in 1966 and 1967 and returned in 1968 to take a class trophy. They regularly appeared at the World Championship series drags at Cordova; they took A/G class honors three years running starting in 1967.

By 1969, the guys could see the writing on the wall for these old Willys Gassers and sold the car. They replaced it with a hemi-powered Opel Kadett, a car that brought the Groves much success. The Willys found a new owner locally who dropped in a hemi and ran it for a couple of years before the car eventually disappeared from the local scene. Current owner Ron Normann bought the Willys from a fellow who used to live across the street from the Groves. It seems the fellow was out in Arizona visiting his sister, who unknowingly lived just a few doors down from the then-owner of the Willys. Walking down the road one day, the fellow sees a Willys in a garage. As any car guy would do, he stopped and struck up a conversation with the owner. Looking the car over, he immediately recognized the '58 Chevy taillights that had been frenched into the rear by the Groves. The fellow bought it and brought it back to Iowa where it sat for the next five years as he thought about restoring it to its former glory. Ron finally talked the fellow out of the car and then spent the next three years resurrecting the old Willys.

The car was just a shadow of its former self when the restoration began; it was little more than the original chassis, body, and suspension components. Ron definitely had his work cut out for him. He consulted with the Groves who helped guide the restoration and supplied a number of original parts. J.R. retained the original Moon fuel tank and, once restored, Ron had the Groves sign the tank before clearcoating and installing it. The 427 was built to replicate the original engine and carries many period-correct parts. The Hilborn injector is a brand-new unit; it was purchased by a speed shop but never sold or used. The 427 features a stock bore and stroke and uses TRW pistons as well as Comp Cams camshaft and valvetrain hardware. Plugging the 427 onto a dyno showed it developing 605 hp.

Like any good Gasser, the Willys interior is devoid of frills. The Groves relied on a Sun tach and Stewart Warner gauges to monitor the semi-hemi Chevy. The fabricated firewall accommodates the 10-percent engine setback. (Photo Courtesy Chadly Johnson)

Chapter Four: The Wild Bunch   123

The Willys makes use of a TurboHydramatic 400 transmission as it did previously and the original, leaf-sprung 1960 Oldsmobile rear end. Mike Slaughter prepped the Willys body and applied the star mist candy paint.

For decades, the Willys was lost but not forgotten by those who watched it dominate all those years ago. Ron wowed the crowd when he debuted the restored Willys at the O'Reilly Auto Parts 60th World Series of Drag Racing held at Cordova in August 2013. The restoration was a true labor of love and the crowd's reception made it all worthwhile.

From any angle, this Willys is a knockout. A Don Long axle carries Americans wheels up front, while timeless Cragar S/S rims carry the rear load. Glass panels have replaced the front clip, doors, and fenders. The custom frenched taillights are from a '58 Chevy, something the competition became familiar with. (Photo Courtesy Chadly Johnson)

Jack Merkel's 1933 Willys

At Indy in 1966, Jack seems to tower over his low-slung '33 Willys. He bucked the trend of high center of gravity and built his all-glass Willys close to the ground. In its day, Jack Merkel Automotive built more national champions and record holders than all other New York shops combined. (Photo Courtesy Richard McKinstry)

In the early 1960s, drag racing was still in its infancy and trying to shake its bad boy image. Jack Merkel never fit that stereotype. You see, Jack owns a pair of engineering degrees and approached drag racing in a very businesslike manner. He opened Jack Merkel Automotive in Ridgewood, New York, during the late 1950s and saw many young hot rodders come through the doors. Jack realized that building a drag car was a great way to expand his clientele. He had raced a couple Chevys before building the more familiar 1939 Willys, which bought him plenty of recognition. It was the A/Gas cars that got the ink and in 1965, the B/G '39 gave way to a '33 Willys powered by a supercharged small-block Chevy.

The Willys was a lightweight screamer that topped out at more than 148 mph and give the hemis fits. Ohio George was one constant rival that Jack didn't need. When George signed with Ford, he replaced his Chevy mill with an SOHC Ford. It was time for Jack to head back to the drawing board. He faced George and the competition with the '33 Willys pictured here, a car he began constructing in October 1966. The car features an all-glass shell, 3-inch top chop, and one-piece lift-off front end. Subtle changes such as a flush-mounted windshield, molded fenders, and body channeling were incorporated to cheat the wind.

Jack had Charlie Doerkin spray on the heavy metallic, chartreuse yellow paint while Jack made himself busy assembling the 427 Chevy. Jack's 427 incorporated

The 427 Chevy could rev to 8,500 rpm and ran a best of 8.70 through the quarter. Class rules dictated that you had to run a radiator, although they didn't say anything about circulating coolant through it. Jack's radiator consisted of two tanks; the top one was for fuel while the bottom one was the overflow tank for the coolant that circulated through the engine. Thompson water fills were added to the front of each cylinder head. Jack considers the chopped '33 as the most comfortable and straightest car he ever drove. (Photo Courtesy Richard McKinstry)

aluminum heads, a GMC 6-71 blower topped by a Hilborn fuel injection, and a bug catcher. He made use of Crower camshafts and worked closely with the manufacturer, experimenting with numerous profiles. Frank Cali performed a lot of the fabrication work on the new car including boxing the stock 1933 frame rails. The 1960 Oldsmobile rear end houses 4.56 gears and is supported by coil-over shocks, a Panhard bar, and a unique traction arm based loosely on a 1940s Jaguar design.

Jack was required to research and develop a thesis for graduation from the Pratt Institute. He based his thesis on the arm and came up with a mathematical equation that worked flawlessly when put into practice: The length of the arm/bar divided by the rear gear ratio equals the distance between the driveshaft and the tip of the torque arm. If you deviated from this formula, the bar wasn't as effective. Jere Stahl studied the arm while building headers for the Willys and marketed his version of the bar to the Junior Stock crowd.

Rounding out the drivetrain was a Vitar Turbo 400 transmission and torque convertor. The Willys rode on Halibrand quick-mount rims up front and 10-inch American Torque Thrusts out back. Ready to race, the featherweight Willys weighed a measly 2,135 pounds.

In August 1967, the fresh AA/GS Willys made its first trip down the tarmac and cranked out a respectable 9.30 at 149 mph. By the time Jack retired the Willys, he had the car hitting 8.70 times at more than 156. Jack built his cars to promote his business and had no emotional ties to them. Once they were sold and were no longer making money for him, he forgot about them.

The Willys was sold in 1968 and continued to run Gas as the *Glass Slipper*. It passed to a person on Long Island who did little with the car. In 2002, Vinnie Muscaro came to the rescue. Vinnie cherished the Willys and spent a lot of time and money on the car. He went through the painstaking chore of duplicating the original metallic chartreuse paint; he realized that the color did not turn out as close to the original as he had hoped, so he

Jack was very methodical when building his race cars and every part on his cars proved itself. A Schiefer magneto lit the mixture that traveled through a Hilborn flat-foot injection unit and GMC 6-71. Chrome-plated headers are exact duplicates of the original Stahl units. Vinnie Muscaro restored the Willys and even though he trusted storing the car in his home garage, he never trusted leaving the one-off headers on the car. He kept those locked in his bedroom closet. (Photo Courtesy Chadly Johnson)

Gold metalflake coats the all-fiberglass body while the interior features black Naugahyde. Jack and the Willys entered the 1968 New York Coliseum Custom Car Show and, going up against 240 others cars, won the award for outstanding competition car. (Photo Courtesy Chadly Johnson)

The magnesium rims are showing their age but along with the tires, they are original to the car. The trunk houses little more than a semi truck battery, which Jack mounted on a roller, allowing him to move it to improve traction. Stopping power came courtesy of a Deist chute and rear brakes only. A single wheelie bar prevented Jack from standing the car on its rear bumper. (Photo Courtesy Chadly Johnson)

stripped it and did it again. The Willys was, for the most part, complete when Vinnie purchased it but the one-off Stahl headers were missing. At some point they ended up on the Vitar Transmission–sponsored '33 Willys. Vinnie couldn't talk the owner into selling him the pipes, but he convinced the owner to allow him to borrow the headers so that he could make a duplicate pair.

Sadly, Vinnie passed before he could complete minute details of the restoration. The Willys was left to his sister to sell and she knew immediately where the car had to go. She contacted Ron Normann, the owner of Jack Merkel's 1939 Willys, and the pair struck a deal in 2012. The car new resides in Illinois and joins Ron's small but growing collection of significant cars.

Jack operates Jack Merkel Performance Engines in New Jersey with his son. He has warmed to his old cars and was there with Vinnie to fire up the Willys for the first time.

Mike Gish's Fiat Altered

It seems that for every Borsch or Mondello Altered built, there were dozens of lesser-know Altereds terrorizing dragstrips across the nation. Jerry Adams' Fiat was just one of them. Jerry hailed from Kenosha, Wisconsin, and built his Altered in 1964. He purchased a 96-inch-wheelbase chassis from Lakewood and an all-glass body from the Hot Rod Shop. For power, a 348 Chevy topped by a Hilborn injection was chosen to propel the 1,640-pound Fiat. Backing the W engine was a Chevy 3-speed transmission and an Olds rear end.

The Fiat made its first trip down the track in 1966 at the famed Union Grove against the dominant Willys of Stone, Woods & Cook. In 1967 Jerry swapped the 348 for an injected 427, which propelled the Fiat to a best clocking of 9.80. Looking elsewhere to get his kicks, Jerry put the rolling chassis up for sale at the end of the season and the car quickly found a new owner in Mike Gish. (Photo Courtesy Paul Zielsdorf)

Jim Luker of Magnum Racing Engines in Milwaukee built Mike a Hilborn-injected 301 Chevy engine that made use of an Isky roller cam, aluminum rods, and forged-domed pistons topped by ported and polished 461-casting heads. The Chevy transmission remained along with the Chevy rear end. The rear houses 4.56 gears and features Olds axles machined by Henry's. A handheld brake and Airheart disc brought the Fiat to a stop. The wheels were magnesium American Racing Torque Thrusts in the rear and spindle-mounted 12-spokes up front. Steering was handled through a Corvair box.

The Fiat was built for show-and-go and when raced, it was driven by either Mike or his nephew Dave Straw. The car ran in A/Altered through 1972 and cranked out a best of 10.17. It toured the northeast ISCA show circuit during the same period and in 1973, it took third place overall in the competition category.

The fancy ribbon paint was applied in 1971 and remains on the car today. The ribbons were smoked into the paint with an acetylene torch and cleared with pearl lacquer. After racing A/A in 1972, the engine was pulled and never reinstalled. From there, the car sat neglected and was moved from one storage area to another. *(Photo Courtesy Paul Zielsdorf)*

Paul Zielsdorf spotted the Fiat at a friend's house and knew he had to have it. He purchased the car and restored it in 2008. Although neglected for a number of years, the car retains a surprising number of original parts. The rear tires have been updated and are 10.00-15 Mickey Thompsons. The tires give great traction during Paul's banzai starts. The unique doghouse for the parachute was installed by Roger "The Mole" Jackson in 1971. *(Photo Courtesy Chadly Johnson)*

The interior remains true to form retaining its original upholstery, Ansen bellhousing, and Stewart Warner gauges. The master cylinder is a Triumph Spitfire part and is controlled by a hand lever. A modern safety harness has replaced the 1957 military belt used by the original builder. *(Photo Courtesy Greg Rourke)*

Paul rebuilt the original engine with the help of Donerite Automotive in Mosinee, Wisconsin, and hit 11.0 ETs at Great Lakes Dragway. The Altered remains a push-start car and has no battery on board. Previous owner Mike Gish provided much help throughout the restoration and gave up the original tool tray with orange balls on it that sits in the injection stacks. The paint was applied by Roger Burchak in 1971 and looks just as good today. *(Photo Courtesy Chadly Johnson)*

Kohler Brothers' *King Kong*

Initially, short-wheelbase Supercharged Anglias were deemed illegal in Gas so that left them to either run unblown or Altered. The Kohlers chose to run AA/A with their blown big-block Chevy at the 1967 NHRA Winternationals. They downed the defending champ, Hugh Tucker, in the Super Eliminator final with a 9.42 at 145.63 clocking. The Kohler Brothers won big on their initial investment of $75 in 1967 as they also won the supercharged class at the AHRA winter meet. (Photo Courtesy Dottie Plumer)

Between 1964 and 1968, few Gassers were as feared as Ray and Ed Koehler's California-based 1951 Anglia. Appropriately named *King Kong*, the Anglia was the brothers' first venture into the world of drag racing, and boy, did they build a winner. Painted a brilliant Tahitian Candy Orange, the Anglia looked as good as it ran. The car hit the Fontana track in 1964 and in 1965, took A/G at both the NHRA and AHRA winter meets, and followed up with a class win at the Smokers Meet in Bakersfield. By May, the stroked and injected 388-inch Chevy was propelling the Tahitian treat to record-setting times of 9.97 at 136.

In AHRA trim, the Anglia's numbers were more impressive, setting the record with a 9.85. Switching back and forth between a small-block Chevy and a blown and injected 427 big-block stroked to 454 inches, the Anglia ran both Gas and Altered categories. Running A/GS in 1966, the brothers dropped an astounding 9.23 at 152.54 mph. A late arrival to the camshaft wars, the *King Kong* Anglia relied on a Sig Erson cam to open and close the valves of the semi-hemi Chevy. The bottom end was sturdy, thanks to crank, pistons, and rods from Crankshaft Co. A Schiefer magneto lit the fire.

As you can see, the Anglia was built using proven parts of the day and has been restored the same way.

When Chevy introduced the 396 and 427 the team got to work with new engines. The current blown 454 houses an 11.7:1 compression ratio. Demar Ray helped with the original engine, blowers, and swaps. George Britting also helped with the original build. (Photo Courtesy Carlos and Mary Cedeño)

Backing the big Chevy is an Art Carr Chrysler Torqueflite transmission. The Koehlers' *King Kong* is reported to have been the first Gasser to make use of this popular transmission. The tall first gear helped to minimize wheel spin, which was caused by inadequate tire technology. A Chevy rear end carries 4.56 gears and Henry's axles and is supported by quarter-elliptic springs. The front suspension consists of a standard straight axle with transverse leaf springs while a Volvo box handles steering. Cal Automotive fiberglass fenders, grille, doors, and trunk lid help get the total weight down to 2,260 pounds. Painting the car for the Kohlers in 1965 were the Martines Brothers in Azusa, California.

The *King Kong* Anglia was very popular during the height of the Gasser Wars and spent plenty of time through 1968 traveling the country match racing, taking on drag racers including Stone, Woods & Cook, Ohio George, and Big John Mazmanian. Playing up the part of the *King Kong* namesake, they often arrived at the track with a crewman dressed in a gorilla suit. Driving chores were often split between Ed and Ray; Ed took the wheel at most major events.

Chuck Pacini bought both the Kohlers' *King Kong* and the side-venture *Thames* of Kohler/Vasser at the end of 1968. He repainted the Anglia green and tagged it with

In 1979, Carlos Cedeño found the Anglia for sale at a swap meet in Niagara Falls. The seller told him it was previously the Kohler Brothers' car, but it had a gunslinger on the nose. Carlos bought the car and discovered that after the Kohler Brothers, it was raced by Chuck and Joe Pacini as Showdown, *with a gunslinger painted on the nose. (Photo Courtesy Carlos and Mary Cedeño)*

The second rebuild took place in 2006 when the car was finally retired from drag racing. The frame is the original Anglia and has been boxed. Stopping power comes courtesy of Airheart discs up front and Lincoln brakes out back. (Photo Courtesy Carlos and Mary Cedeño)

A four-point roll bar surrounds the twin glass bucket seats and a Naugahyde interior. The firewall is aluminum and held in place with Dzus fasteners. King Kong is along for the ride. (Photo Courtesy Carlos and Mary Cedeño)

The Cedeños raced the Anglia from 2004 to 2006 using a big-block Chevy. Beautifully restored to original King Kong *status, the Cedeños have done the Kohlers proud. Underpinnings include a chrome John Troxell front axle, while rolling stock includes timeless Cragar wheels. (Photo Courtesy Carlos & Mary Cedeño)*

the name *Showdown*. With improvements of the day, Chuck turned a best of 8.67 at 167, besting the Kohlers' low-9-second times. Chuck got tired of replacing broken Chevy rears and installed the Chrysler 8.75 rear from the Kohler/Vasser *Thames*. At the same time, George Britting and Ray Kohler helped replace the long ladder bars with a "lift bar" setup.

Ed occasionally raced *Showdown* because Chuck was a commercial pilot, and had schedule conflicts. Chuck parted with the car and its whereabouts was unknown until current owner Carlos Cedeño discovered the car at a Niagara Falls swap meet in 1979.

When Carlos bought the car, it was painted black with green flames. Although reasonably complete, the car definitely needed a top-to-bottom rebuild. Carlos and Mary Cedeño went through *King Kong* not once but twice. The first time was from 2001 to 2004. In 2004 the Cedeños took *King Kong* drag racing, turning 9-second times with a big-block Chevy and a Powerglide transmission. They raced the car through 2006 when it was restored to the condition in which the Kohler Brothers raced it. Blown big-block Chevy and all.

It's unfortunate that the brothers who made the car famous have both passed on; Ray died in 1989 and Ed in 2012. Before his passing, Ed confirmed that the restoration was nearly back to the way it was when he had raced it. Dewey Dilcher, a friend of the Cedeños from Byron, New York, painted the car and Dan Delaney (Dan the Sign Man) added the lettering and gorillas.

The Cedeños acknowledge that it was Ed and Ray Kohler who created the Gasser legend and who deserve the credit for the history of the car. The Kohlers stopped racing in 1968 when family and business interests took priority. The Cedeños have ensured the legend lives on. In 2006 the car was recognized by the NHRA as one of the 33 most historic Gassers in the nation. In 2007 Ed Kohler was inducted into the Drag Racing Hall of Fame in Henderson, North Carolina, and in 2010 the car was again recognized for its unique history at the 50th anniversary of the Winternationals at Pomona.

Jim Oddy's AA/GS Austin

As this 1970 image shows, it's always a busy time at Indy and the bleachers are at capacity. This was one of the Austin's final appearances as Jim switched to an Opel Gasser in 1971. (Photo Courtesy Michael Mihalko)

Jim Oddy is one of those drag racers who has done it all, and one of few who has been doing it all for more than 50 years. Hailing from upstate New York, Jim has been a car owner, paint and body man, fabricator, and engine builder at one time or another. As late as 2008, he was polishing his skills as a crew chief in Pro Mod. He's come a long way since 1960 when he took his first trip down the airstrip at Dunkirk, New York. He won E/Gas with his modified Chevy, which only fueled the fire in him to keep going back. A trip to the NHRA Nationals in 1964 showed him his path in life. Watching Don Garlits grab Top Fuel and Joe Lunati take Street, he knew this was the life he wanted.

The following season Jim returned to Indy to compete with a small-block Chevy–powered Anglia and captured B/Gas honors. Getting his doors blown off by the competition in eliminations only fueled his desire to go faster. How do you go faster in Gas? Add a blower, of course.

Knowing his Anglia didn't meet the category wheelbase requirement for blown cars, Jim went in search of a late-1940s Austin and found one close to home. He tore into the car during the winter of 1965–1966, taking over his parents' garage while he shoehorned a blown Hemi into the British import. Talented as he was, Jim prepared the stroked engine himself while holding down the position of manager at Gor-Den Automotive. Backing the mill was an Art Carr–prepped Torqueflite transmission, which is believed to be one of the first used during the Gasser Wars. He installed an Anderson one-piece fiberglass front end and modified the rear fender openings for additional tire clearance. Suspension modifications included a tube front axle with Willys spindles and an early-Oldsmobile rear end out back. Once the mechanicals were complete, Jim sprayed the Austin 1957 in Oldsmobile sapphire mist blue.

Jim debuted the AA/G Austin in May 1966 when he defeated the Willys of K. S. Pittman at a Niagara match race. To Jim's surprise, the car ran .2 off the record on its first pass, hitting a 10.10. From that point forward, Jim had no problem picking up match-race dates where he usually pocketed an average of $500 for a day's work.

The Austin was hauled back to the family garage at the end of the season for further modifications. Jim pieced together a fresh 480-inch hemi, making use of Venolia pistons, Mickey Thompson rods, Engle cam and valvetrain, Mondello heads, and Hilborn four-port injector sitting atop a GMC 6-71 blower. The proven Torqueflite remained intact while the Olds rear end was narrowed and carried Summers axles and 4:30 gears.

Jim performed the original body mods and paint in 1968. Restoration of the body was carried out in Trouble's home garage. (Photo Courtesy John Cassiol)

The 392 features a 0.030 bore, Venolia pistons and rods, and an Isky valvetrain. The blower is a GMC 6-71 and features a Delta drive and pulleys. The fuel tank is by Moon, while Jim fabricated the trick aluminum radiator back in the day. A Chrysler Torqueflite transmits the power to the early-Olds rear. The frame itself is the original '48 Austin, boxed and strengthened. (Photo Courtesy John Cassiol)

Restoration of the Austin was extensive because it had to be. The car was pretty rough when Trouble purchased it. Bob Labuszewski and Al Niespodzinski handled newly fabricated tinwork and chassis prep. The gauges are Stewart Warner "green line" series water temperature and oil pressure. (Photo Courtesy John Cassiol)

The suspension was reconfigured to lower the car and get it out of the air. To further reduce drag, extensive body modifications were made including molding the rear fenders and a well-proportioned 4-inch roof drop performed by Ron Gerstner. Ron completed the task by making use of a second A40 top. The metal doors were replaced with fiberglass units before Jim once again sprayed on his favorite sapphire blue mist paint.

Jim had a banner year in 1969 when he took home the Division 1 Comp Eliminator points championship after winning three points meets and hitting a best of 8.82 at 162.74 mph. Adding to his accomplishments were both Driver of the Year and Mechanic of the Year.

By 1970, the face of the Gas category was changing; racers were turning to newer body styles, which offered greater aerodynamics and high-speed stability. All of a sudden, Mustangs and Opels were stealing the show and the old boxy Austins and Anglias were being cashed in. In 1971, Jim followed suit, selling the Austin in favor of an Opel.

Like many old race cars, the Austin changed hands a number of times over the years, even going to Canada at one point and finally showing up on Long Island, New York. That's where current owner John "Trouble" Cassiol discovered the car. Or rather, what was left of it. Even though the body was in pretty good shape, the car as a whole was little more than a shadow of its former self.

Flipping the Anderson Industries fiberglass one-piece front clip reveals the stout Hemi built by Jim in 2006. This may just have been the last Hemi he built before retirement. In its heyday, the Austin held class records of 9.43 and set the NASCAR record for A/GS at 145.16 mph. (Photo Courtesy John Cassiol)

The Austin was painted a beautiful sapphire mist lacquer by George Oliver back when and duplicated by Greg Labuszewski in 2011. Jim ran AA/GS through 1968 and often ran in BB/A at NHRA meets. (Photo Courtesy Bob Wenzelburger)

Long gone were the fiberglass front clip, roll cage, and interior. A small-block Chevy now rested in place of the blown Hemi. The car was hideous looking; it sported a bright yellow paint job and motorcycle fenders.

With the help of friends including Bob Labuszewski, Al Niespodzinski, Pat Snyder, and Jeff Cryan, restoration of the body and frame began in 2001. All the while, Trouble hunted hemi parts for a fresh 392, and called upon Jim Oddy to build it. Once the body was prepped and a fresh Anderson Industry fiberglass front end was procured, Greg Labuszewski went about spraying on the custom mix of PPG blue, duplicating the original sapphire blue mist. The lettering and silver leaf was handled by Dan DeLaney.

Like most of us, Trouble has had to make his dollar stretch and the Austin restoration has been a slow process. Finer details are yet to be completed, but Trouble can't resist taking the Austin to nostalgia meets throughout the Northeast where it's always a crowd favorite.

Current owner John Cassiol shows the Austin regularly and thoroughly appreciates the attention the car receives. He grew up admiring the Gassers and understands the awe shown by most onlookers. A 14-foot Simpson chute frenched into the original trunk lid helped bring the Austin to a halt. Total weight is a measly 2,420 pounds. (Photo Courtesy Bob Wenzelburger)

Fred Hurst's A/GS Barracuda

Fred Hurst gained fame wheeling a Willys Gasser but as times changed and the Gassers evolved Fred's Willys chassis adapted a 1968 Barracuda shell. The same chassis found its way under Fred's 1970 'Cuda. (Photo Courtesy Geoff Stunkard)

Most of us can recall a Fred Hurst car or two, whether it's the Willys, his Opel, or a Barracuda. Maybe even a few of you old-timers can still recall the days when Fred was slinging the gears in a Pontiac. All of Fred's cars were standouts; they were meticulously maintained and were some of the best-constructed cars in competition. His 1970 A/GS Barracuda pictured here bears that out.

Fred began racing A/G in 1963 with a Pontiac-powered 1940 Willys. In 1965, he began an alliance with Chrysler, replacing the Pontiac engine with a Hemi. The following season, he earned the A/G national record with a 9.87 at 138.89 clocking. In 1968, with the financial support of Chrysler, Fred exchanged the aerodynamically challenged Willys body with the sleek shell of a '68 Barracuda. The face of the gas category was changing as more teams saw the advantage of running the newer bodies. Change was definitely in the air after Fred won the 1968 Street Eliminator title at the NHRA World Finals. The following season he took the same combination to an A/G class win at Indy.

In 1970, Fred swapped bodies once again, exchanging the old Barracuda for a new 1970 Barracuda shell. The car retained the Jim Thorpe–prepped 1941 Willys chassis, which today still resides under the unrestored car. Bill "Short Round" Rowell applied the candy apple red paint and Jim "Dauber" Farr applied the intricate graphics and lettering. The fact that the paint has held

This is an all-original steel car and retains the paint applied by Short Round and Dauber" in 1970. The gorgeous color is a deep candy apple red lacquer with underlying Plymouth logos visible in bright light. (Photo Courtesy Geoff Stunkard)

Hilborn, Hooker, and TRW are just a few of the goodies that made Fred's A/G Barracuda fly. The headers are fabricated and like all of Fred's cars, this one is spotless. Times of 9.0 at 150 were common. (Photo Courtesy Geoff Stunkard)

The all-original red anodized aluminum carries through the car and adds to the beauty of the beast. The no-frills interior features Hurst shifter, water temperature gauge, oil pressure gauge, tach, and seating for two, if you dare. (Photo Courtesy Geoff Stunkard)

up so well for 40 years is a testament to the skill these men processed.

The 480-inch Hemi that Fred relied on to lay down low-9-second times was the only thing missing from the car when the current owner Clark Rand purchased it. To make the car as authentic as possible, Clark went with period-correct parts to build a fresh 480 Hemi. Topping the engine are Hilborn injector stacks jutting through the original fiberglass front clip. Tucked below is a Crane camshaft, TRW pistons, Hooker headers, and a Vertex Magneto. Backing the potent Hemi is the original B&M ClutchFlite transmission that transmits power to the original Dana 60 series rear end. Ladder bars and Monroe shocks support the rear, while a leaf-spring straight axle carries the load up front. The driver's compartment houses the original red

"Evil, Wicked, Mean, & Nasty" proclaims the tag on the trunk lid. How many competitors do you think came to realize this? Fiberglass makes up the front end, doors, and deck lid while the glass is Lexan. Fred was honored in 1971 as Car Craft magazine's NHRA Competition Eliminator Driver of the Years. (Photo Courtesy Geoff Stunkard)

Chapter Four: The Wild Bunch   133

The rare Halibrand spindle mounts are original to the car as is the majority of paint. The doors were touched up to add the Fred Hurst name, which was covered-over years ago. Fred used rear brakes only and a chute to bring the car to a halt. (Photo Courtesy Geoff Stunkard)

anodized-aluminum paneling along with original fiberglass bucket seats and the original Stewart Warner gauges.

Says Clark, "This car has a multitude of totally original parts making it a real survivor. We simply cleaned it up and added a period-correct injected 480 Hemi to make a lot of noise."

With Chrysler factory support waning in 1974, Fred built himself a brand-new Opel to run A/G and the Barracuda was sold as a "roller" to Canadian racer Brian Wall. However, Brian never raced the car. He never got beyond painting his name on the doors. The car sat in Brian's garage for 20 years, untouched, before being sold to Jack Schiffer in Wichita, Kansas.

As unbelievable as it sounds, Jack parked the car in his garage and there it sat for another 14 years. Clark Rand purchased the car in 2009 after responding to Jack's ad in *Hemmings*. As Clark recalls, the ad said nothing about the car's history; it only stated that it was an old Ohio Gasser. A special thanks has to go out to AAA Restorations in Adams, Minnesota. AAA coordinated completion of the Hemi along with all of the many elements that brought this "barn find" back to life.

Mondello & Matsubara AA/FA

Sush Matsubara made more than his share of trips down the Wilmington strip better known as Lions. The track was sanctioned by the AHRA, which was the first to give a home to the fuel-burning altereds. The team's second Fiat, seen here in 1969, was feeding 95-percent nitromethane to the Mondello-built 427 Chevy. (Photo Courtesy Karpo Murkijanian Collection)

It was Sush Matsubara who first hunted down Joe Mondello in 1963 to have him prep a pair of cylinder heads for his high-flying Studebaker. Each man's reputation was on the rise at the time, Sush because of his driving skills and Joe for his machining abilities. The pair joined forces and, in 1965, Sush purchased an Ed Weddle–built Fiat Altered.

An injected 327 Chevy engine assembled by Mondello powered the all-fiberglass Fiat. With a healthy dose of methanol and 20-percent nitro, the small-block eventually banged-off a best of 9.32 at 154 mph. The car won its share of comp eliminators at such legendary West Coast tracks as Lions and served the pair through 1968. The Fiat took on many guises; before being sold, it was gulping air through a blown 427 and hitting 8-second times.

A new Fiat was in order for 1969 and Ron Scrima at Exhibition Engineering was hired to build it. Equipped with the same blown 427 Chevy, this car was the first Fuel Altered to run in the 7-second bracket. These ETs didn't come overnight and the team ran through numerous setups, including injected gas, injected alcohol, blown gas, blown alcohol, and finally, blown nitro. An interesting side note is that at the time, it was the only big-block Chevy–powered Altered able to crack 200 mph.

The candy-colored Fiat Topolino of Mondello & Matsubara was and is a beautifully constructed car. Before its retirement in 1970, the Fiat was knocking out low-7-second times on a consistent basis. (Photo Courtesy Karpo Murkijanian Collection)

As she was found, the Fiat retained enough original parts to easily tell it was the real deal. The only key pieces missing were the engine and transmission. (Photo Courtesy Karpo Murkijanian Collection)

At the 1969 NHRA Nationals the pair dropped the hammer and set the AA Fuel Altered national record to a stunning 7.25 at 213 mph. To put that amazing feat into perspective, the low ET for Funny Cars at the event was a 7.22 turned in by Don Schumacher's Hemi Barracuda.

As these pictures acknowledge, the car was beautifully built and restored. The chassis is unique even to an old Fuel Altered; it was designed in a fashion similar to the early Funny Cars. One of the special features of the car was its live rear axle. The setup didn't last long and in short order they were back to a solid axle; you can see the "outside of the box" thinking that went into this car.

Joe Mondello was asked what made the car so special. One of the things he mentioned was the open-chamber heads he had developed with extremely large open combustion chambers. He referred to the design as "monoflow." Joe acknowledged that downsizing the intake valves from 2.19 to 2.0 and running exhaust valves of equal size is what really helped to push the car over 200.

Joe and Sush were really ahead of the competition when it came to engine and chassis development. Through 1969, they toured the country with the Fiat and defeated many unsuspecting competitors. Joe knew that with the power they were making and with Sush behind the wheel, nobody was safe. Joe's building and tuning abilities were recognized in both 1968 and 1969 when he earned a spot on the *Car Craft* all-star team as Engine Builder of the Year and then Crew Chief of the Year.

Joe and Sush went their separate ways in 1970. Joe dipped further into research and development for the manufacturers, while Sush hooked up with Joe Pisano and took the wheel of a Camaro Funny Car. The Fiat passed on to Rick Picard and eventually disappeared, its whereabouts seemingly unknown until 2005.

John Carambia sprayed the restored Fiberglass Trends body. An acetylene torch's smoke and a steady hand were used to create the look. Larry Fator lettered it. (Photo Courtesy Karpo Murkijanian Collection)

The Ron Scrima chassis was nearly complete when the car was discovered in 2005. Here, the restoration of the Funny Car–style chassis is nearly complete. Koni rebuilt the original front shocks while the original springs were rechromed. The wheels are original spindle-mounted 12-spokes by ARE. (Photo Courtesy Karpo Murkijanian Collection)

The restoration is first-rate throughout as evidenced by the rear suspension detail. The rear end is a solid-mounted Olds with adjustable ladder bars. It's simple but effective for 7-second quarter-mile passes. (Photo Courtesy Karpo Murkijanian Collection)

An Autolite sticker on a big-block Chevy? Blasphemy, I say! The stout 427 houses 8.0:1 compression, Venolia pistons, Howards rods, a billet crank, and a camshaft featuring .708 lift. The engine was installed like the original, set back 25 percent of the wheelbase. Behind it sits a TurboHydramatic 400 transmission assembled by John Funakoshi. This car was done right! (Photo Courtesy Karpo Murkijanian Collection)

While talking of the old days and Fuel Altereds, Karpo Murkijanian and Pete Eastwood started the search for the Mondello and Matsubara Fiat. The pair came across a recent photo of a Mondello & Matsubara car while surfing the Internet; it had been shot at a track in New England. The trail was heating up. They contacted the track owner who told them that the car was located in Rhode Island and passed along the owner's name. These amateur sleuths had hunted down a missing Mondello & Matsubara car, but which one? Contacting the owner, Karpo discovered that the car was indeed the 1969 Fiat and that it was for sale. Within days, Karpo had flown to Rhode Island, checked the car, and had it back home in Southern California.

Karpo says, "The car was remarkably complete for its age, and still had the original chassis, wheels, seat, seat belts, fuel tank, and much more. Only the engine and transmission were missing."

Karpo, Pete, and Derek Bower set out to resurrect the old Fiat. Karpo spoke with the car's original painter, Bill Carter, who still recalled the specific colors used on the car. John Carambia was given the task of applying the fresh coats of candy cobalt blue, purple, and red graphics over a base of pearl lavender. When it came to engine choice, the guys stuck with a 427, which mounts a 6-71 Bowers supercharger and a Hilborn injector. Just as it was in 1969, the Hilborn scoop has been cut down to make barrel-valve adjustments easier.

Topping the semi-hemi heads are Moon valve covers with Stellings/Hellings breathers. The transmission is a Turbo 400, which B&M had supplied new to Mondello & Matsubara on a weekly basis as the guys were carrying out experimental work for the company. The live Ford 9-inch rear end was originally fitted with coil-overs and then strutted. Rear Hurst Airheart brakes in conjunction with a Simpson chute were relied on to bring the car to a halt.

The restored Altered made its debut to a throng of onlookers at the 2008 California Cacklefest. With nothing left to prove, the car that was once billed as the World's Fastest Fuel Altered is back, and it's still wowing the crowds. Fuel Altereds Forever indeed.

Meticulously restored, the Mondello & Matsubara Fiat never lacked in the performance or looks departments. A ride like this was not for the faint of heart and took real skill to handle. Sad to say, Sush, the one man who could handle it, passed away in 2006. Joe, who was a great help throughout the restoration, passed in 2011. (Photo Courtesy Karpo Murkijanian Collection)

Nanook Fuel Altered

The original Nanook Altered debuted in 1965 and drew its name from the Inuit word meaning master of bears, and this altered was a bear! The first Nanook was based upon the steel shell of a 1929 Model A Roadster and was initially powered by a carbureted Oldsmobile. The Olds was replaced by a Charlie Brent AA/FD hemi, which probably contributed greatly to the car's known ill handling. Nanook met its demise after bouncing itself off a guardrail in 1968. Nanook 2 was campaigned from 1968 through 1970 and was often referred to as the World's Fastest Altered. With John Hough behind the wheel, speeds in excess of 219 mph were common. (Photo Courtesy James Handy)

Nanook 2 features a CCE tube chassis, Donavon Hemi, and a Cal Automotive '23 T fiberglass body. Nanook was often housed at Donavon's and played the role of test mule for his aluminum hemi development. The car was sold in 1973 and ran largely as a bracket car through 1988. It was sold again to Mike Karels who displayed the car in his North Dakota museum until 1995. Geno DeBortole became the next owner in 1995 and began the process of returning the Altered to dragstrip competition. The body and drivetrain were restored and the 392 hemi rebuilt. The engine features Brook rods, Mickey Thompson pistons, and a Chris Neilson cam. A Bower/Mooneyham 6-71 blower and Hilborn four-port injector feed the air/fuel mixture. In 1996, the new combination hit mid-8-second times at 180 mph. (Photo By Doug Huegli, Courtesy worldofspeed.org)

Nanook 2 was purchased complete from Bucky Austin of Tacoma, Washington, for display at the World of Speed museum in Oregon. Even though the Fuel Altered category itself may have died in 1972, the cars never really went away. Today's Nanook is piloted by a third-generation Hough and cranks out times of more than 230 mph. (Photo By Doug Huegli, Courtesy worldofspeed.org)

Ron Bizio's AA/GS 1933 Willys Pickup

Chuck Finders originally built the Willys in 1965 and sold it to Ron in 1967. The pickup dominated match racing around Southern California through the late 1960s and never failed to entertain with on-track antics. Aftermarket suppliers included Mickey Thompson, Henry's, B&M, Mondello, and Engle.

John Willys, founder of Willys Overland, has to be smiling down from above. After all, few cars have enjoyed as much quarter-mile popularity as the 1930s and 1940s cars that bear his name. The Willys was the "go to" car during the Gasser Wars of the mid-1960s, defending its supremacy on a weekly basis against equally competitive Anglias, Austins, early Fords, and Chevys.

In 1965, Chuck Finders used one of Mr. Willys' '33 pickups to build a small-block Chevy–powered Gasser. Chuck, a legend in his own right, had won A/GS at the 1962 Winternationals and had caught a ride with Stone, Woods & Cook driving their *Dark Horse* '33 Willys. He was a terror around the Southern California tracks wheeling his own truck, which featured a 4-inch chop, Cal Automotive glass panels, and a fabricated aluminum box. As trick as the truck was, it wasn't the prettiest in black primer but the bored and stroked Chevy mill got the job done.

Bellflower, California, resident Ron Bizio became the new owner of the pickup in 1967 and painted it an eye-popping candy blue. With the help of Chuck, Ron yanked the small-block Chevy and in its place went a poked and stroked supercharged hemi measuring 448 inches. The reborn Willys was good for 8.60 quarter-mile times thanks in part to Mondello heads, an Engle cam, Mickey Thompson rods, and Venolia pistons. A Don Hampton 20-percent overdriven 6-71 blower with a Hilborn injector fed the fuel, while a Cirello magneto helped to light the pump gas. Backing the potent hemi was a bulletproof Torqueflite, which transmitted power to an Olds rear end that housed 4.56 gears. All that new-found power would be wasted without the right chassis prep so Bizio called upon S&R Race Cars to add some stiffness.

Although the truck dominated Southern California match-race action through 1969, Ron chose to put the

The 1957, 392 hemi has been punched out to 398 inches and features a magnesium 6-71 blower, homemade zoomies, and Hilborn injector. Oddy Automotive freshened the engine in 2010.

Still running AA/GS, current owner Jeff Cryan keeps himself busy running as many nostalgia meets as time permits. Interest in the old Gassers continues to grow. Look for more new and old cars to appear in the future. (Photo Courtesy Bob Wenzelburger)

"for sale" sign out so that he could pursue his dream of running a Funny Car. The Willys remained in Southern California where it was bracket raced into 1984. It's believed that the truck sat for a few years before showing up on a used-car lot in Southern California in 1986. Tom Wilford spotted the truck and, even though it sported a multicolored psychedelic paint job, recognized it as the former Finders/Bizio truck and purchased it.

Tom hauled the Willys home to Washington where he performed a functional restoration with the help of his son. The pair then raced the truck occasionally at nostalgia events. The truck switched hands once again, going to Wendel Paulson in 1997. Wendel updated the roll cage to meet the current safety standards and assembled a fresh .030-over 392 hemi. The engine remains in the truck today and makes use of Venolia pistons, a reground Isky cam, magnesium 6-71 blower running 20-over, and Hilborn injection. Backing the 392 is a GM Turbo 400 transmission as well as the truck's original '58 Oldsmobile rear end and ladder bars.

Wendel raced the truck into the early 2000s before current owner Jeff Cryan came calling. Jeff continues to race the truck today where eighth-mile times of 5.27 at 140 mph are the norm. The 1967 Little John candy lacquer blue paint was rematched and painted by Dan Leuthold in the 1980s using a House of Kolor candy blue. Jeff Harley and Dan "The Sign Man" of Buffalo, New York, applied the gold-leaf lettering. The interior consists of 1960s Cal Automotive fiberglass seat and black Naugahyde.

Jeff has probably put more miles on this Willys than all previous owners combined and has no intention of stopping now. I think Mr. Willys and Mr. Finders would be proud.

George Montgomery's AA/GS 1969 Mustang

Ohio George is all smiles posing proudly with the lovely Miss Linda Vaughn after winning his first Gatornationals in 1973. George had defeated Steve Woods in the Comp Eliminator final. This was the first time a Boss 429 had won a major NHRA event. (Photo Courtesy Michael Mihalko)

Ohio George was tagged with the title "King of the Gasser" in the early 1960s thanks in large part to a pair of Little Eliminator wins at the NHRA Nationals in 1959 and 1960. George and his small-block Chevy–powered '33 Willys A/GS always seemed to be one step in front of the competition. When he hooked up with Ford Motor Company in 1966, bolting in a SOHC 427, it seemed that there was no stopping him.

George recalled that Ford had hoped to get him under its belt in 1964 to run one of the 289 engines. But George already had a winning combination and had no interest in parting with his blown Chevy. Then he lost at the 1965 Nationals. For a guy who was used to winning, and winning a lot, he took the loss hard and realized it was time for a change. He contacted Ford, which gladly signed him under the Mercury banner. Class wins followed at the Nationals in 1966, the winter meet in 1967, and again at the Nationals in 1967 where he cranked out an 8.93 at more than 162 mph.

Looking to get the most bang for their sponsored buck, Ford pushed for a switch from the Willys to a Mustang and provided George with a fiberglass body to slip over his Willys chassis. George and the *Malco Gasser* (as it was dubbed) forever changed the face of the category. It was the first modern-bodied Gasser and today's fans look back on this Mustang and see it as the car that spelled the beginning of the end of the category.

George spoke highly of his Mustangs, characteristically stating that he never realized how poorly his Willys handled until he hopped into the Mustang. As more competitors picked up on the advantages of the sleek body styles, George searched for ways to stay on top. Ford saw that he did stay on top and provided a prototype 1969

The metal-flaked Mustang features a stretched Willy's chassis and carries a 110-inch wheelbase. George did the machining and assembly of the 429 in his own shop. The suspension consists of a tube axle up front with Logghe adjustable shocks while adjustable ladder bars and coil-overs carry the rear. The suspension was adjustable at all four corners. (Photo Courtesy Jerry Heasley)

Mach 1 so that George could have a fiberglass shell laid up.

The new body was positioned over the same '33 Willys chassis that had been stretched to a 110-inch wheelbase. Supporting the car was a ladder-bar rear suspension and a tube axle up front. The suspension featured coil-over shocks at all four corners that allowed George to fine-tune to specific track conditions. A blown SOHC 427 producing 1,200 horses was initially used and was backed by a beefed C-6 transmission and 9-inch rear end. All were courtesy of the Ford Motor Company, which watched as the car dominated during its Indy debut.

George backed up his Malco Mustang Springnationals win by taking class and winning Super Eliminator in 1969. He defeated Ron Ellis in the final at the Nationals and set the AA/GS class record in the process with an 8.59 at 164.23 mph. George stuck with this combination until 1971 when he made the switch to a Boss 429. Not satisfied with the run-of-the-mill 6-71 blower setup, George took it to the next level and installed twin Schwitzer Turbochargers.

Although Ford had pulled its racing support by this point, George enjoyed back-door assistance from Ford Indy expert Danny Jones. The pair relied heavily on the manufacturer's defunct Indy program for turbo parts and technology.

George has stated that it took a couple of years to work out the bugs but once the car was sorted out, it cranked out times of 8.40 at 175 mph. As turbo technology was lagging (no pun intended) at the time, the trick was to kill some of the top end and try to compensate for the turbo lag. The guys downsized the fuel nozzles and modified the stock Boss heads, taking the 2.28 intake valves down to approximately half the size.

George says, "We killed 400 to 600 top-end horses in an attempt to overcome the initial lag. Each blower was putting out more than 30 pounds of boost and we were beating everyone." Due to the car's killer mid-range and top end, they just drove around cars that were quicker off the line.

A highlight of George's career was winning the NHRA Gatornationals in 1973 and 1974, which didn't seem

Flipping the glass front end reveals a sight that would make many mechanics consider another trade. But not George; he thrived on mechanical ingenuity. With the support of Ford Engineer Danny Jones, George dipped into the manufacturer's Indy parts bin to come up with this twin-turbo 1,800-hp bomb. The blowers are Schwitzer units and even though each was set up to feed a 4-cylinder, two of the cylinders were on the opposing bank of the engine. The fuel delivery system is by Bendix, which relied on a Mallory ignition to light the fire. By necessity, compression was in the neighborhood of 7.0:1. (Photo Courtesy Jerry Heasley)

The shell of the Mr. Gasket Gasser is all-fiberglass and was formed in 1968 using a 1969 Mustang prototype. George's Mustang debuted running AA/GS but by the time the car was retired, the Gasser classes had fallen by the wayside and the car was relegated to BB/AT. (Photo Courtesy Jerry Heasley)

The all-original interior is like a step back into 1969. The floor tin remains flawless thanks in part to the fact that George placed mats before hopping in the car. The candy-striped seats, like the exterior, feature heavy metalflake. (Photo Courtesy Jerry Heasley)

Peeking through the domed hood where a 6-71 blower once resided are the top of the Boss 429 intake plenums. Says George, "Relying on Indy technology, the engine was engineered to think it was twin Offys." Best time for the setup was an 8.22 at 173.75 mph. (Photo Courtesy Jerry Heasley)

to make the NHRA too happy. Not fully understanding turbo technology, the association felt that George was holding back on power and penalized him for it by forcing him to run off a handicap. Eventually George's combination was outlawed.

"They didn't understand turbos and were afraid of them. In not so many words, they let me know that the car was no longer welcome." George parked the car at the end of 1975 and went on to campaign a single-turbo 4-cylinder Pinto. He retired from racing in 1985 and settled down to build engines with his son.

The twin turbo Mustang lived on, surviving in a sealed container inside his shop in "as raced" condition. For those who don't know George, "as raced" means spotless. Throughout his career, George was as well known for his beautifully detailed and maintained cars as he was for going fast. As seen here, the Mustang is unrestored and 100 percent original.

Bob Perkins, the third and current owner of the car, says, "All the car needed was a quick cleanup. As you see, this is just how it was when George retired the car in 1975."

Schley Brothers' *Lightning Bug*

The late Don Kirby laid on the paint in 1970 while Nat Dick did the lettering. Body panels were hand-laid fiberglass while the sunroof opening and windows were filled with Lexan. (Photo Courtesy Schley Brothers)

In 1963, young Mark and Paul Schley set out to buy themselves a twin 4-barrel 413-powered Plymouth but giving in to pressure from the salesman and the neighbor they brought along, they did a complete flip-flop and came home with a VW Beetle. Influenced by local race legend Dan Gurney, the boys from Costa Mesa, California, made the best of their Bug. They gradually turned the Beetle into a quick street car and eventually an all-out I/Gasser.

Their first *Lightning Bug* didn't last long as it was lost in a horrific crash at Orange County in October 1969. The crash left driver Mark banged, bruised, and with 80 stitches. Eager to get back onto the horse, the boys had the second *Lightning Bug* ready for the 1970 NHRA

One of the Bug's countless victories came at the 1972 NHRA Summernationals at which it captured H/G. Note the stylish pants provided by sponsor Lee. Paul recalls, "Lee paid for our gas and our trips to national events. In return we pushed their products at supermarts on our days off." In 1972, Lee paid the guys to travel the country putting on clinics, much the same as Sox & Martin and Dick Landy had done for Chrysler in the late 1960s. (Photo Courtesy Schley Brothers)

Winternationals. A 1960 Bug was purchased and immediately stripped and acid dipped. Except for the center tunnel, the floorpan was cut out to make room for aluminum flooring. Joining the pan on the cutting room floor was the frame head, which gave way to a fabricated tube axle.

While employed by Dean Lowry the boys designed the axle; it was attached to the main unibody by two 10-inch-long modified torsion springs. Fabricated adjustable upper control arms were attached to the tube axle and main center bar. Steering relied on a stock VW box, while the tie rods were converted to a cross-steering design using a drag link bolted to the passenger-side spindle. A pair of VW steering dampeners took the place of shock absorbers. Going to extremes in weight reduction, the dampers were drained of their fluid.

Paul recalls the total weight of the front suspension was a mere 28 pounds. "We had removed 130 pounds." Helping to reduce the total weight to a slim 1,064 pounds were hand-laid fiberglass fenders, doors, hood, and trunk lid. Add 250 to 260 hp to the equation and you've got yourself the first H/G Bug to crack the 10-second quarter-mile barrier. The boys accomplished the feat in October 1972 at Freemont running a 10.97 and backing it up with a 10.94.

Propelling the *Bug* to 23 national records between 1970 and 1972 was an owner-built 2,180-cc engine. The VW engine case was extensively modified and welded. In addition, a homemade cradle was fabricated to help hold it all together. Shuffle pins were added and the oiling system was modified to keep the pistons cool. Says Paul, "The oiling system squirted oil to the bottom of the pistons because with 15:1 compression, so much heat was being generated."

Additional supports were added to the block where it cracked, which was usually around the flywheel, inside the bellhousing. The *Bug* went through plenty of rod bearings, which required replacing every five runs. The boys got so quick at changing the bearings that they actually pulled the engine in the staging lanes at the

Shortly after running the first 10-second time, the Bug was sold to a gentleman in Puerto Rico. Christened *Magnificent Banana*, the Bug proved to be the quickest car in the nation during 1973. (Photo Courtesy Schley Brothers)

The original gold-anodized aluminum paneling survives and is in great shape. For safety purposes, the roll cage had previously been updated. As allowed by NHRA Gasser rules, the seats were pushed back 10 percent of the wheelbase, or 9.4 inches. Outside of modern gauges, the interior remains as it was in 1970. The glass seats are by A&A and the brothers fabricated a shifter when they worked for Deano Dyno-Soars (Photo Courtesy Schley Brothers)

This is the engine that could. The "little" 2,180-cc pancake-4 was built back in the day by the Schleys and pumped out in the neighborhood of 250 horses. (Photo Courtesy Schley Brothers)

NHRA U.S. Nationals to replace them and had the car ready to go by the time they were at the front of the line.

The heads were ported and the exhaust valves' guides moved so that larger valves could be fitted. The intakes measured 48 mm while the exhaust valves measured 42 mm. To help reach maximum RPM quicker, the pushrods were drilled out and lightened. Shift points came at 8,000 rpm. The Weber carbs started out as 48 mm but were opened up to 51. Lighting the fire was a Joe Hunt magneto. The VW gearbox was swapped for a rare Porsche 741 box, which, unlike the VW box, had individual gears sets that allowed the Schleys to mix and match to suit conditions. The flywheel weighed 7 pounds and the one-two shift didn't happen until you were past the Christmas tree. M&H provided the traction while the rims were welded two-piece spun-aluminum made by the boys while employed by Lowry's Deano Dyno-Soars. The front wheels weighed a mere 3 pounds each while the rear rim and tire combination weighed 9 pounds each.

Feeling they had reached the limit with the *Bug* and still wanting to go faster, the Schleys sold the car in January 1973 and built themselves the first VW-powered, 9-second dragster. *Lightning Bug* went to Diego Febles in Puerto Rico with the promise that if he were to ever sell it, the Schleys would have first dibs. Christening it *Magnificent Banana*, Diego raced the Beetle for 37 years, made few modifications to it, and earned a lot of money with it. In 1973, the "Banana Bug" was the fastest car in the country. By 2010, Diego had retired and true to his word, placed the long-awaited call to the Schleys. The guys wasted little time in making arrangements to bring the car home.

Thankfully Diego kept the few original parts that he had removed from the car, which made the planned restoration process much easier. The Schleys hired Romance with Rust of Orange, California, to do the restoration and once stripped, the body was acid dipped to clean it up and remove the surface rust. The restored Beetle was painted by Pete Santini of Santini's Painting in Westminster, California. Pete found a sample of the original paint from inside the car that had not faded from the sun. He used a custom combination of House of Kolor paint to come up with a perfect match to the original blue. The Schleys themselves rebuilt the drivetrain and chassis. The total restoration took a year and a half and as you can see, it was time well spent.

Romance With Rust and Chris Albright helped along the restoration of the Bug. *In 1970, the Schleys took it upon themselves to chop 4 inches out of the roof. It was the teen boys' first chop and when the body was stripped in 2010, it showed. Additional metal work and rewelding cleaned it up nicely. (Photo Courtesy Schley Brothers)*

A single master cylinder was used for rear brakes only. The plastic gas tank you see up front was pulled from a riding lawn mower. The fenders weighed 5 pounds each; garden lights replaced the standard headlights. Weight of the lights? A mere 9 ounces each. (Photo Courtesy Schley Brothers)

Kroona & Sandberg

The team of Sandberg, Kroona & Crandell's first serious drag race effort was this record-holding A/G Anglia. With Crandel behind the wheel, the car ran consistent 9.30 times and was a record holder into the early 1970s. The car is thought to be the first tube-chassis Gasser. (Photo Courtesy Dave Davis)

Hailing from St. Paul, Minnesota, the team of Bruce Crandall, Dave Sandberg, and Dave Kroona took their drag racing seriously. Crandall and Sandberg partnered in the early 1960s and campaigned a number of Modified Production Chevys before Kroona joined the show. It wasn't until 1967 that the guys really got serious about their racing and built themselves an A/Gas Anglia. It was a beautiful car that featured one of the category's first tube chassis.

Dave Kroona recalls, "Actually, we had just completed building the car using the stock frame when the NHRA changed the rules allowing the tube chassis. This set us back a few months while we fabricated a 2 x 3 frame." Driven by Bruce, the big-block Chevy–powered Anglia took class at its first Indy appearance in 1969. It set the A/G record during the early 1970s before Bruce left the team; he sold the Anglia to build himself a Pro Stocker.

Kroona and Sandberg carried on with a second Anglia, which they debuted in 1969. Like the first Anglia, the car pictured here was purpose-built with the intent to do battle in AA/GS. Jim Oddy's blown Austin was a big influence and Kroona notes that, like the first Anglia, the guys had a game plan and stuck to it. A 2 x 3 chassis was built and fashioned with a Don Long front axle and ladder-bar rear suspension. Nestled between the rails was a 30-over 354 Hemi built by the legendary Jack Wheeler.

Located in Blaine, Minnesota, Jack has had his hands in more national event winners and record holders than most and was a mentor of sorts to Division 5 racers. He stuffed the Hemi with ForgedTrue pistons, Howards rods, Airflow Research heads, and topped it off with a Donavon-prepped under-driven GMC 6-71 blower. A Hilborn four-port injection fed the fuel while a magneto fed the spark. Numerous grinds of the camshaft were trialed before the guys settled on a Norris shaft.

Backing the engine initially was a B&M ClutchFlite. However, the car seemed to go through these on a regular basis. They tried a B&M Hydro and, finally, in 1973, a 4-speed Lenco. The Lenco did the trick, and driver Kroona recalls that it was a handful. "Steering the short-wheelbase car, watching the track, and pulling levers; after the first run I was ready to pull the transmission." That was before he saw his time slip. The

The team's second Anglia was completed in 1969 and raced into 1974. Best clocking was a 9.02 at 156 mph. The car features the standard fiberglass parts, along with plexiglass windows and a 3-inch top chop. Darrell Hanson sprayed the original black lacquer. (Photo Courtesy Dave Davis)

The 359-inch Hemi is based upon the old 354 of the late 1950s and was assembled using period-correct parts and lots of compression. Kroona, Sandberg & Crandell did a lot of their own fabrication, including the headers. (Photo Courtesy Dave Davis)

The all-business interior features blue anodized tin, which was laid out by Kroona, Sandberg & Crandell in 1968 and looks like new today. How many Gassers have you seen with a Lenco 4-speed? The Anglia was bought in 1968 from Winnipeg, Manitoba, Canada, for $100. (Photo Courtesy Dave Davis)

transmission had dropped .3 off of his elapsed time. Rounding out what proved to be a bulletproof drivetrain was a Dana 60 rear end.

Supporting the 2,700-pound Anglia were American five-spoke rims up front and 16-inch Halibrands out back. Even though these gave way to Super Tricks later on, the car was restored using the original rims and tires, which had been stored in Sandberg's garage.

The guys made it to many national events with the car; the final one was Indy in 1974. They met Bob Panella there; Bob happens to have a soft spot for the Anglia. Until a couple years before, Bob campaigned an Anglia of his own and with Ken Dondero behind the wheel and had won Super Eliminator at the 1969 NHRA Winternationals. Bob was now fielding a sleek little Opel Gasser. He had dominated with a controversial turbo setup in the Opel before rules forced him to switch to a blower.

With Kroona and Sandberg looking to build a lower car, Bob and driver Phil Featherston hastened the decision when they laid down a blistering 8.88. At the time, the Kroona & Sandberg Anglia was hitting a best of 9.02. Shortly after Indy, they sold the Anglia as a rolling chassis to someone in Ohio while the short-block went to Jim Oddy in New York. The two Daves found themselves an Opel and started the build early in 1975. While thumbing through a copy of the *National Dragster* they came across Bob's "The Chance of a Lifetime" Opel for-sale advertisement.

Unable to say no to a proven winning combination, a deal was struck to buy Bob's car and their project went on the block. Once the guys had the Opel home in Minnesota, they immediately started stripping the Fiberglass Trends body and repainting it their signature black while Jack Wheeler went through the destroked 354 Hemi. Before reassembly, the Ron Scrima chassis was sandblasted and every nut and bolt was replaced.

Bob suggested they bring the car west for the 1976 NHRA Winternationals, something Kroona and Sandberg

Larry Dahl prepped the body while Ron Gorrell at Unique Body & Paint in Blaine, Minnesota, sprayed the black. All the stickers are reproductions while the classy wheels and tires are original to the car. They had been in "forgotten" storage for approximately 40 years. (Photo Courtesy Dave Davis)

Chapter Four: The Wild Bunch 145

To the crowd's approval, Kroona and Sandberg had both restored cars on hand at Bowling Green in 2012. The former Panella Opel was brought back from a near basket case whereas the Anglia was 90-percent complete and retained most of its original parts when found. Both restored cars were finalists for the Bob Daniels Award at Bowling Green and invited to Indy for the final pick. It was the only time two cars by the same owner were ever selected to compete for this prestigious award. (Photo Courtesy Dave Davis)

were reluctant to do as Kroona had yet to drive the car. Bob suggested that Phil drive for them. Phil had some pretty good luck with the Opel; he played runner-up in Comp Eliminator at the 1974 Winternationals and returned in 1975 to run CC/A and win it all. The Daves agreed, and Phil won the meet again.

The basic Panella engine and drivetrain combination remained the same, and why not? Bob had the car cranking out a best of 8.30 times. Kroona and Sandberg ran the car into 1978 before selling the rolling chassis; they had thoughts of building an alcohol Funny Car. They followed the sport and attended the big meets, but the alcohol Funny Car just never materialized.

That's what has happened to many of us. Priorities take over and things like building a race car move into the back seat. "Before you know it, 40 years have passed." That's exactly what happened in the case of Kroona and Sandberg. During those years, the Anglia was always in the back of their minds and they wondered what became of it.

Unbeknownst to Kroona, his good friend Boyd Harlan had placed ads in trade papers and posted flyers at every track he visited in search of the Anglia. Finally, a response was received from a gentleman in Nebraska. Recalls Kroona, "Boyd called me up one night and told me he had found the car. I say, 'What car?' 'The Anglia,' he says. He was a bit of a prankster and I thought he was pulling my leg so I threatened to hang up on him." Boyd finally convinced Dave that he was telling the truth and gave him the current owner's phone number.

How did the owner know it was the old Kroona & Sandberg Anglia? Easy. It still carried the original paint, decals, and the majority of its original parts. As was told to Kroona, the fellow had grown up in Iowa; he and his dad used to watch the car race when it came to town. His dad was in love with the car and bought it when it went up for sale.

The Anglia was nearly complete but it now sported a small-block Chevy. With a family to raise, the gentleman was prepared to sell and Kroona was eager to buy. The car came "home" in the early 1990s where it sat for the next dozen or so years before he found the motivation to restore it. The Anglia was missing a few parts and needed a fresh hemi and 4-speed Lenco. The previous owner retained all the parts he had removed from the car and that included the original plexiglass windows (with stickers), which he had replaced years before with glass.

The car came with all the original spare parts it was sold with, including extra headers, track bars, and a bent tube axle. Kroona must have caught some serious air back in the early 1970s and the team had to replace the axle after he came down hard. The original black lacquer was showing its age so the car was taken down to bare metal by Larry Dahl who prepped the body before Ron Gorrell of Unique Body and Paint laid on a fresh coat of black. Kroona & Sandberg debuted the Anglia at the GSTA Car Show in 2006. An invitation to Indy the same year brought the car plenty of accolades along with a number of "Where's the Opel?" from knowing fans.

The pair hadn't given much thought to the Opel; they last saw the car in the 1990s on the West Coast where it had been running Super Gas. To their surprise, they found out while at Indy that the Opel had just sold on eBay. This really piqued the pair's interest so they contacted the buyer. Yes, he was willing to sell them the car but at an overinflated asking price. The pair decided to hang on to their money and passed on the car. Kroona

Running CC/A in 1975, the Kroona & Sandberg Opel was wheeled by Phil Featherston. He drove the Opel to three Winternationals wins. The first one came while driving the car for Bob Panella. It's believed the Opel was raced into the 1990s running Super Gas with a single 4-barrel big-block Chevy. (Photo Courtesy Dave Davis)

Phil is all smiles, taking the seat of the Opel for the first time in 35 years. He first drove the Opel for Bob Panella and won three Comp titles at the Winternationals, the first one while competing in BB/GST with a turbo. He twice set BB/GST record in 1973, first with an 8.98 then an 8.64 at 159.26. The Opel held both ends of the national record with an 8.44 at 163.33 before the class was killed. The destroked Hemi (301 inches) features a 4-inch bore and 3-inch stroke. (Photo Courtesy Dave Davis)

kept in touch with the owner and in 2009, he was ready to sell at a more realistic price.

Unlike the Anglia, the Opel was in pretty rough shape. At some point the flip-up body was cut off at the firewall and the main body permanently attached to the chassis. A hood opening was cut into the front end that was now removable. Thankfully the chassis, roll cage, and the majority of the Tom Hanna tinwork remained intact.

Again, as with the Anglia, Kroona purchased the Opel as a rolling chassis so a fresh 301 Hemi had to be built. Instead of the original 3-speed Lenco, a 4-speed was found and bolted in. Larry Dahl and Ron Gorrell were once again called upon to piece together the body and lay on the fresh paint. With the restoration complete in 2012, Kroona and Sandberg debuted the Opel at the Bowling Green Hot Rod Reunion, finally putting to rest the question, What about the Opel?

The Opel passed through four or more owners before coming home to Dave Kroona. Body and paint were handled by the same person who took care of the Anglia. Dave Sandberg helped extensively with the restoration, returning the car to better-than-race condition. Who wouldn't love this one parked in their drive? (Photo Courtesy Dave Davis)

Chapter Four: The Wild Bunch 147

CHAPTER FIVE
DOOR SLAMMERS GALORE

The name "door slammer" refers to stock-bodied cars that competed in categories such as Stock, Super Stock, and Modified Eliminator. At one time, these were considered entry-level categories, as they were generally the least expensive cars to build and to compete with. Although the majority of competitive cars in these categories were dedicated race cars, many of the early door slammers were licensed and street driven.

The Stockers and Super Stocks still battle it out today. However, in 1981 the NHRA unceremoniously axed Modified Eliminator, and the screams can still be heard. Why the NHRA did away with the category, which was popular with both fans and racers, is still unclear. The excuse given was low overall contestant participation. This excuse is just as hard to accept today as it was in 1981. At almost every major event, more cars showed up for the Eliminator than the field allowed.

The final race for Modified Eliminator came at the season-ending World Finals. However, it was at Indy where racers voiced their disapproval. One hundred fifty cars showed up for the Eliminator and in silent protest, the majority of these modified cars clogged the return road in a slow procession.

> **IN 1981 THE NHRA UNCEREMONIOUSLY AXED MODIFIED ELIMINATOR AND THE SCREAMS CAN STILL BE HEARD.**

Above: Restored by John Accarino in 2010, Bill Blanding's line of Modified Production MIMI Camaros was a dominant force in the late 1960s. Bill shared driving duties with Rich Mirarcki and set many national records including 137.40 mph at Raceway Park, New Jersey, and 10.03 at Sanair in 1971. Bill retired this car in 1973 after building a Pro Stock Vega. Restoration was extensive, requiring floorboards, firewall, and many body panels. Powerhouse Hot Rods performed the work. A ZL-1 built by John is now in the works.

Dave Strickler's *The Old Reliable II*

Dave and Grumpy pose proudly with The Old Reliable II. *The pair has a reason to smile. Can't say the same for their competitors. (Photo Courtesy Mike Strickler)*

As with so many postwar teenagers, hot rodding seemed to run through Dave Strickler's veins. By his mid-teens, he was racing the back roads of York, Pennsylvania, in his father's workhorse Chevy truck. He used his part-time work earnings to modify the truck; he installed twin carbs and a split manifold. Eventually Dave graduated to racing the local dragstrips and honed the skills that led to 16 NHRA class Championships, 41 National Records, and a World Champion Title in 1968.

Dave hooked up with Grumpy Jenkins in 1959 and by 1961, they were partners in campaigning the first *Old Reliable* Chevy, a 409-powered Biscayne tuned by Grumpy that gave them the first Optional Super Stock record, turning in a 13.24.

A 409-powered 1962 Bel Air was special-ordered from sponsor Ammon R. Smith late in 1961 to replace *The Old Reliable I* Biscayne. Because of delays in delivery, hopes of making the NHRA Winternationals were fading fast so a change of plans saw a 409-powered Bel Air pulled from the showroom floor.

Initially rated at 409 hp and developing 420 ft-lbs of torque, the engine was balanced and blueprinted. It included late-1961 twin Carter 4-barrel carbs, large-port cylinder heads cc'd by Grumpy, along with power slot-cast pistons. Completing the drivetrain of *The Old Reliable II* was a Hurst-shifted BorgWarner 4-speed transmission (sporting a 2:20 first gear) and a rear end that housed 4:56 gears. To help strengthen the notoriously weak third member, the rear center pot was drilled opposite the pinion gear, tapped, and a threaded bolt inserted. The bolt had a built-up brass tip and rode an approximate .005 off the ring gear to eliminate excessive movement. Additional modifications included carrier cap braces and over-the-counter service package spider gears. In examining the restored *The Old Reliable II*, Grumpy noted that the nonoriginal rear end (as the housing) was missing the bolt hole.

To aid in weight transfer, a pair of nine-passenger station wagon springs was installed up front with a set of stiffer, shorter coils in the rear. In a move to improve traction, the body was moved back on the frame mounts, which placed greater weight on the rear wheels. Grumpy had previously credited the Ford ace Dick Brannan with this idea.

In mid-January, Dave and Grumpy headed for sunny Southern California and the NHRA Winternationals. Their first stop was a lead-up race at San Gabriel at which, on the first pass, the Bel Air "puked the motor." Scrambling to find a block and pistons 2,600 miles from home was no easy task. Grumpy recalled having to belt-sand the new pistons down to size because they were too large. "The car ran pretty good considering the mess it was when it went together."

At the Winternationals, the Bel Air competed in Super Super Stock (SS/S). Dave set the lowest elapsed time of the meet with a 12.55 but lost class honors to Hayden Proffitt in his Carroll Cones–sponsored Chevy.

In the Mr. Stock Eliminator run-offs, Dave lost to Don Nicholson in a nearly identical Service Chevrolet–sponsored Bel Air. Ironically, some felt that Dave had the title wrapped up as Don failed to make the initial call to

The Old Reliable II is looking a little worse for wear sporting a crunched fender after an accident falling off the trailer ramp. (Photo Courtesy Mike Strickler)

The aluminum inner fenders were hand-fabricated after the 1962 units that were installed disappeared before the current owner took possession of the car. The heart of Old Reliable II *was its 409 ci, developing well over the 409 rated horsepower. Note the quick-disconnect on the generator.*

the line. Because Dave dreamed of defeating Don, he and Grumpy made the fatal decision to wait until Nicholson's car was ready. Don then went on to defeat Carol Cox for the Mr. Stock Eliminator title. As proof that the sport of drag racing was still in its infancy, National Dragster reported in winning the battle, Don's take included a color television donated by Mr. and Mrs. Sopps of Sopps Car Wash in Los Angeles.

At the NHRA Nationals in Indianapolis, Dave captured its first national event win to earn Super Stock honors by wading through six rounds of eliminations to meet and defeat Hayden Proffitt with a time of 12.97 to Hayden's quicker but lagging 12.83.

Mr. Stock Eliminator run-off pitted the 50 fastest Super Stocks at the Nationals against one another. It again found Dave and Hayden meeting up. Hayden, who had accused Dave of leaving the line too soon during the Super Stock final, exacted a measure of revenge by eliminating Dave while on his way to the Stock Eliminator finals. (Hayden defeated Jim Thornton in the Ramchargers Dodge to take the Mr. Stock Eliminator crown.)

In a Petersen Publication article covering the Nationals win, Dave described how he came off the line at the drop of the flag between 2,200 and 2,500 rpm and ran the Hurst shifter through the gears between 6,500 and 6,800 rpm. In reality, Dave rarely watched the tachometer; instead he chose to drive by the seat of his pants. This frustrated the technically minded Grumpy as he wanted to know how the car ran, at what RPM he shifted, what RPM he went through the traps, etc.

With NHRA's realignment of classes in 1963, *The Old Reliable* Bel Air now competed in A/Stock. In January, the Bel Air was once again towed west to Pomona for the winter meet where it captured class with a 12.66 at 114.58.

In July, *The Old Reliable II* was set up to run B/FX with the aluminum front clip installed and proceeded to set both MPH and ET records at York. Later the same month the car was match raced at Mason-Dixon and produced the first 11-second track time for a stocker. Dave and *Old Reliable* defeated Bud Faubel's 413-powered *Honkin* Dodge running times as quick as an 11.86 at 120.80 mph.

At the 1963 NHRA Nationals, Dave spent most of the day bouncing back and forth between *The Old Reliable II* and *The Old Reliable IV,* handling the driver chores of both. It had been awhile since he last drove in competition; Bill was briefly called upon to climb behind the wheel of *The Old Reliable II* as eliminations wound down. His time away from the driver's seat found him a little rusty and he was eliminated in the semi-finals.

In one of its final appearances, *The Old Reliable II* match raced against Arlen Vankes' A/FX record-holding 421-powered Pontiac Tempest at Cecil County, Maryland. In defeating Arlen in three straight, *The Old Reliable* turned a quick 11.73. Later in the day, Dave returned for an exhibition run and banged-off a crowd-pleasing 11.58 at 123.28 mph.

By the end of the 1963 season, *The Old Reliable II* was transformed back to street status, at least in appearance, and placed on the used lot of Ammon R. Smith. It sold quickly to Maryland resident John Chapel. The car passed through numerous hands before being purchased in 1983 by current owner Larry Brinkley. Larry took on the daunting task of restoring the car to its former A/Stock status.

During the restoration, he had to make extensive repairs because a previous owner had backed the car into a lamppost. Larry also discovered to what extent Dave and Grumpy had gone to in order to get weight off the car. It was obvious that the torches had come out and anything that could be removed was removed. Frame rails were drilled with lightening holes, springs were removed from the rear seat, and (although invisible with the fenders installed) the lower cowl had sections of metal removed.

Dave's proficiency behind the wheel, courtesy to others, and friendly disposition are legendary. He retired from drag racing in 1974 after campaigning a mildly successful Pro Stock Vega. Sadly, we lost Dave to a heart attack at the age of 44.

Larry makes an easy pass on Old Reliable *during an early-1990s muscle car show. Larry spared no expense to restore the car correctly and has met the approval of the Strickler family. In its heyday, Dave and the Chevy ran Stock, Super Stock, and Factory Experimental classes.*

Dave Kempton's Plymouth Fury

Dave's 1962 Plymouth Sport Fury, originally labeled San Gabriel Dragstrip Special, *was really shaking things up in the mid-1960s, as it practically owned C/SA. With the NHRA adjusting the weight breaks in 1966, the Plymouth, sporting a single-4-barrel 305-horse 361, ran D/SA. A later upgrade to a 343-horse 383 put the Plymouth back into C/SA.*

To say that Dave Kempton had himself a pretty good career in drag racing would be an understatement. The man campaigned his cars on a part-time basis; he rarely traveled outside of Division 7, but still managed a win percentage that was the envy of his peers. He won three National events between 1965 and 1968 and remember, this was back in the day when there were only four events per season. Class wins came at the NHRA Winternationals in 1963, 1965, 1966, 1967, and 1968. He was the Division 7 points champion in 1964 and was runner-up to Jay Hamilton's Pontiac in 1965. The one rare occasion when Dave did travel outside of his time zone was in 1966 when he headed for Indy and won the whole thing.

A late bloomer in the world of drag racing, Dave's first pass down the quarter-mile was at the ripe old age of 27, when he took his flathead 6 '49 Plymouth down the old San Gabe in the mid-1950s. One of the first strips in existence, Dave found part-time work there classifying cars and teching in the stockers. Until the gates closed in 1963, his spare time was spent at the track, either working or running one of his Plymouths. I don't know where he found the time but he still managed to hold down a 9-to-5 hanging billboards and was also the competition director for the *Drag News* magazine. All in the name of fair play, Dave never raced his Plymouths on the days he was working the strip but still managed to stockpile well over 400 trophies throughout his career.

His wife, Norma, proved to be a worthy opponent herself; she added more than her share of trophies to the family mantel. Norma later worked the tower at Irwindale while their son Mark worked the pits and time-slip booth. For a family of enthusiasts, the Kemptons seemed to have had found the ideal way to spend quality time together.

The renowned *Shaker* Sport Fury was purchased new in 1962 from the Milne Brothers in Pasadena and initially saw double duty as the family's daily driver and the

Chapter Five: Door Slammers Galore

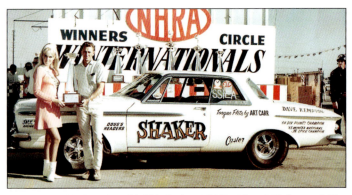

Dave tried his hand at SS/EA during 1967 with a 343-horse 383 and started the year off right by taking class at the NHRA Winternationals with a 12.70 at 111.15. Back in the Stock ranks with a 383-ci Sport Fury in 1968, Dave enjoyed a C/SA class win at the Winternationals, where he knocked the Ford brass on its collective ear by defeating their Cobra Jet Mustang. Dave joined AMC in 1968 and the Plymouth made its way east after being sold to the team of John Pratt and Bob Burkitt.

Before the Nationals in 1966, Dave swapped the 361 for a 343-horse 383 and won C/SA. Here, he polishes his skills against Eddie Schartman's 390 Comet.

weekend racer. Mark recalled more than one trip to the market with Mom engaging those who tried to entice her into a little stoplight action. The 361-powered Sport Fury proved to be a perfect fit for C/SA and was aptly named *Shaker* because of the fear it struck into its opponents.

The single 4-barrel 305-horse 361 saw little initial tweaking, relying only on a quick cleanup of the Doug's heads, recurved distributor, and adjustments to the Carter carburetor to win its first Winternationals with a 13.68. Art Carr prepared the Torqueflite transmission while out back, 4:88 gears filled the 8¾ rear. Casler tires holding approximately 12 pounds of pressure were relied on to get the power to the ground. Before moving the car into SS/EA in 1967, Dave had the Plymouth running a best of 12.83 at 110.15 after installing a fresh twin 4-barrel 343-horse 383.

His Super Stock success with the car, although limited, caught the attention of AMC who offered Dave a factory deal in 1968, something he never enjoyed while running his Plymouth. Competing in SS/F, Dave's AMX received only the best parts and cranked out 12.30 times. Nevertheless, as with the preceding Plymouth, Super Stock success was fleeting and Dave returned to the stocker ranks late in 1969; he built a G/SA '62 Plymouth wagon dubbed *Shaker Maker*.

The Sport Fury was sold to Ronnie Beech and later to Kenny Ford, who painted the car black and continued to race it with the 383. Current owner Artie Fulcher purchased the Sport Fury in 1984 with no idea of the car's original history. His raced the car through 1987 when it was retired. Artie had discovered the car's historic significance and felt it was too valuable to continue racing.

Even though the car retains some of its later performance cues, surprisingly it still has many of its original race parts, including the trick Art Carr Torqueflite transmission and convertor. Dave was a great help with the restoration, sharing plenty of information to ensure the restored race car is true to its origins.

Artie Fulcher's *Shaker* Plymouth was confirmed by the late Dave Kempton as the real deal. Although the Sport Fury retains a number of its later styling cues, many of the original parts remain or have been installed. (Photo Courtesy Artie Fulcher)

Dave's Sport Fury had been raced into the late 1980s and at one point featured black paint. The original teal interior has been dyed black by a previous owner to match the paint. (Photo Courtesy Artie Fulcher)

Frank Sanders' Z-11 Chevy

Frank Sanders was a popular West Coast racer in the early 1960s. He won class at the NHRA Winternationals three times and the AHRA Winter Nationals twice. Racers also relied on the additional horsepower provided by Sanders' S&S headers. (Photo Courtesy Nick Smith Collection)

The year 1963 could be considered the peak of Detroit's involvement in organized drag racing as each of the Big Three offered all-out drag-race–specific vehicles. This was the last year for General Motors' direct involvement; early in 1963, they pulled out of racing to reaffirm their commitment to the 1957 AMA ban on involvement in organized racing. All American auto manufacturers signed this agreement and they appeared to have adhered to it, initially. However, embracing the mantra "Win on Sunday, Sell on Monday," the manufacturers caved to the lure of the exploding youth market and, within a few years of the ban, the factory wars were on again.

Chevrolet introduced the 348 "W" engine in 1958 as a big brother to the 283. Its inherited design gave it loads of torque and by 1960, the early big-block was battling Ford's 352 for on-track supremacy. In 1961, the 348 was redesigned and stretched to 409 inches. Arizona's Frank Sanders, setting the tone for the year, drove his Rudolph Chevrolet–sponsored Dyno Don Nicholson–tuned 409 Biscayne to Super Stock honors at the season-opening NHRA Winternationals.

As the factory wars continued to escalate, Chevrolet introduced mid-season upgrades, bringing the 409 engine's horsepower rating up to an equal of its displacement, 409. In a preview of things to come, Chevrolet introduced 20 aluminum-nose 409 Impalas in July 1962, which were quickly followed by the availability of over-the-counter large-port heads, a two-piece aluminum intake manifold, a .507-lift camshaft, and matching valvesprings. In the B/FX class final at the NHRA Nationals, Dyno Don and Dave Strickler faced off in a pair of these specially equipped Impalas with Don taking the win with a 12.93 to Dave's 12.96.

The icing on the 409 cake was the introduction of 50 1963 RPO Z-11 Impalas. At the heart of the $1,240 Z-11 package was the 409-derived 427 engine. Conservatively rated at 430 hp, the 427 was a stroked 409 fitted with large port heads, 13:5.1 compression, a camshaft featuring .556 lift, and a two-piece aluminum intake manifold. Perched on top of a pair of Carter AFB carburetors was a specially designed air-cleaner housing that funneled fresh air from the cowl.

Lightweight aluminum fenders, hood, splash pan, fan shroud, bumpers, and brackets (20 aluminum pieces in all) helped bring the curb weight down to 3,405

Frank entered a contract with Arizona-based Rudolph Chevrolet on January 16, 1963, which lasted through September 1, 1963. The Chevy passed through a few hands before Roger Sortino had the car restored in 1999–2000. Here Frank accepts the gold for taking Limited Production class at the 1963 NHRA Winternationals. Frank had defeated the similarly equipped Z-11 car of Terry Prince with a 12.01. The NHRA created the Limited Production class for the Super Stock racer whose manufacturers failed to show proof of the minimum 50 units sold. Frank was later tossed as his GM camshaft did not meet the specs the manufacturer had given to the NHRA. As was the rule of the day, no class winner was designated. (Photo Courtesy Nick Smith Collection)

Chapter Five: Door Slammers Galore 153

The Z-11's restored chassis and drivetrain awaits the body. The frame of the Z-11 cars was standard 1963 Chevy while driveline components, including the exhaust system, were 409 goods. (Photo Courtesy Nick Smith Collection)

GM ship manifests show a total of 50 427s were shipped to Flint, Michigan, in August 1962 to be installed in the special-edition Z-11 1963 Impala. In addition to the initial 50 engines, another 20 half-engines were shipped through July 31, 1963. The Z-11 was the winningest stock-class drag car in 1963. Horsepower of a well-tuned engine was estimated to be in the neighborhood of 550 to 575 while today, dyno pulls show a stocker to be capable of 485 to 500 horses. The cowl induction, rocker covers, and aluminum water pump were unique to this engine. (Photo Courtesy Nick Smith Collection)

The Z-11 package consisted of 20 different aluminum parts including hood, fenders, and bumpers. Weight savings equated to approximately 200 ponds. (Photo Courtesy Geoff Stunkard)

The austere interior is all-original and features a Hurst Shifter and a Sun tachometer that was installed by Frank in place of the factory original. Frank was a master fabricator and built his own clutch scattershield. Underdash gauges were limited to oil pressure and water temperature. For the intended application, little else was needed. The odometer in this car shows an original 3,500 miles. (Photo Courtesy Nick Smith Collection)

pounds. Additional weight saving was found by omitting the sound deadener, radio, and heater. Metallic brake linings with vented backing plates helped to bring the Impalas to a stop from 120-mph charges.

Frank's Z-11 was one of the more successful stockers of 1963; it won Limited Production at the NHRA Winternationals along with being the first Z-11 car to top 120 mph. Frank went on to attain the number-1 position on the Drag News Top Stock Eliminator list. It was one of only two cars that spent the entire year on the list and won 19 of 20 races. Closing the season, Frank's car was the overall points champion.

Willie Smith completed an extensive frame-off restoration of the car in the late 1990s, but it is still considered to be one of the most original Z-11 cars in existence. Having spent its life in the dry climate of Arizona and California, it retains all the original rust-free sheet metal

Willie Smith is responsible for restoring the Chevy. Panels are all-original and required minor tweaking as the Chevy saw little abuse over the years. The fresh coat of Azure Aqua covered the pristine sheet metal. (Photo Courtesy Nick Smith Collection)

and aluminum panels. The engine and BorgWarner transmission are original to the car along with Frank's own S&S Headers. Excluding the carpet, the interior is as delivered to Rudolph Chevrolet in 1963. If a limited run of 50 isn't rare enough for you, how about the only one painted Azure Aqua?

Frank, like many GM racers, switched brands when the manufacturer dropped out of racing. He took to an SS/A Plymouth in 1964 and called AHRA's Beeline Dragway home. By the end of the decade, Frank was out of racing and into aeronautics. Sadly, he died in 1990 when his vintage Korean trainer jet crashed over Roswell, New Mexico. Frank's Z-11 Chevy is a fond reminder of days gone by and today the car resides in the open collection of Nick Smith.

From any angle, this Chevy looks great. NOS Firestone cheater slicks are mounted out back while up front, 7.10 x 15s fill the bill. Magnesium rims by American Racing was Frank's wheel of choice. (Photo Courtesy Geoff Stunkard)

Osburn Trucking's Lightweight Ford

Although they raced all over the Midwest, Detroit was the home track for Osburn's A/Stocker. Fresh-air tubes fed the Holley carbs through the factory-modified grille work. The Ford weighed 3,740 pounds and cost the dealer $3,950 (automatic cars cost $4,150). This price was $170 more than a Thunderbolt. (Photo Courtesy Nick Smith Collection)

The lightweight Ford Galaxie was the big brother and protector of the Fairlane Thunderbolt. These Galaxies were built in case the 427-powered Thunderbolt was not accepted by the NHRA for Super Stock competition at the 1964 NHRA Winternationals. History shows the 'Bolts were accepted and owned Super Stock. The Galaxies initially ran B/FX class but once the 50 units were built, the green light was given to run AA/S and AA/SA.

All 50 cars were built at Ford's Atlanta assembly plant and production was split evenly between automatic- and standard-transmission cars. All but six of the cars were delivered between February and June and if you can believe it, the remaining six cars had to be sold at a reduced price late in the year.

These were unique cars from the get-go; they were assembled on a lighter frame and were not subject to sealant, sound deadener, radios, or heaters. Even more weight was saved by using lightweight bucket seats, an RC aluminum bellhousing, and a scooped fiberglass hood. The mandatory twin 4-barrel 427 was backed by either a Toploader 4-speed featuring a 2.36 first gear or a 3-speed automatic. Out back, the 9-inch housing carried 4.71 gears and hefty 31-spline axles.

The Osburn Trucking car has a 4-speed; Dale Osburn purchased it from dealer Bob Ford in Dearborn. Dale had bought the car as a means of keeping his son Dan from street racing. As Dan recalls, "The car initially ran 13-second times but through the help of a third party, we had Bill 'Grumpy' Jenkins go through the engine, which got the car down into the 11-second bracket. Bill had the engine about three weeks and when we got it back, the car was a completely different animal." Dan had the fastest car in class and set the class record in Ohio with an 11.49.

Ford Motor Company paid Dan and his helper, Jack Schick, to travel west for the NHRA Winternationals and had the car shipped there by train. The car was

An old hot rodder's trick was to move the battery to the trunk where the added weight did some good. The manufacturers picked up on the idea in the late 1950s. The Autolite dropped 50 pounds from the front end and placed it over the rear wheels for added traction. (Photo Courtesy Nick Smith Collection)

Even though the car shows a documented 20 miles on the odometer, it has gone through two restorations. In 2011–2012, the body came off the frame, was stripped to bare metal, and restored to better than new. (Photo Courtesy Nick Smith Collection)

tied down along with a number of Mustangs destined for Holman-Moody. When they arrived on the West Coast, the Galaxie needed all its drag shocks replaced. Apparently, tying the car down ended their usefulness. Fontana Ford was the go-to place when the Ford contingency needed repairs so the pair headed over and the shocks were replaced. They were back at Fontana's shortly to replace the transmission that blew before Pomona during a warm-up race. Once at Pomona Dan had the field covered but his luck continued to run south. His day came to a quick end when the rear end let go during class eliminations.

With match racing all the rage in the 1960s, Dan did his fair share of it and, as he recalls, won more than he lost. With 10-inch Race Masters bolted on the rear, the Ford reportedly cranked out consistent 10.50 times. All racers had their speed secrets and Dan was no exception. Tucked under the passenger seat was an oxygen tank that fed highly pressurized air through a tube to the twin carbs. "A homemade blower setup seemed to help," says Dan. "You couldn't turn it on at idle as it would kill the motor."

By the late 1960s, Dan had found true love and the Ford went bye-bye. Billy Pearson purchased it and reportedly swapped the twin 4-barrels for a single Holley and

The 9-inch rear features 4.71 gears and 31-spline axles. The traction arms were installed by the Osburns in 1964 and are similar in design to those used on Thunderbolt Fairlanes. In the foreground is a part of the car's exhaust, an NHRA requirement back in the day for stock class cars. (Photo Courtesy Nick Smith Collection)

The high-rise 427 was blueprinted by none other than Chevy legend Bill "Grumpy" Jenkins and by the owner's guesstimate, put out 600 hp. "It went from a 13-second car stock to mid-11s." NHRA rules required the retention of the factory valvetrain, which limited RPM to 6,500. (Photo Courtesy Nick Smith Collection)

All 50 of the lightweight Galaxies featured red interiors (code 75) and Wimbledon white exteriors. A Hurst shifter controls the Toploader 4-speed. Bucket seats are lightweight, whereas the rubber floor matting is sans any underlay. Although not present today, the Osburns had a lever beside the driver's seat, which was connected to the emergency-brake cable. This was used as a primitive line-lock, holding the car on the line while the tree ticked down. (Photo Courtesy Nick Smith Collection)

continued racing it. It switched hands once again, this time in a trade for a Ram-Air Comet. Don Gillespie took a divisional race at Milan with the Ford in 1969 and raced it through 1974. A few more owners came and went before the Ford ended up in Florida with current owner Nick Smith.

The Osburn Galaxie was purchased through Bob Ford by Dale Osburn as a means of keeping his son from racing on the street. Bob Ford sold five of these lightweights, two 4-speed cars and three automatics. In its heyday, the car was maintained and driven by both Dan Osburn and friend Jack Schick. (Photo Courtesy Nick Smith Collection)

Golden Commandos' Barracuda

Mrs. Gene Meyers, the wife of one of the Commandos, poses proudly with the Barracuda back in its heyday. The car was built by the Golden Commandos to demonstrate that racing could be done, and fun, on a budget. (Photo Courtesy Bruce Lindstrom)

The Golden Commandos was a Plymouth factory-backed drag team consisting of engineers who first came together in 1962. After successfully campaigning a number of Factory Experimental and Super Stock cars, the guys decided to wet their hands in Junior Stock with this featherweight Barracuda. Years later, the Commandos admitted to the thrill that was making the little 273 perform. And it did perform. At the 1965 NHRA Nationals, driver John Dallafior won F/S class and in the process, set the class record with a 13.47 at 103.68 mph.

The Commandos started with an assembly-line Barracuda, stripping all the dead weight from the car and running the fenders, hood, radiator support, and doors through an acid bath. The 150 pounds shaved off the front was strategically located to the rear of the car by way of filling the spare tire with water and adding lead weight to the rear-seat trunk divide area. As rules limited rear tire width to a maximum of 7 inches, this added weight really helped the M&H slicks bite.

Stifling rules also limited what modifications were allowable to the little 273. You knew the guys were really pushing the envelope to produce an estimated 100 horses more than stock. For match-race purposes,

Chapter Five: Door Slammers Galore 157

The Barracuda looks ready to race, and it is. The current owner built the car to compete. Currently, the odometer shows just 352 original miles. The driver-door window was replaced with Lexan by the Golden Commandos in 1965 as body flex and the acid-dipped doors caused the door glass to break. Total vehicle weight is a mere 2,900 pounds. (Photo Courtesy Bruce Lindstrom)

The current 273 features fabricated headers, a 650 Holley on an Edelbrock manifold, 11.2 compression, .040-over JE pistons, W heads, and a .557-inch-lift roller camshaft. Dyno results show 380 horses and 337 ft-lbs of torque. (Photo Courtesy Bruce Lindstrom)

the Commandos built a .040-over 318, which ran twin Carter 4-barrels, ForgedTrue pistons, and a Racer Brown camshaft. Match-race clockings were pegged at 11.57 in the quarter-mile.

Backing either engine was a 2.69:1 first gear A-833 4-speed while the rear end of choice depended on where the car was being raced. For NHRA competition, the Barracuda was forced to run the weak-kneed 7.75 rear end while racing with other sanctioning bodies and match racing, an 8.75 rear end with 4.89 gears was used. Super Stock–style springs supported the rear end and to aid traction, the bottom leaf was pulled from the driver-side spring, cut in half and bolted to the front of the passenger-side leaf-spring bundle. Mounting the springs to the chassis was a prototype set of offset spring hangers.

The Commandos ran the Barracuda up to 1969 and won 90 percent of their races. The car passed to sponsor dealership Hamilton Motors, which enjoyed factory support through 1971. With a change in Chrysler focus, support of the car ended and the dealer sold the Barracuda. It passed through another four owners before landing in the lap of current owner Bruce Lindstrom in 1999. Bruce had a blown 440 Mopar that needed a home; he called a friend who happened to have a car Bruce could take. The Barracuda had been sitting for the past 11 years and seemed like an ideal candidate to Bruce. That is until he realized the significance of the car.

A little digging and Bruce was in touch with chief Golden Commando Ray Kobe who authenticated the car. Bruce indeed owned the one and only Golden Commando Barracuda and the last fully documented Golden Commando car in existence. He spent close to 15 years restoring the Barracuda, relying on the help of Ridge Reamer of Colorado to build the fresh .040-over 273, and Bruce's Body shop to perform the body, paint, and interior as well as install a new wire harness. Topping the candy coat is a duplicate of the original lettering, which has been applied by Chris Miller signs.

The surviving members of the Golden Commandos were overwhelmed to see the car for the first time in 45 years. Fan appreciation really showed during the car's first outing in 2013 when it took Best of Show honors at Henderson, North Carolina. Plans call for more shows and a return to the quarter-mile where, no doubt, the Golden Commando *Goldfish* will lead the way.

Although the Barracuda traveled the nation doing damage, it called Detroit home. The Golden Commandos disbanded by 1971 but left a lasting legacy, winning 90 percent of their matches. (Photo Courtesy Bruce Lindstrom)

AHRA Record-Holding Dodge

The folks at Chrysler had their bases covered in 1965. While guys such as Landy were tearing it up on the match-race circuit, you had approximately 204 lightweight Coronets and Belvederes dominating Top Stock. These A990 cars featured such items as lightweight panels, a race-bred Hemi, and slightly altered wheelbase. This particular car was sold new from Chicago's Grand Spaulding Dodge to a gentleman in Los Angeles. Almost immediately, the owner defaulted on the loan and the car was repossessed. Engine Masters' Ray Alley became the new owner and ran the car briefly before selling it to a gentleman in Texas, who failed to make payment. Ray called upon customer Kenny Bernstien (yes, that Kenny) to repossess the car. Kenny, who was a college student at the time, was racing a small-block Anglia and was sponsored by Joe Muscanaro's restaurant. Kenny talked Joe into buying the Coronet. It passed through four more owners before Pat Lobb purchased the car in early 2010. (Photo Courtesy Pat Lobb)

The race-bred Coronet features this factory-applied disclaimer on the glove box door. Like the rest of the car, it's in mint condition thanks in part to the fact the car sat in storage in west Texas for approximately 35 years. Today it's believed only 49 of the original A990 cars remain. (Photo Courtesy Pat Lobb)

Although the odometer reads just 268 miles on this Coronet, it was necessary to replace the interior as rodents had made a home of it. The column-mounted shift lever notes the reverse pattern of the Torqueflite transmission. Total weight of the Coronet is a shade over 3,000 pounds thanks in part to aluminum door hinges, and lightweight A-100 cargo van seating and brackets. There were no options available with the A-990 cars, which were devoid of such frills as radio, heater, insulation, and sound deadener. (Photo Courtesy Pat Lobb)

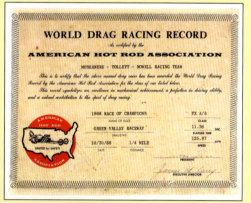

The Coronet was a regular AHRA combatant and in 1966, set both ends of the class record. In what should be considered a rarity for a factory race car, this one retains most of its original parts. The car was parked in storage in 1976 with just 108 miles on the odometer. (Photo Courtesy Pat Lobb)

The Hemi features twin Holley carburetors on a magnesium cross-ram intake manifold, aluminum heads, and 12.5:1 compression. Even though the car was original when purchased by Lobb, many of the little, hard-to-find parts weren't right. Plug wires and firewall-mounted regulator are unique to the '65 Hemi cars. (Photo Courtesy Pat Lobb)

Tender fender says it all. Fenders, bumper, hood, and scoop were pressed from thin gauge steel and were unique to the A990 cars. Note the absence of the second headlight, which was standard Coronet fare but deleted to save weight on these factory racers. Color on the car duplicates the 1965 paint scheme. (Photo Courtesy Pat Lobb)

Sox & Martin 1967 Plymouth

Sox & Martin joined the Chrysler camp in 1965 and earned factory backing on this altered-wheelbase Plymouth along with a Super Stock car. Paper Tiger *earned the pair a lot of dough on the match-race circuit and helped solidify them as Chrysler's drag racing front men.*

The Sox & Martin team came together out of necessity during the early 1960s. Buddy Martin couldn't beat Ronnie Sox on the track so the best way around the situation was to hire him to drive his car. The pair initially campaigned a Z-11–powered 1963 Chevy before moving on to a factory-backed 1964 A/FX Comet. Ronnie drove the car to a Factory Stock eliminator win at the NHRA Winternationals and holds the honor of being the first Factory Experimental car to crank out a 10-second ET. The pair moved on to Chryslers in 1965, beginning an almost decade-long partnership.

Chrysler threw their full support behind the team and in 1967 identified a great marketing opportunity by creating the Plymouth Supercar Clinic. They placed Sox & Martin at the helm. The clinics featured first-hand racing knowledge aimed at the grassroots racer. Ronnie and Buddy promoted Chrysler performance at more than 100 Chrysler-Plymouth dealerships throughout the East and Midwest. All the while, the pair managed to run a business and maintain an on-track winning record of more than 80 percent.

The same year, the NHRA created a new Super Stock category and Chrysler produced a limited number of "WO" and "RO" production-based drag cars to fit the category. The Sox and Martin car pictured here is one of approximately 55 Hemi Belvedere IIs produced. These drag cars were built in special runs on the factory production line specifically to run Super Stock/B competition. The engines were essentially the street Hemi design with intake and carburetor modifications, a dual-point distributor, and transistorized ignition, and were rated at 425 hp. When Sox & Martin's mechanic Jake King was through with the Hemi, it produced about 500 horses.

In the transmission department, either a Hurst slick-shift 4-speed or a manually shifted Torqueflite 727 automatic was available. The automatic transmission–cars carried an 8.75-inch sure-grip rear end, which housed 4.86 gears while the 4-speed cars received the Dana 60 rear end and 4.88 gears. No optional equipment was available and the cars came sans radio, heater, insulation, sound deadener, sway bar, and hubcaps. The hoods were steel with a bolt-on fresh-air hood scoop and carburetor-to-hood sealer. For better weight distribution, a 135-amp battery was mounted in the trunk. The cars were all painted white (WW) with cloth and vinyl black interior (H4X). Sox & Martin added their own blue and red paint; these were Ford colors that the team had been using since 1964.

Looking to push sales of its GTX model higher, Chrysler requested that Sox & Martin update the trim on their S/S Belvedere to "GTX." The guys then converted a stock street Hemi GTX to be used as a second race car. This Belvedere has been documented and verified to be the only factory-supplied Super Stock Belvedere campaigned by Sox & Martin during 1967 and 1968.

On March 29, 1967, the Sox & Martin Plymouth was shipped to Gate City Motor in Greenboro, North Carolina. Titled to Buddy Grey Martin on May 23, 1967, this is believed to be the only Sox & Martin car actually titled to Buddy. The manufacturer suggested retail price was $3,875. No team was more feared in early Super Stock than the pairing of Ronnie and Buddy. In 1967 and 1968, the pair fielded multiple cars and at one point hired Old Reliable *Dave Strickler to drive for them.*

The car was shipped new to Gate City Motor Company on March 29 and titled on May 23, 1967. The team had two successful years with the car: They took many class wins including Super Stock eliminator titles at the NHRA Spring Nationals in 1967, the 1967 NASCAR Heads Up Eliminator, and Super Stock Eliminator runner-up at the 1967 Super Stock Nationals. The car was reclassified SS/D in 1968 and continued on its winning ways by taking Super Stock honors again at the NHRA Springnationals before it was replaced by the team's new Hemi Barracuda.

The car is owned today by Clark Rand, who discovered the car complete, minus engine. All of the original panels, parts, and interior were included and fortunately, the car had not been updated or cut up at all. Engelhart Performance and AAA Restorations in Adams, Minnesota, performed a very thorough cosmetic restoration utilizing correct NOS parts. This car's "sister" '67 Plymouth exists today and is owned by John Mahoney of Kansas City.

"The Plymouth Win You Over Beat Goes On" was the manufacturer's sales slogan for 1967 and seeing how Sox & Martin and the Hemi were mowing down the competition, muscle car buyers didn't need much persuasion. (Photo Courtesy Geoff Stunkard)

Sox & Martin Supercars earned four NHRA World Championships between 1968 and 1971, a pair of Super Stock crowns in 1968 and 1969, and Pro Stock honors in 1970 and 1971. The pair proved to be an equal threat in both AHRA and IHRA competition.

Built to spec, the Wheelers Machine Hemi dynoed out at 520 horses. Modifications are true to form and include a Crane cam, TRW pistons, Dykes rings, a 9-quart oil pan, Hooker Headers, and twin Carters modified by Arlen Vanke. A Hayes clutch fills the void between the engine and A833 transmission, while 4.56 gears fill the Dana rear. (Photo Courtesy Geoff Stunkard)

Sitting pretty on Keystone Classics, the original Plymouth white and Ford colors were beautifully rematched and sprayed by Jim Remlinger in Winona, Minnesota. Don Dennis duplicated the lettering and silver leaf. Restoration of the car was three years in the making. At one time, Ronnie called this car his favorite. (Photo Courtesy Geoff Stunkard)

The interior retains the factory-installed vinyl and cloth and looks quite plush when compared to today's Super Stock cars. Stewart Warner gages monitor the engine while a Hurst Shifter (model DP-FX-65) was standard to the RO-23 cars. (Photo Courtesy Geoff Stunkard)

Al Joniec's Cobra Jet Mustang

Al had the deadliest Cobra Jet in the nation and ran an easy 11.83 at the Winternationals on an existing 11.93 record. Recalls Al, "Ford engineers feared the Cobra Jet cars would run too fast, forcing the NHRA to lower the class index." The initial run of Cobra Jet cars all featured Wimbledon white paint and black interiors. Al's car differed from the others as he used his own painter, Ralph Hart, to stripe and letter his car. (Photo Courtesy Nick Smith Collection)

History books show that the Ford flathead V-8 ruled the performance roost for a number of years and has powered everything from pre–World War II jalopies to 1950s Bonneville record holders. However, with the introduction of the overhead-valve V-8 in the late 1940s, the tide began to turn. By the mid-1950s, General Motors (Chevrolet, specifically) was the king of the hill and Ford was left to play catch-up. They strung together a number of dominant drag cars in the early 1960s with their limited lightweight Galaxies and 427-powered Thunderbolts.

It wasn't until 1968 that they hit a home run with the masses when they built the 428 Cobra Jet–powered Mustang, a car that might never have been built if it weren't for the efforts of Rhode Island's Bob Tasca. It was late in 1967 and Ford's share of the performance market had dwindled to less than 8 percent; Bob could see they needed a car that would put them back on top. Enter the Tasca-built "King of the Road 428."

The KR-8, as the Mustang was dubbed, was based upon Bob's personal 390-powered '67 Mustang coupe. When the engine "suddenly" expired, Bob took the opportunity to drop in a Police Interceptor 428. It proved to be an easy swap and was accomplished using off-the-shelf 406 and 427 parts. In November 1967, *Hot Rod* magazine ran a feature on Tasca's Mustang and encouraged its readers to contact Henry Ford II directly to have this solid 13-second car built.

Early on, Bob had taken the car to Michigan where the brass and engineers thoroughly examined it. Between *Hot Rod* readers and Bob's influence within Ford, production of the Cobra Jet Mustang commenced on December 13, 1967. Based upon the 2+2 platform, the initial 50 cars were lightweights assembled specifically for drag racing. Omitted from the initial assembly were radios, heaters, sound deadeners, and other power-robbing accessories.

Six of these cars were delivered to Holman-Moody/Stroppe in Long Beach, California, for additional modifications including high-flow aluminum intake manifold, tube headers, three-point roll bar, blue-streak slicks on Cragar S/S rims, and battery relocated to the trunk. As the Super Stock category allowed the use of any camshaft, Al chose to install a Crane bump stick. It proved to be the

Al is all smiles after his Winternationals victory. He put his Super Stock win down to a combination of luck and consistency. "I never opened my hood all weekend and stuck with my combination." (Photo Courtesy Nick Smith Collection)

Dick Esteves became the second owner of the Cobra Jet and enjoyed Super Stock success of his own into the 1980s. The car adapted to the ever-changing rules and at some point, rear wheel tubs were installed. (Photo Courtesy Nick Smith Collection)

The first six Cobra Jet Mustangs were released to Holman-Moody on January 5, 1968, and prepared by the group specifically for Ford's team drivers. The car competed in both Stock and Super Stock. Today, the Cobra Jet makes the rounds of East Coast shows and is housed in the collection of Nick Smith's Factory Lightweights. (Photo Courtesy Nick Smith Collection)

The dominant 428 Cobra Jet was a favorite with the Blue Oval crowd from the get-go. Al's winner carries a factory 735 Holley, 11.6:1 compression, and .600-lift Crane camshaft. Underrated from the factory at 335 horses, the NHRA refactored the combination to 360. (Photo Courtesy Nick Smith Collection)

To say the restoration was a major undertaking would be an understatement. The floorboards were replaced through to the rear wheel tubs, undoing years of modification and minor rust. Randy Delisio's Performance and Restoration was responsible for performing much of the work. (Photo Courtesy Nick Smith Collection)

ticket as the car was hitting 11.20 times, which were consistently .3 quicker than the other Cobra Jet cars. Recalls Al, "We rented Lions and held practice one week before the Winternationals. Chuck Fulger coordinated the practice and kept the speeds a secret but told me I had the fastest car."

Hubert Platt introduced the Cobra Jet Mustang to the world when he debuted his C/Stocker at the AHRA winter meet at Lions in January 1968. Showing plenty of promise, Hubert red lighted away a healthy 12.63 time. The six specially prepared cars made their debut at the NHRA Winternationals in 1968 and dominated SS/E. It was a win-win situation for Ford Motor Company as the class final boiled down to the Cobra Jet cars of Al Joniec and Hubert Platt. It was a battle to the finish with Al taking the win with an off-pace 12.12 at 109.48. Al drove around all the Chevys and faced Dave Wren's Mopar in the category final. It proved to be an anticlimactic final for the fans as Al, who was driving the slower car, received a handicap start over Wren. Dave and his quicker SS/DA Plymouth had to wait and watch the taillights of Al's Mustang pull away. Feeling the pressure and knowing he was going to have a tough time playing catch-up, Dave cut the light a little too quick and fouled away any chance of winning. The race was over on the starting line and Al and his Ford were the new Super Stock Champions.

After taking the win, Al spent the remainder of the year match racing the car, swapping the 428 for a tunnel port 427. "We were matching racing the car running 10.20s at 138 mph. We raced the car once more in Super Stock, at the Summernationals, where the 428 broke an exhaust valve and that was it." At the end of the season, Al bolted the 428 back into the car and sold it to

Dick Esteves for a cool $3,000. Dick had his own success running Super Stock with the car into the 1980s before retiring it.

In 1990, Randy Delisio was approached by Dick who showed an interest in selling the Mustang. Randy was interested in buying the Mustang, but a deal couldn't be reached and the car was passed over. Turning the calendar ahead to 1995, Randy once again spoke with the owner but this time, he was bargaining on behalf of Don Fezell. A deal was struck in November 1995 and after approximately 25 years of on-track abuse; it was time for a complete overhaul. Randy, owner of Randy Delisio's Performance and Restoration, was given the job of restoring the Mustang to its 1968 Winternationals status. Today, the legendary Cobra Jet lives in the Nick Smith collection along with a number of factory lightweights.

The Mustang is right at home on the start line. The restoration is true to the original setup and has done Al proud. He fondly recalls many match races in the car, using a 427 to defeat the likes of Grumpy Jenkins. With a Boss 429 in the pipe, Al knew the engine would never fit the Cobra Jet engine bay so the "for sale" sign went up. (Photo Courtesy Nick Smith Collection)

Larry Griffith's Super Stock 1968 Hemi Dart

The Dodge logo on the quarter panel denotes Larry's Hemi Dart as a team player. Approximately 80 of these Darts were produced in nearly race-ready form. Larry added the paint, deep sump oiling, and M&H tires to turn mid-10-second times. (Photo Courtesy Joe Hilger Collection)

As the 1960s were winding down, so were the days of the muscle car. It seemed that Detroit was getting its final "yah-yahs" out before the government and insurance companies inevitably stepped in and slammed the door shut on the performance market. Before they could, however, each manufacturer produced its own limited run of all-out race cars. Without a doubt, the quickest of them all were the 1968 Hemi-powered Barracuda and Darts produced by Chrysler and built by Hurst.

There was nothing civil about these brutes. They came equipped with aluminum heads for the Hemi, a cross-ram manifold bolting twin Holley carbs, 12.5:1 compression, and Hooker Headers. The fenders and the scooped hood were lightweight fiberglass, the side windows were lightweight Lexan, and the window cranks were omitted. Quarter windows were fixed while door glass was raised or lowered by the use of a strap.

To further reduce weight, the bumpers and doors were lightened and bucket seats from the A-100 series van were installed. Of course, such frivolous things as heater, wipers, radio, sound deadener, rear seat, and exhaust systems were omitted. You could get your Dart or Barracuda with either a 4-speed transmission or automatic. The 4-speed cars received the Dana 60-series rear end, which housed 4.88 gears, while automatic-equipped cars received the 8.75 rear with 4.86 gears. Mounting the rear ends were Super Stock springs that featured relocated perches. Buyers could forget about color choices; all cars were sold in just a primer coat.

Now if all this didn't clue you in to the car's full intent, the disclaimer sticker attached to each car would: "This vehicle is equipped 426-ci engine (and other special equipment). This vehicle is intended for use in supervised acceleration trials and is not intended for highway

It's 1968 and Larry poses proudly with his Dart on the return road at Cordova. The car rode on timeless Cragar S/S wheels. Note the fabricated deep-sump pan. The K-member was lowered to gain additional room for the Hemi installation. (Photo Courtesy Joe Hilger Collection)

or general passenger car use." The good folks at Chrysler and Hurst had left little for the racer to do. A blueprinting of the bottom end, a camshaft of choice, a deep sump pan, and slicks and these cars were hitting mid-10-second quarter-mile times at more than 130 mph.

Larry Griffith is a long-time drag racer who has been running Mopars since 1963. He started his affiliation with a Max Wedge car in 1968; his success had earned him a factory deal and a new Hemi Dart. One of the most beautiful Hemi cars to grace the quarter-mile, Larry's multi-hued and laced Dart competed strongly in UDRA competition.

One of the oldest drag racing organizations in the nation, the UDRA was formed in late 1963 by a group of Southern California racers. As told by *Drag Racing Online* magazine, the organization was formed to foster and promote better competition. By 1967, the organization had expanded to cover all corners of the country. Competing in the organization's Super Stock circuit, Larry and his Dart were knocking out 10.40 times on 11-inch M&H tires. His consistency behind the wheel helped him earn the points championship in 1968, 1969, and 1970.

Bolting on larger tires and slipping in a taller 5.12 gear, he had the Dart dipping into the 9s during an AHRA race in Kansas. At Chrysler's direction, Larry turned to the new Pro Stock category in 1970 and gave his Dart a facelift by installing a 1970 Dart front clip and tail-panel pieces. Retaining the same gorgeous paint, Larry added a Weiand intake manifold and a pair of Holley 4500 carbs, which dropped speeds into the 9.80s at more than 140 mph.

Recalling a career highlight, Larry fondly remembers taking Pro Stock honors over Ronnie Sox at the 1970 Super Stock Nationals. That year, Larry parted with the Dart, selling it to longtime friend Larry Pontnanck to help finance his latest Pro Stock effort. Larry shared driving duties with Pontnanck in 1971 and again the Dart captured the UDRA points championship. Pontnanck sold the car in 1974 to Gil Kirk of the Rod Shop but before doing so, converted it back to its 1968 appearance. Even though the Dart had more or less fallen off the radar at this point, it showed up on occasion during the 1990s. In December 1999, the car was featured in *Mopar Muscle* magazine.

In 2002, Chrysler's vice president of Global Service, Joe Hilger, came across the car for sale in a *Hemmings*

The Dart appeared in Mopar Muscle magazine in the late 1990s sporting gloss-black paint. This is how the car appeared when purchased by current owner Joe Hilger. Through connections within the Chrysler dealer network, Joe was able to track down Larry Griffith, who performed the restoration. (Photo Courtesy Joe Hilger Collection)

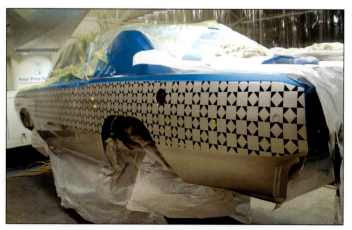

The restoration of the Dart was well under way by early 2007. Ralph Eckler applied the original paint and lace. Ralph's wife picked out the pattern to lay the lace. Greg Clause and Bill Shambauch of Joe's Paint & Body repeated the task 40 years later. (Photo Courtesy Joe Hilger Collection)

Chapter Five: Door Slammers Galore 165

Now that's a Hemi! Twin Holleys on a magnesium cross ram, aluminum heads, and a Cam Dynamics .700/.680 lift camshaft help produce an estimated 535 horses. (Photo Courtesy Joe Hilger Collection)

Larry restored the car, which debuted in 2007 at Cordova Dragstrip. The Dart called Cordova home back when and to this day Larry maintains his shop just a few miles down the road. (Photo Courtesy Joe Hilger Collection)

ad. Joe, a kid at heart, had pined for a Hemi Dart since their introduction in 1968 and now jumped at the chance to finally own one. Through his connections within Chrysler, Joe was able to contact Larry Griffith who would perform the majority of the restoration when the time came. That time came in 2005 when Joe retired from his duties at Chrysler.

Larry called upon Greg Clause and Bill Shambauch of Joe's Paint & Body in East Moline, Illinois, to perform the bodywork and duplicate the original blue, silver, and lace. The Hemi has been bored .060-over and squeezes out 13.0:1 compression. It relies on the original 770-cfm Holleys for fuel and a Cam Dynamics cam featuring .700 lift to actuate the valves. Many of the original race parts found their way back onto the car, including the deep-sump oil pan that was fabricated by Larry, the Hurst shifter with the reverse lock out. Even the original spark plug wires were dug out and used.

The anticipated unveiling of the restored Dart came in 2007 at its old stomping grounds, Cordova Dragway in Illinois. Larry had managed to keep the restored car's final appearance a secret from Joe until that moment and you couldn't have removed the smile from his face with a two-by-four.

Larry hasn't missed a beat in 40 years of competition. With Charlie Fitzsimmons behind the wheel of Larry's new, A/SA Challenger, the car has clicked off 9.50 times. Larry received the second new Challenger behind Don Garlits. (Photo Courtesy Joe Hilger Collection)

Anderson Oldsmobile's W-31 Cutlass

Between 1969 and 1971, the Anderson Olds W-31 was a regular winner at tracks such as Capitol and Cecil County. A total of 112 W-31-powered post cars were produced in 1969. This one compiled 499 miles before its retirement, many of which were recorded a quarter-mile at a time.

In the late 1960s, Doctor Oldsmobile and his band of misfits gave us the potent line of W machines. These 350-, 400-, and 455-powered muscle cars proved to be both boulevard bruisers and dragstrip terrors. Dave Siltman of Sparks, Maryland, has plenty of fond memories of this specific W-31–powered dragstrip terror, which he proudly calls his own today. Sponsored by Anderson Oldsmobile of Baltimore, Maryland, the Cutlass was the dealership's answer to "Win on Sunday, Sell on Monday." Not only had Dave watched this car terrorize such memorial tracks as York U.S.-30 and Cecil County, but also his family happens to have direct ties to the dealership. You see, Dave's family has called Anderson an employer for more than 50 continuous years.

This was Anderson's fourth and final race car; it was preceded by a '65 442 and both a 1967 and a 1968 car. Driven by both Terry Becker and Sonny Freeman, the 3,465-pound Cutlass fit nicely into NHRA F/S where it easily cranked out consistent 12.40s times through the 1970 season. At the heart of these near-record times was a 350 engine conservatively rated by the good Doctor at 325 horses. Limited by the restrictive category rules, the 350 relied on blueprinting, an aftermarket "cheater" camshaft, headers, a mild rework of the heads, and a reworked carburetor and distributor. The dealer had two successful years with the car before the decals were stripped off in 1971 and the car was placed back on the lot.

With the ever-increasing insurance rates applied to big-block muscle cars, they were losing popularity as the youth of the day turned to small-inch cars such as the W-31. Needless to say, the Anderson's drag winner didn't stay long on the dealer's lot. With its reputation and just 499 miles showing on the odometer, it sold in a hurry. The car passed through a number of hands over the years before Dave purchased it in 2003. Remarkably, the car had remained intact and had accumulated just 11,000 miles. To this day, the car retains the majority of its original Aztec Gold paint along with the original interior, engine, and drivetrain.

Dave strayed a little from the usual show-and-shine routine, which befalls many muscle cars, and instead chose to wet his feet on the quarter-mile. He had the engine rebuilt by Aaron Shipley of Baltimore, who performed a mild reworking of the heads and installed a Comp Cams camshaft and Diamond pistons. The intake is an aluminum 1970 W-31 piece mounting a reworked Quadrajet carburetor. The original Muncie M-21 was beefed up and shifts by way of a Hurst Competition Plus. Out back, the 12-bolt houses 4:33 Richmond gears. The suspension reads like a 1969 parts catalog. Out back Air-Lift air bags reside inside the rear springs and 50/50 shocks help control the bounce. Up front, 90/10 shocks

The majority of paint is original to the Cutlass as are the stripes. Note the underbumper air inlets that were standard equipment on the $205 W-31 package. In stock form, the W-31 was capable of 14-second ETs. Frank Augustine, who wrenched on the car in 1969 and 1970, confirms that the Cutlass ran a best of 12.38. (Photo Courtesy Geoff Stunkard)

Chapter Five: Door Slammers Galore 167

Factory rated at 325 horses, the 350 has been reworked with aftermarket goodies from Hooker, Brooks, Milodon, and Comp Cams. The estimated 450 horses should get the Olds into the bottom 12-second bracket. The car is devoid of power brakes as the engine with its 308-degree camshaft couldn't make enough vacuum. Making use of the Ram Air tubes forced the relocation of the battery to the trunk. (Photo Courtesy Geoff Stunkard)

It's 1969 all over again. Stepping into the black vinyl interior is like stepping back in time. Upholstery is all-original and is complemented by a Hurst shifter and aftermarket gauges. (Photo Courtesy Geoff Stunkard)

allow maximum lift for optimal weight transfer. The car is dressed in period-correct Cragar S/S rims while M&H 27 x 9 slicks on the rear get the power to the ground.

The near-mint interior takes on a day-two appearance with the addition of a Sun Tachometer and aftermarket Stewart Warner gauges. Dave has returned to the car's old stomping ground of Cecil County where he has soft-pedaled the Olds to bottom 13-second times. The Cutlass is a regular show winner and Dave has amassed a healthy share of trophies, all to the good Doctor's approval.

With performance in mind, the Olds sports a W-27 12-bolt rear cover, which hides 4.33 gears. Getting the power to the ground are slicks by M&H. Dave called on Delco Signs in Hanover, Pennsylvania, to rematch the car's original 1969 lettering. (Photo Courtesy Geoff Stunkard)

AMX-1 Super Stock 1969

AMX-1 was one of the more successful S/S AMX cars on the track running under or near the SS/E record in 1969. In 1970 it took the SS/D record from Shirley Shahan's AMX, turning a 10.81. More records followed through 1974. (Photo Courtesy Carl Rubrecht)

With the youth-driven performance market in full bloom by 1968, the once-stodgy American Motors Corporation set out to grab themselves a piece of the pie. Known more for its commitment to the human race through safety and economy, AMC saw the light and

The Hurst-prepared Super Car Rambler Rogue was an instant hit in 1969. Powered by a warmed-over 390, this predecessor to the S/S AMX was guaranteed to knock out 14.30 quarter-mile times. (Photo Courtesy Carl Rubrecht)

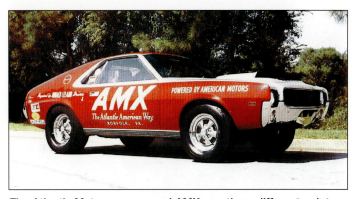

The Atlantic Motors–sponsored AMX saw three different paint schemes throughout its racing career, this one being the first. (Photo Courtesy Richard Riley)

introduced the performance-oriented Javelin and AMX. The Javelin was categorized as a pony car and competed head-to-head with the Mustang, Camaro, and Barracuda while the AMX (a two-seater built on the Javelin platform) was marketed as a poor-man's sports car. Power for the two cars came courtesy of a standard-equipment 225-horse 290 while the option list gave you the choice of either a 290-horse 343 or a 315-horse 390.

AMC left no doubt as to the AMX's intended use by revealing the car in February 1968 at the Daytona Speedway. To further enhance American Motors' newfound performance image, Bill McNealy, vice president of marketing, approached Dave Landrith, vice president at the Hurst Performance Centre in the summer of 1968. As described by Mark Fletcher and Richard Truesdell in their book, *Hurst Equipped*, McNealy had hoped to persuade Landrith to join AMC's new performance group. Landrith declined the offer but did recommend fellow Hurst employee Walt Czarnecki. Looking to follow up on the success of the Hurst-prepared Chrysler Hemi Barracuda and Dart, George Hurst and Doc Watson met with the AMC performance group and out of that meeting came the groundwork for the SC/Rambler and Super Stock AMX. Hurst was contracted to modify a limited run of 390-powered 1969 Rambler Rouges, which proved to be a $2,998 bargain.

The SC/Rambler could hold its own on both the street and the dragstrip, where the lightweight could bang off 14.30 times all day. Following in the *Scrambler*'s footsteps was the Super Stock AMX. Once dealer commitments were in, 52 frost-white cars were shipped from Kenosha, Wisconsin, to Hurst's rented facility in Ferndale, Michigan. All cars were equipped with the 390 engine, a BorgWarner 4-speed transmission featuring a 2.64 first gear, and a rear end that housed 4.44 rear gears and Henry's axles. Such standard equipment as heater, wipers, and radio were omitted along with the insulation and sound deadener.

Once in the capable hands of Hurst, the modifications were completed in assembly-line fashion. Engines and transmissions were pulled for the installation of J&E 12.3:1 forged pistons and Crane modified cylinder heads. Valve sizes were a healthy 2.06 and 1.74. Holley 4584 carburetors on an Edelbrock STR-11 cross-ram manifold topped the engine. The connecting rods, crank, and camshaft remained stock AMC pieces. A Mallory dual-point tach-drive distributor provided the spark while Doug Thorley 1-7/8-inch-diameter headers took care of the spent gases. Backing the engine was a Schiefer flywheel and Borg & Beck 10-inch clutch wrapped in a Lakewood hydroformed bellhousing. Gear changes were controlled by a Hurst Competition Plus shifter, which featured a reverse lock out.

Modifications to the body were limited to stretching the rear wheel wells 3 inches for tire clearance and opening up the hood and installing a scoop. All 52 of the S/S AMX interiors were charcoal colored while the majority of exteriors remained white. Rumor has it that a few of the cars did receive the AMC red, white, and blue paint scheme prior to shipment.

According to superstockamx.com, the cars retailed for $5,200, some $1,500 over the cost of a standard loaded AMX. A buyer would have to spend additional money to add paint, wheels, and an engine blueprint. (Photo Courtesy Richard Riley)

Chapter Five: Door Slammers Galore 169

The all-business interior features just the bare necessities. No heater, radio, clock, or insulation. A Hurst shifter controlled the gear changes while Stewart Warner gauges monitored the engine. (Photo Courtesy Richard Riley)

NHRA factored to 420 horses, the 390 featured a standard bore and such goodies as an Edelbrock cross-ram intake, Holley carbs, Crane reworked cylinder heads, and ignition by Mallory. As part of the Hurst conversion, the battery was located in the trunk. Don Leland was the mechanic and later the driver. (Photo Courtesy Richard Riley)

The AMX pictured here is number 31 of the 52 produced and went to Sam Vanderslice, owner of Atlantic Rambler in Norfolk, Virginia. The car was campaigned by the dealership and driven by Nat Thompson and Don Leland. Bill Gwyn was responsible for blueprinting the 390, which propelled the car to numerous IHRA and NHRA record times including a SS/C mark of 10.65 in 1973. The AMX was sold by the dealer in the mid-1970s and eventually ended up in the hands of Dave Lesick, who completed a restoration in 2007.

The car is currently owned by Richard and Paulette Riley. The way they came about the car is an interesting story. In 2009, Richard and Paulette owned S/S AMX number 19, on which *Hemmings Muscle Machines* magazine did a feature article. A person who knew Joel Sporn, the son of the original owner of Westbury Rambler (where the AMX was sold new) brought the article to his attention. Joel had fond memories of AMX 19 and set out to return the AMX to his family. Joel contacted Richard but unfortunately, old number 19 was not for sale, but if it ever were, Joel would be the first to know.

The day came in 2012 when *AMX-1* went on the block. Richard contacted Joel and told him that if the Sporns purchased it, he would trade him their number-19 car for it. It took several months but the deal was finally realized with each partner getting the car they wanted. Says Richard, "It's very rare in life when everyone gets exactly what they want. This was one of those instances. Of course, none of this could have happened without Dave Lesick and his outstanding efforts in researching and restoring *AMX-1*. We plan to be good guardians of his legacy to the SS/AMX racing."

Dave Lesick carried out the restoration in 2007. Dave started with a solid body that required minimal work. All panels and scoops are factory-original steel. The Cragar S/S rims were installed by the dealership. (Photo Courtesy Richard Riley)

From any angle, the AMX looks stunning. Rear wheel openings were enlarged by Hurst to accommodate racing slicks. This car held numerous class records in NHRA and IHRA competition. (Photo Courtesy Richard Riley)

McMaster & Gunning 1957 Chevy

Grin & Bear It with Courtney Nelson behind the wheel. This N/S Chevy won class at the Nationals in 1967 and 1968. In 1967, the Chevy held the class record with a 13.73. MPH records followed in 1968 and 1969 with Ken Gunning at the wheel. (Photo Courtesy Ken Gunning)

The NHRA Junior Stock rules of the 1960s were quite restrictive and turned building a winning stocker into a science. The record books show that Division 1 had more than its fair share of competitive cars and always near the top of the list were Jack and Ken Gunning. The Gunnings' *Jolly Green Giant* '57 Chevrolet wagon was meticulously built and set class record numerous times. In 1967, Ken propelled the *Giant* to runner-up at the NHRA World Finals, missing the crown by just hundredths of a second.

The Gunnings parted with the wagon during the 1968 season and continued on their winning ways by joining forces with McMaster & Nelson in campaigning the *Grin & Bear It* M/S '57 Chevy four-door hardtop. As points were awarded to the driver and not the car, Ken Gunning crawled behind the wheel to close out their Division 1–winning 1968 season. In 1969, the Gunnings became regular partners in the car after owner Alan McMaster bought out Courtney Nelson. The rare four-door hardtop Chevy, rescued from a salvage yard, was meticulously prepared; the bottom side was sandblasted before being coated in white. The *Grin & Bear It* red, applied by Ken, was repainted red, white, and blue by Ken in 1969 using Camaro colors. Even 45 years later the paint still looks great.

Bill "Grumpy" Jenkins built the 220-horse 283 in 1967, which the Gunnings freshened up in 1969, switching the Jenkins-blueprinted cam with an allowable aftermarket General Kinetics number-6 camshaft. Backing the 283 was a BorgWarner 4-speed transmission featuring a 2.54 first gear. Filling the rear were stronger Chrysler axles, spider gears, and a 5.13 ring and pinion. Getting the power to the ground was a pair of M&H tires. Jere Stahl provided the single rear traction arm and front tires while his totally tuned headers were passed over for a set of Hooker adjustables.

Ken commented on his borderline phobia for cleanliness, saying the Stahl tires looked "cleaner" with the lettering to the inside. Jere, looking for maximum publicity, cringed at the thought and halfheartedly give Ken an earful.

In 1970, the NHRA tightened the category rules and outlawed the use of the 4-speed transmission in any pre-1959 Chevrolet. Except for the Corvette, the 4-speed was not even an option in these cars so, really, they shouldn't have been accepted in the first place. To remain competitive with the Chevy, Alan and Ken tried their luck with the 3-speed standard transmission. Grumpy Jenkins showed Ken what needed to be done to make the venerable transmission survive the rigors of drag racing abuse. As Ken recalls, by the end of 1970, he had built more 3-speeds than he cared to recall. "Too many" he repeated in anguish.

With new rules in 1970, the 4-speed transmission was no longer allowed for use in 1957 to 1959 Chevys. The team switched to an automatic and again grabbed the class record. (Photo Courtesy Ken Gunning)

And the winner is . . . A casual-looking Ken Gunning holds the class trophy after taking O/SA at the 1971 NHRA Summernationals. Ken defeated the '57 Chevy of Malone, Rodriguez & Kennedy. Both Ken and the record-holding Chevy retired not long after. (Photo Courtesy Ken Gunning)

A Bob Beckhart–built 2-speed Powerglide featuring a Vitar torque convertor was later trialed along with a pair of sticky Firestones and 5:38 gears. This combination took the team to a class win at the 1971 NHRA Springnationals. With the NHRA implementing a 10-year rule (no cars older than 10 years) for 1972, the Chevy was retired from competition at the end of the 1971 season.

Although the whereabouts of the Gunning original wagon is unknown, Ken purchased the hardtop in November 2012 from the McMaster family. "Alan passed a few years back and the car languished in a garage, untouched." The Gunnings hauled the Chevy home and began the restoration by rebuilding the engine and brakes. A good cleanup and the car was ready for its debut at the 2013 York Reunion. At the same event, Jack and Ken became members of the York Legion of Honor, joining Don Garlits, Bill Jenkins, and Jim Liberman.

The 283 engine was rebuilt by Jack and Ken Gunning and retains all the Jenkins Competition goodies originally installed in 1967. Excluding a mouse, which made it home in cylinder number-1, the engine was in surprisingly good condition. Although last run with an automatic, the car has been restored with in its original 4-speed configuration. (Photo Courtesy Ken Gunning)

McMaster & Gunning's 1957 Chevrolet as it appeared when uncovered in 2012. The car was parked at the conclusion of the 1971 season (inside a single-bay garage) and remained intact. (Photo Courtesy Ken Gunning)

The Gunnings debuted the Chevy at Darwin Doll's York Reunion in 2013 and was an instant hit with onlookers. The Ken Gunning paint has survived remarkably well after all these years. (Photo Courtesy Ken Gunning)

Hubert Platt's Ford Drag Team Mustang

Hubert poses proudly with his eastern Ford Drag Team match racer. The '69 Mustangs received 1970 sheet metal when the new year rolled around. Hubert headed the East Coast drag team while Ed Terry spearheaded the West Coast team. There were six cars in total: The eastern cars were blue with white accents and the West Coast cars were the opposite, white with blue accents. (Photo Courtesy Jerry Heasley)

Georgia Shaker was born in the Myrtle Beach area of South Carolina in 1931. Not exactly drag race central for someone with Hubert's skills but in the mid-1950s, there was as much demand for fast cars and good drivers as there was plenty of bootleg liquor to be transported. Hauling moonshine earned Hubert a few bucks but the one last haul cost him his car and a hefty fine.

Late in 1958, he moved to Atlanta where he discovered his real talent was on the quarter-mile. He caught the attention of Don Nicholson in the early 1960s and teamed with him in 1963, running Chevys before General Motors pulled out of racing. The first car to carry the *Georgia Shaker* name was a Z-11 Chevy but it was all Ford after that.

A Frank Vego Ford–sponsored Thunderbolt preceded the now-famous *Georgia Shaker* Falcon, which debuted in 1965. Hubert earned a factory deal in 1966 and ran the gamut of Ford-backed cars, starting with a long-nose Holman-Moody Mustang followed by a 427-powered Super Stock Fairlane. He took delivery of one of the original Cobra Jet Mustangs that debuted at the 1968 NHRA Winternationals.

Late in 1968, Ford decided to follow in Chrysler's footsteps and start a drag clinic program of their own. The idea, similar to Chrysler's, was to create two "Drag Teams" with each visiting dealerships during the week, pushing the manufacturer's muscle parts, drawing crowds, and setting up Ford drag clubs. On the weekend, they'd visit the local strip for some match-race or Super Stock action. On the West Coast, the program was headed-up by Ed Terry in conjunction with Dick Wood while Hubert led the East Coast team with Randy Payne. Ed and Hubert each campaigned a Cobra Jet Mustang in Super Stock and a second SOHC Mustang for match races. Dick and Randy each wheeled a Super Stock Cobra Jet Torino.

Even though the cars fared well in Super Stock competition, the match-race cars were the ones that really turned heads. The February 1970 issue of *Super Stock & Drag Illustrated* reported that Hubert's match racer was good for 9-second 140-mph quarter-mile times. Not your typical drag 'Stang by a long shot. The Holman-Moody–prepped 427 car was built around a 428 CJ, sport roof body, and featured such lightweight items as fiberglass fenders, hood, Boss scoop, doors, trunk lid, and lightweight side-window glass. Of course, the car was delivered sans radio, heater, and all those other ET-robbing add-ons.

Hubert's 427 featured a Crane cam, ForgedTrue pistons, 12.5:1 compression, Mallory ignition, and Doug's Headers. Helping to drop some of the 427's 680 pounds were

The SS/HA Mustang was powered by a 428 Cobra Jet that Hubert drove to a class win at the 1969 NHRA Winternationals. Seen here at the later Nationals, Georgia Shaker *failed to repeat. (Photo Courtesy Jerry Heasley)*

Chapter Five: Door Slammers Galore 173

factory-supplied aluminum heads, water pump, balancer, and tunnel ram manifold. The *Georgia Shaker*'s original SOHC engine disappeared years ago; current owner Bob Perkins went to Ohio George Montgomery for a replacement. Backing the 427 is a rare, close-ratio Toploader transmission and a 9-inch rear end containing 4.86 gears.

The Drag Team Mustangs were given a face-lift in 1970; they took on the new Mustang front clip and taillights. Hubert ran the Mustang in the new NHRA Pro Stock category through spring 1970 before debuting his purpose-built Maverick at the Nationals. When Ford pulled the plug on its racing activities in 1970, Hubert sold the match racer and focused his attention on his Pro Stocker.

The Mustang went to Tom Sutton of South Carolina, who continued to race the car into the late 1970s with a 428 Cobra Jet. Bob Perkins purchased the car from Ford enthusiast Jacky Jones who, with word from a truck driver hauling new cars, discovered the car wasting away in Tom's shop. Bob has owned the car since the mid-1990s and completed the meticulous ground-up restoration on the rust-free body. Bob got lucky with this one as many of the factory trick parts and original race parts remained with the car.

Through Tom, Bob was able to retrieve the original tempered windows, tach, and formula race seat. Through Hubert, Bob was able to obtain the original headers and tunnel ram manifold. In 2012, the restoration was completed and *Georgia Shaker* made its debut at the Mustang Club of America Grand Nationals held in Mustang, Oklahoma, of course.

Nicely restored, Hubert's match-race car retains all of the factory-installed lightweight components including fiberglass doors, fenders, hood, and trunk lid. Current owner Bob Perkins has noted that the fiberglass panels were formed using factory sheet metal and even the stamped date codes transferred into the fiberglass pieces. All the team cars sat on classy American Torque Thrust rims. (Photo Courtesy Jerry Heasley)

The twin 4-barrel race-bred 427 SOHC produced an estimated 675 hp and propelled the match-race car to ETs in the high-9-second range at more than 140 mph. Even though the original engine was long gone when purchased by Bob, Gasser legend Ohio George was able to provide him with what he needed. Holley 780-cfm carburetors feed the hungry beast. (Photo Courtesy Jerry Heasley)

Today's Cobra Jet drag cars have nothing on Georgia Shaker. This car looks flat-out mean and has performance characteristics to back it up. In its day, the match racer faced and defeated many top Chevy and Chrysler opponents. Inner headlights were replaced with air tubes feeding the Holley carburetors. (Photo Courtesy Jerry Heasley)

Goodyear 12 x 15 Blue Streak slicks in conjunction with Holman-Moody & Stroppe ladder bars helped get the power to the ground. Rear springs are heavy-duty Ford. Paint is pearl white and blue matched to Gordon Smith's original. (Photo Courtesy Jeff Heasley)

Scotto & Blevins Chevy Nomad

Ready to race in 1968, the '55 Nomad initially housed a 327. It wasn't until Joe Scotto and Paul Blevins hooked up with the Duffy gang and built a 283 that the wins started coming. A string of national records and Division 1 crowns followed. In 1971, the Nomad took Modified Eliminator at the first running of the NHRA Grandnationals. (Photo Courtesy Carl Rubrecht)

Joe Scotto and Paul Blevins, high school chums from New Jersey, chose to go modified drag racing in 1966 using a salvaged Nomad. The '55 Nomad pictured here served them well through 1971 before the pair focused all their attention on an equally successful modified Corvette. Joe rescued the Nomad from a wrecking yard by for the paltry sum of $50. The car needed little more than a couple of fenders, which Joe replaced before laying on the white paint.

Recalling the pair's early days, Joe says, "Paul and I were there when the Napps were clearing the forest for Englishtown Raceway. That's when we made the decision to go drag racing. While Paul was in Turkey serving Uncle Sam, reading all the American car magazines he could get his hands on, I was home preparing the Nomad."

The pair initially relied on a warmed-over 327 to do battle but got nowhere until hooking up with Danny Jesel and the guys at Duffy's. The year was 1968 and with a fresh .030-over 283, the Nomad was, more often than not, tripping the win light. Agreeing that one driver got to know the car better than two (and improve consistency), Paul became the permanent driver and set the G/MP record at York in June 1968 with a 12.16. He retained the class record through 1972, lowering it twice. Although the 283 could rev to 10,000 rpm and usually came off the line at 9,000, the engine and drivetrain were remarkably reliable and rarely broke.

Driven by Paul, the Nomad was an unbeatable record-holder in both AHRA and NHRA competition. In UDRA competition, Scotto/Blevins practically owned the modified circuit. In 1971 Paul dropped his G/MP class record from a 12.16 to an 11.91 and finally to an 11.44 before retiring the car in 1972. (Photo Courtesy Carl Rubrecht)

Backing the 283 was a beefed-up BorgWarner 4-speed featuring a 2.54 first gear; out back was an unbreakable '57 Olds rear that housed Summers axles and anywhere from 5.12 to 6.17 gears. An Air-Lift air bag mounted on the rear passenger's side aided traction along with traction bars that Paul had modified to follow the curvature of the springs.

With the Nomad winning on a consistent basis, sponsors who wanted their names on the car hounded the pair. As Joe recalls, "This led to plenty of free parts and led directly to us building the World Championship–winning Corvette." The Nomad was raced into 1972 before energy was focused on the new car. Bill Izykowski was hired to drive the Corvette, which took runner-up at the World Finals in 1971 before winning it in 1972. Joe retired from racing in 1972 to focus on his car sales business and gave both cars to Paul.

Eventually both cars were sold to support Paul's Pro Stock effort. The Nomad went to Fred Egloff (Fred's Speed Shop, Yonkers, New York) in mid-1972, who raced it briefly, no doubt piling up wins before parting with it. It passed through a number of hands before finding

The heart of the Scotto/Blevins Nomad was a punched-out 283. The 660 Holleys were fed by a pair of Carter fuel pumps. Danny Jesel did the block machining while Paul did the final assembly. About 9,000-rpm launches were the norm and recalls Joe, "We only broke one engine, and Dave Strickler offered to tow the car back to the pits with Grumpy Jenkins' Pro Stock Camaro." (Photo Courtesy Bob Destalto)

The beautiful Scotto/Blevins interior was replicated by Gary Egan. The bench seat was notched to clear the Hurst Super Shifter. A Moroso cable-drive tach and Stewart Warner gauges keep tabs on the engine. (Photo Courtesy Bob Destalto)

current owner Richard Rudolph. Richard wasn't looking for the car but a gentleman who was looking to buy a '32 Ford roadster made him an offer he couldn't pass up. He contacted Richard who told him he had a '32 coupe but would only sell or trade it for either a '55 Chevy ragtop or Nomad. It took a year of bargaining before they worked out a deal and Richard got the Nomad he wanted. "I use to go out of my way to watch this car race back in 1971 and 1972," he says, never dreaming that someday he'd actually own the Nomad.

At some point a previous owner had painted the car black and added a black diamond-tuft interior. The original engine was long gone; a warmed-over 283 with a single 4-barrel replaced it. Before purchasing the car, Richard contacted Paul to confirm the car was the real deal. The Nomad retains the Olds rear end and the modified traction bars Paul had installed. Other telltale signs included the spark plug holders in the radiator support, Bondoed-over holes in the dash, and the air-valve hole in the quarter panel (Bondoed) drilled for the air bag line.

The rules dictated 10.5 maximum-width drag slicks, so it was important to get as much of the car's weight over the rear as possible. During the ground-up restoration, Richard came across a few hidden gems, which were obviously placed many years before to aid traction. While refurbishing the interior, he found lead weights tucked behind the rear paneling and a logger's chain, weighing approximately 100 pounds, buried in the tailgate. At least they remembered to remove the manhole cover from under the floorboard. Joe Scotto recalled having to add weight at some point but obviously, someone forgot to remove it all. Richard, a paint and body man, stripped the exterior before laying on the fresh white paint. He relied on a friend, Don Conklin, to duplicate the lettering.

The Nomad no longer makes quarter-mile passes; instead, Richard gets the historic race car out to as many shows as time and weather allow.

After surviving years as a street rod, the most-renowned Nomad in drag racing history was finally restored at the turn of the millennium. Both Joe and Paul were called upon to ensure the job was done right and in the end, both gave it a thumbs-up. (Photo Courtesy Bob Destalto)

High School 1957 Chevy

Originally built by John Cesareo's students at Western High School in Anaheim, California, this 1957 Chevy was driven by Bill Allen to an M/S win at the 1971 NHRA Winternationals. The winning time for the Tom Neja 283-powered Chevy was 14.40. The car is believed to be the first high school drag race car in the United States to race at a national event with the school name on it. (Photo Courtesy James Handy)

Going to high school usually entails taking at least one elective subject related to industry. I suspect that like most of you holding this book, I chose Automotive. Even though Mr. Berg always kept class interesting, we never had the pleasure of taking on a project such as the one John Cesareo's students enjoyed.

John taught at Anaheim's Western High and as a means of deterring kids from street racing, he purchased a dilapidated '57 Chevy, which the class could build to compete with in the High School Scholarship Drags. Sponsored by Ford Motor Company, the program worked, for a while, as other Southern California High Schools were quick to join. John's Chevy was discovered in the weeds behind a radiator shop in Buena Park and purchased for the paltry sum of one dollar. However, before they could cart the Chevy away, they had to wait a couple weeks for the litter of puppies just born in the trunk to mature.

Once the Chevy finally found its way to Western High, the members of the newly formed auto club began the task of rebuilding the old Chevy from top to bottom. The complete drivetrain was first to go, which actually belonged to the previous owner. Seven different '57 Chevys were stripped of useable parts for salvage to keep the project going. Retailers within the community were quick to throw their full support behind the project, including Henry's Axles and Mickey Thompson, who opened his parts catalog and told John, "Whatever you need."

To raise additional funds to keep the project rolling, the team members held fundraisers, slurred driveways, pulled weeds, and painted. The car initially competed in 1969 and was driven by two different members judged by John as the best. There were plenty of growing pains that first year and plenty of experience gained. The car didn't look the greatest in its primer and the team struggled with a junk engine. Things changed in 1970 as West Coast Junior Stock racer Tom Neja assembled a fresh 270-horse 283 for the Chevy and Stylers laid on the pearl and candy paint, while Ken Young followed up with the lettering.

A new member, Bill Allen, joined the team in 1970 and earned himself the driver's seat. He had the honor of driving the Chevy at the first and second High School Drags held at Orange County. As the pessimist within would say, "No good deed goes unpunished." Once the school board realized that the car was actually being raced, they shut the team down. Recalls John, "It was a liability issue. We could show the car but they couldn't risk student lives by allowing us to race it." And on that note, John sold the car, trailer, and spare engine to driver Bill for $1,200.

Once a magazine feature car and cover car, Pioneer I had been beaten by the ravages of time. When it appeared for auction in 2003, it was but a shadow of its former self. John had his work cut out for him. (Photo Courtesy John Cesareo)

The classic lines of a '57 Chevy are hard to beat. The paint was laid on by the legendary Danny D and accentuates the 150-series styling nicely. (Photo Courtesy Roger Rohrdanz)

Bill continued to compete with the car and, with the help of the Neja brothers, won M/S class at the 1971 NHRA Winternationals. John lost track of the Chevy after he sold it and last saw it around 1974 for sale on the lot of Stick City on Whittier Boulevard. To his surprise, it showed up on eBay in 2003. The seller had owned the car for approximately 18 months and told John that before purchasing it, the car had sat in an El Cajon carport for 22 years.

Power is provided by a 270-horse 283, which was originally assembled by Tom Neja in 1970. Vangordon Race Engines were called upon to rebuild the engine, which is topped with a pair of Carter carburetors. (Photo Courtesy Roger Rohrdanz)

Looking much worse for wear, John purchased the worn Chevy and spent the next nine years performing a frame-off restoration. The number of original race parts that remained with the car after all those years surprised John. The biggest change seems to have been the installation of a Dana 60 rear end at some point. John sold the rear for a pretty penny and, just as in the Junior Stock days, installed a '57 Chevy rear with 4.56 gears.

While the chassis was out from under the old body, John sent it to PSC Powder Coating in Chino for cleaning up. Much to his surprise, the owner of the company happened to be one of his former students. The chassis was reassembled with all-new components while

The all-business interior once sported the handiwork of Kat at Pennys Auto Center but 40 years of misuse and abuse called for some new threads. John went with reproduction 150-series panels and seat covers, which were installed by Jimmy Z. A Hurst shifter rows the 3-speed while gauges are the original Stewart Warners. (Photo Courtesy Roger Rohrdanz)

The timeless Sun Super Tach resides where it has on countless '57 Chevys over the years, on top of the dash, right in the driver's sight line. This tach is original to the car and was installed in this location in 1968. (Photo Courtesy Roger Rohrdanz)

polished centerlines on Mickey Thompson rubber were used to replace the old chrome slotted rims. Under the hood resides the original Tom Neja 283, which has been refreshed and is backed by a 4-speed.

As for its appearance, the car is a flat-out knockout. Tom Rodriguez at Cypress Auto Body can take pride in bringing the panels up to snuff and applying the 2002 Infinity White Pearl. Topping the pearl is Danny D–applied light blue lace paneling that features royal blue borders. The finishing touch came courtesy of Larry Fator at Quicksilver who applied the gold-leaf *Pioneer 1* logo.

John enjoys getting the restored Chevy out for cruise nights as it's enabled him to reconnect with a number of former students. Many students contributed to the project, which left plenty of fond memories, and kept the majority of them from street racing.

John Cesareo, or "Mr. C," as his students knew him, spared no expense in bringing the *Pioneer 1* Chevy back to its former winning status. He shows the car regularly, frequenting cruise nights, which has brought him back in touch with a number of former students who helped build the car in 1968. (Photo Courtesy Roger Rohrdanz)

Granny Goose II 1969 Camaro

***In the early 1970s**, Granny Goose owned D/MP. Its screaming small-blocks (the size varied) built by car owner Dave Lewis guaranteed mid-10-second record times. (Photo Courtesy Karl Thiele Collection)*

One of the most recognized modified eliminator cars in existence, *Granny Goose II* set the drag race world on fire in the early 1970s. Built by Cincinnati-based Dave Lewis with help from partner Bruce Scott, the Camaro's outstanding performance was matched equally by its good looks. Dave and Bruce had initially teamed in the late 1960s campaigning a Modified Production Corvette. Looking for a new car in 1970, Dave talked Woody Bateman out of this 1969 Camaro.

An original Fathom Green L-78 4-speed car, Woody bought the Camaro new from Glenway Chevrolet and put a little more than 11,000 miles on the odometer before choosing to modify it for a life on the dragstrip. That's when Dave came along. Following a similar path, Dave built the car to fit D/MP production with a healthy .030-over 302 and immediately made an impact. The Camaro debuted at Edgewater on Easter Sunday in 1971, Dave playing runner-up in eliminations. The Camaro earned the class record shortly after with an 11.11 and backed it up with a WCS win at National Trail Raceway in Ohio.

The familiar multihued blue paint came in 1971 courtesy of Bill Roell and Jim "Dauber" Farr. The paint, referred to as Bill Roell Blue, consisted of multiple shades including Royal, Chinese, and Aqua Blue laid over a pearl base. Barely noticeable, the paint fades from light to dark from front to rear. Hidden under the clear were ghost stripes. Speaking volumes of a job well done, upon entering its first World of Wheels car show, the Camaro took best of show.

On the track, Dave continued to rack up wins through 1973. He took D/MP at a points meet in Indy and repeated at the Blue Grass Nationals, the Summernationals, and the U.S. Nationals. Changing owners in 1974, the Camaro never lost a step. Renamed *Golden Goose*, Jerry Coley won a pair of points meets along with class wins at both the Winternationals and Gatornationals. He closed out the season by taking the Division 2 modified crown. Jerry may be remembered by some as the person who

Jerry raced the Camaro into 1975 but fighting a losing battle against the fiberglass Corvette grew old. The car sat a number of years before Karl came to the rescue. (Photo Courtesy Karl Thiele Collection)

Dauber and John Bastian were responsible for body prep and rematching the original paint. Colors included four shades of blue over two shades of pearl. The paint fades from light to dark starting at the front. Photos do not do this car justice. (Photo Courtesy Karl Thiele Collection)

formed the United Sportsman Racers Association in 1981 and his failed attempt to bring litigation against the NHRA for dropping Modified Eliminator.

In 1975, the NHRA changed the rules and allowed fiberglass Corvettes into Modified, and the category was never the same. Feeling that the car could no longer compete, Jerry parked the Camaro after an Indy loss to the Thompsons' Corvette. And there she sat until Karl Thiele came along in 1988. Karl remembered the car from Edgewater. "It was the car's home track and I only lived about a mile away. I watched the car regularly and fell in love with it."

Karl hunted the car down, and found it in Alabama still in Jerry's hands. It was for the most part complete with the majority of its original race parts intact but the memorable paint was long gone. The car had spent some years sitting in the Florida sun, which baked the clear coat and turned it yellow. When Karl found the car, it was in a primer coat. It didn't matter to Karl; he loved the car and hauled it home, minus engine and transmission. With the help of Steve Glasgow he began a thorough restoration.

He debuted the restored car in Cincinnati in 2002. Once again, wherever the car went, it was the center of attention. Karl is quick to give credit where credit is due and thanks Bob Martin and Cleon Short who helped with photos and information.

A financial setback forced Karl to sell the *Goose* and in 2005, James Payne became the new owner. Not content to restrict the Camaro to showings, James went about preparing the car for a return to the dragstrip.

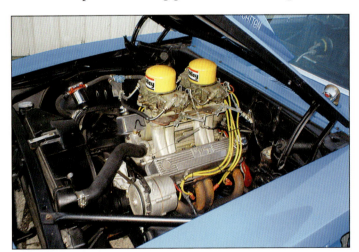
Dave played with multiple-size small-blocks but generally ran a bored and stroked 283 or a destroked 327. Karl restored the car with a healthy small-block while current owner James Payne relies on a 331 to crank out 10.20 times. (Photo Courtesy Karl Thiele Collection)

The austere yet functional interior needed little attention by Karl. The Hurst shifter controlled a BorgWarner transmission (later a Nash) and a six-point cage protected the driver. (Photo Courtesy Karl Thiele Collection)

He built a 331 that propels the Camaro to 10.20 quarter-mile times. Long gone is the BorgWarner transmission and in its place is a G-Force box. A Dana 60 rear rides on the same suspension that supported the car in the 1970s. The Camaro continues to rack up wins but, unlike life with Karl, the wins are once again coming on the race track.

The Goose is just as comfortable on the show circuit as it is on the race track. The stance and wheels-up launch have been helped along by original modified A-arms and custom springs. (Photo Courtesy Bob Wenzelburger)

Dianna & Ripes Corvette

John and Marv joined forces in 1970 and quickly became the scrooges of Division 7 stock. Their subrecord Corvette won the NHRA Supernationals that year with the help of a 283 borrowed from Tom Neja. (Photo Courtesy Tom Ordway)

Marvelous Marvin Ripes, former proprietor of A-1 Automatic Transmissions gained national attention driving his '57 Chevy sedan Junior Stocker to a win at the 1970 NHRA Springnationals, a win he attributed to the use of his recently installed Opel 8-inch torque convertor.

To refresh the memory, Opel was a brand of automobile manufactured by General Motors Germany. The car was imported to America in 1969 to sell through the Buick dealer network. For a Buick dealer to be approved as an Opel franchise, they were required to stock one of every Opel part. Legendary drag racer and friend of Marv Ripes, Bob Lambeck, worked in the parts department of Cummings Buick in Santa Monica at the time and came across one of these convertors. "It was in a tiny box labeled in German "Konverter." I couldn't believe the size of it."

Bob, who had been hired to drive a Dick Landy Dodge, initially showed the convertor to the Mopar group but they weren't interested, so Bob called Marv. Immediately the wheels in Marv's head started turning. He could see the potential in the little "Konverter" and paid Bob the dealer price of $50 for it.

To make it work in his cast Chevy powerglide, it was necessary for Marv to modify the turbine hub, bolt pattern, and pilot hub. So that the transmissions could withstand the forthcoming 4,000-rpm launches, Marvin increased the line pressure and installed a clutch pack designed for Powerglides, which backed the stout 348 engine. "The 348 Powerglides featured a heavier hub and you could put five clutches in them rather than the standard Powerglide, which used four." Installing the reworked transmission and convertor, Marv saw an immediate reduction in ETs and, once traction issues were resolved, the old Chevy pushed wind to the tune of 13.80s on a 14.50 record.

Marv switched rides mid-season in 1970 and teamed up with *Hot Rod* magazine's editor John Dianna in campaigning this first-generation Corvette. A 1956 model tagged as a '57, the car was the terror of I/SA with its 250-horse fuel-injected 283. Recalled Marv, "John supplied the car while I supplied the ramp truck, Powerglide, and 283, which I built with the help of Joe Allread."

The first pass in the Corvette was on the street in front of A-1 Transmission. And boy, did she light 'em up! The first race came the next night at an NHRA points meet at Bakersfield where the car defeated Dave Kempton in the

Chapter Five: Door Slammers Galore 181

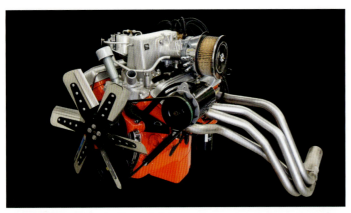

The 283 has been built to NHRA stock specs and features items such as Stahl totally tuned headers. Jere has stated that this was the Corvette he used to create the first-generation Corvette small-block headers in 1970. It appears to be the last Corvette to receive Stahl headers as well. Jere is winding down the business after approximately 50 years of outstanding service. (Photo Courtesy Derek Booher)

The multitalented owner came through once again, refurbishing the interior that was a mess when he purchased the car in 1985. Though complete, it was necessary to replace the vintage 1961 seats with proper 1957 units. The fresh upholstery and paint was completed in Craig's spare time. Note the line lock button mounted on the steering wheel and vintage Moroso tach. (Photo Courtesy Derek Booher)

final go. A category win came at the season-ending NHRA Supernationals, where Marv defeated Gary Glover's ailing Chevy.

The Corvette was taken back East in 1971 where it never ran up to expectations, possibly due to the humid air. There it was sold to someone lost to recollection. The Corvette was reportedly raced with success in IHRA competition sometime before current owner Craig Wood came upon it in 1980. At that time it was located in Michigan and belonged to an owner who didn't want to sell. Craig never relented, though, and five years later, he was able to purchase the car.

Craig believed he had purchased a 1 of 102 automatic-equipped injected Corvettes built in 1956 and was initially disappointed when he discovered it wasn't. With help from a friend, he discovered that the car once belonged to Marv and John. The car was in poor shape in 1985; the original 283 and Powerglide was long gone and it appeared at one time there had been a fire under the hood. The interior was a mess and all that remained of the original Joe Anderson paint was on the gas filler door. That's one of the ways Craig finally came to the conclusion he had the Dianna & Ripes car.

It wasn't until 2012 that the restoration began. Craig rebuilt the 283, using a 1962 fuelie unit instead of the 1961 model Marv and John had used as it flows better. Current proprietors of A-1 Transmission in the Northwest built a fresh Powerglide while multitalented Craig fashioned the new interior and paint. The colors consist of a persimmon candy base under a '57 Corvette red topped with a gold pearl.

The Junior Stock set was always an innovative bunch and Marv and John were no exception. During the restoration, Craig discovered a number of "hidden secrets." The control arms had been modified to improve geometry and the lower arms featured spring pockets, something first-generation Corvette control arms didn't have. To aid the bite of those 7-inch slicks, lead weight had been hidden in the rear bumper and frame rails and 25-pound bags of shot were stashed in the quarter panels.

Craig completed the restoration early in 2014 and debuted the Corvette to rave reviews at the Detroit Autorama. Marv, who proved to be an invaluable asset during the restoration, was united with the car at the York Reunion. At the same event, he was inducted into the York Legion of Honor, rightly joining other legends such as Grumpy Jenkins, Big Daddy, and Ronnie Sox.

The success of the Dianna & Ripes Corvette carried over well into the 1970s with new owners Bob Tech and Ron Costello. Running out of Indiana, the car became an IHRA record holder. Current owner Craig Wood performed the restoration of the car starting in 2012. The rematch of the Joe Anderson paint is flawless. (Photo Courtesy Derek Booher)

Stark Hickey's Super Stock Mustang

Tony followed his Summernationals class win with another win at the 1972 Winternationals. Winning time was an 11.40 at 119.04 mph. In 1970, he ran the Mustang in SS/HA, possibly to avoid the confrontation with the Border Bandits and their Mustang from north of the border. Tony went to work for Stark Hickey in Royal Oak, Michigan, in 1971, where he operated the Clayton dyno and where the Mustang spent its down time. The car was also used as a test bed for Ford's high-stall convertors. (Photo Courtesy Lyle Barwick)

It never fails to amaze me when a unique vehicle such as this Mustang pops out of the woodwork. In September 1968, Ford's own engineers ordered this R-code fastback as a test mule. The 428 was pulled and into its place went an early Boss 302. The car was then used for the development of Boss brake components.

This car shouldn't even exist today. Generally, when a manufacturer is finished with these mules, they face a date with the crusher. Not this car. It received a face-lift at some point and was used by Design as a '70 Mustang composite prototype. In 1969, the Boss 302 and transmission were yanked before the car was sold to engineer Tony Rainero. Tony credits Ford engineer Bruce Sizemore as his biggest supporter and the one behind him getting the car. Tony, its said, threw any hope of winning class at the 1968 Indy Nationals where he was running as quick as the factory cars of Jerry Harvey and Dave Lyall.

The Mustang came courtesy of Ford as their way of showing gratitude. The cost to Tony? One George Washington bill. The Stark Hickey sponsorship was something Tony, it's said, enjoyed dating back to 1968 and it came courtesy of Bruce. The sponsorship carried over to the 1970 car. Tony had the Mustang shipped to Holman-Moody/Stroppe in California, minus the engine, where it was prepped to do battle at the forthcoming NHRA Winternationals.

The Mustang was stored 35 years inside a shipping container in Las Vegas by an owner who lives in Hawaii and was restored by a company in Saskatchewan, Canada. What happens in Vegas doesn't necessarily stay in Vegas, thankfully. (Photo Courtesy Lyle Barwick)

While Tony paid to ship the car west, Ford paid for everything else, including having famed engine builder Wally Cartright of Holman-Moody/Stroppe build the 428. Stark Hickey paid the $3,000 bill for the custom paint, which consisted of pearls over royal maroon and gold-leaf lettering in a design created by Ford's styling group. A one-off car such as this is bound to hold many unique features. This one features a prototype '70 Mustang dashboard, seats, and thin-gauge stamped-steel fenders that Tony procured directly from Ford's defunct Trans-Am program in 1971.

Tony had great success with the car through 1974, running both SS/H and SS/HA. He took class at the 1971 Summernationals and in 1972, won class at the

Chapter Five: Door Slammers Galore 183

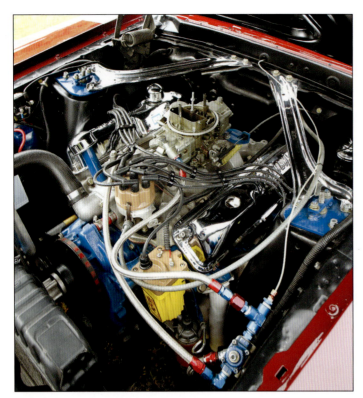

Bob had the foresight to retain the 428 when he pulled it out in 1975. He disassembled the engine and greased every part. It retains all the parts Tony had installed on the engine including carburetor and spacer to oil pan. A manual brake master cylinder was used to gain additional room and save weight. (Photo Courtesy Lyle Barwick)

The test mule Mustang retains its original body panels and Fenton Gyro wheels. The decals are reproduction and are placed to mimic the car's 1970 appearance. In 1971, thin-gauge Trans Am fenders were installed and the car repainted blue. Current owner Bob Wytosky chose the more appealing original colors to paint the car. (Photo Courtesy Lyle Barwick)

season-opening Winternationals. Propelling the Mustang to subrecord low-11-second times was an SCJ428 featuring all the legal (and then some) modifications expected of a mid-1970s Super Stock car. Sitting atop the engine is a modified 735 Holley perched on a sidewinder intake manifold. Internal mods included TRW pistons swinging from SCJ rods, a General Kinetics flat-tappet camshaft featuring .651 lift, and a crank reworked by Moldex. Tony's Mustang generally ran 40 to 42 degrees advance and top-end retard was controlled by a dash-mounted button.

Backing the 428 was either a Toploader 4-speed or a C6 automatic prepared by Winters and incorporating a 5,500-rpm stall convertor. Bringing up the rear was a 9-inch housing with 4.86 gears supported by Mopar Super Stock springs. Up front, Mustang 6-cylinder springs were incorporated along with Koni shocks.

Tony sold the car in 1974 to Larry Thiel of North Dakota who ran it for a season before selling it to current owner Bob Wytosky. Bob chose to run a Carl Holbrook (heavy valve) 428 and disassembled Tony's engine, oiled every part, and put it into storage. In 1977, Bob back-halved the chassis and installed a Max Fulmer 9-inch rear end and four-link suspension. A fresh Holbrook roller engine was built that ran close to the MPH record but by this point, running Super Stock was starting to lose its appeal for Bob. Although the car ran the class index, at the time NHRA was famous for lowering the index or bumping the engine's horsepower. With rumors of further changes coming, Bob felt the little guy was being forced out of Super Stock. He made the difficult decision to retire.

The Mustang was torn down in 1978 and before putting the car into storage everything was greased up. Even the jack stands used to support the car were greased as a means of keeping the rodents at bay. It sat in a storage container until the fall of 2012 when Bob decided something needed to be done with the car. He made

Looks as if owner Bob is raring to take the car for another run through the gears. The interior remains as new with only 833 miles showing on the odometer. Aftermarket accessories include a four-point roll cage, lap belt, aftermarket gauges, and Hurst shifter. (Photo Courtesy Lyle Barwick)

the decision to restore it to its 1970 Stark Hickey livery. Byron Thiessen of Creative Concepts and Restorations was called to do the deed and, as you can see by the photos, they nailed the restoration.

The guys chemically stripped the paint before mimicking the original colors. Says Bob, "We sent something like 16 spray-outs to Tony and his wife, Barbara, to get the pearls and color correct. In the restoration process we only used the pearls that were available in 1969 and 1970." The original Super Cobra Jet engine, which Bob so wisely stored away in 1975, was reassembled and put back into the car. The Mustang is like a step back in time, back to a time when there was still room for the little guy in Super Stock racing.

Bob's Mustang is quite unique because it was a factory test mule that survived the crusher. The Mustang retains its 1969 R-code door tag and a 1970 dashboard and seats. (Photo Courtesy Lyle Barwick)

Arlen Fadely's Super Modified Maverick

Low-10-second times and wheels-up launches were the norm in Super Modified. Although purchased as a 1975 body in white, Arlen's Maverick was built as a 1972; it thereby avoided the large front-crash bumper federally mandated in 1973.

Rick Voegelin and John Dianna of *Car Craft* dreamed up Super Modified as a category in 1974. Feeling that drag racing was in need of an inexpensive heads-up sportsman category, the pair presented the idea to NHRA National Tech director Jim Dale. Jim reasoned that if the pair could get enough racer support, the NHRA would consider it. Using the magazine as their sounding board, Rick and John reached out to their readers who responded overwhelmingly in favor of the idea. The NHRA was in and Super Modified made its debut at the 1975 Winternationals.

Joining the Modified ranks, Super Modified initially consisted of just one class. The base rules for A/SM were minimal: 9 pounds of vehicle weight for every cubic inch with a maximum cubic-inch rule of 366. A minimum weight of 2,850 pounds was dictated with the

Chapter Five: Door Slammers Galore

With Don's chassis work complete, Arlen towed the Maverick back to Michigan just after Christmas 1974. If the car looks a little weighed down, it's because it's packed from trunk to firewall with cases of Coors. At the time you couldn't buy Coors east of the Mississippi, so Arlen had the good sense to stock up before heading home.

total weight of the vehicle divided evenly, front to rear. A single carburetor no larger than 750 cfm and minimal porting of the cylinder heads was required. Rear tire width was kept to a maximum 10.5 inches. Only three cars showed up for the Winternationals but by the time Indy rolled around, more than 20 cars were in the lanes for class eliminations.

With word of the new category coming down late in 1974, Flat Rock, Michigan, resident Arlen Fadely immediately went to work to build this body-in-white Maverick. Laying out $477 for the shell, Arlen arranged to have it shipped directly from Ford's Kansas production facility to Don Hardy Race Cars in Floydada, Texas.

The Hardy crew spent the next two months preparing the chassis. All the factory seams were welded and existing welds were reinforced to meet the rigors of drag racing. Frame connectors were installed along with a six-point roll cage. Preparing the rear suspension, they relocated the spring perches inboard and stretched the wheel tubs. A floating 9-inch rear supported by adjustable coil-over shocks and Hardy's own ladder bars finished the rear suspension. The front suspension remained relatively stock, relying on 90/10 shocks, and trick, lightweight aluminum hubs by Strange Engineering. It was a chore to get as much weight off the front-heavy Maverick and Fadely relied on aluminum bolts throughout, titanium clutch and brakes pedals, and an A&A fiberglass hood and scoop.

Since Arlen worked for Ford's engineering department, it was fairly easy to retrieve a donor Maverick from the company's salvage department. Even though this wasn't necessarily legal, those within the company who supported racing chose to look the other way. A '74 Maverick Grabber was dragged home and gave up all the parts Arlen needed. The paint was (and remains) pearl orange with gold flake and was first applied by Dave Shilk. Jim Hounshell did the lettering and the ghost stripes on the hood.

Arlen built his own Boss-headed 302s and initially ran cubic inches of 318 and 342. He settled on 331, which was derived by increasing the bore of a 302 by .030 and increasing the stroke by .25 inch. Arias pistons supported

Those who read Super Stock & Drag Illustrated *in the 1970s would have caught a few feature articles on this car. The Maverick and its ongoing mechanical refinements were featured at least 18 different times. Arlen's payback was the Super Stock name on the car, which opened a lot of doors to added sponsorship.*

The current owner purchased the Maverick as a rolling chassis. The brightwork had been scuffed by the previous owner and painted matte black. Wherever possible, NOS parts were used in the restoration. Even though the body was solid and rust-free, a number of stress cracks had to be repaired. No expense was spared to ensure the restoration was "right."

The pearl orange paint was applied by Brandywine Coach Works in West Chester, Pennsylvania, while Dan Danzenbaker did a beautiful job recreating the lettering.

The current owner went through painstaking efforts to replicate the Boss, which measures 331 inches. Helping Arlen with the original build was Ted Brann, among others.

by BME aluminum rods squeezed out a healthy 12.5:1 compression. A Race Cams roller shaft actuated the Crane 1.72 rockers. Gapp & Roush provided the fabricated oil pan along with a single-plane intake manifold. A class-maximum 750 carburetor provided by Holley topped the 331.

Arlen initially ran a Toploader transmission that gave way to a Doug Nash at the end of the 1977 season. The 9-inch rear was stuffed with Richmond 5.67 gears and Strange axles. At higher-altitude tracks, Arlen preferred to run 6.0 rear gears, which propelled the Maverick through the traps at 9,200 to 9,300 rpm.

The NHRA expanded Super Modified in 1976 by adding two more classes. Arlen ran his Maverick in C/SM and won class at Indy in 1976, or at least he thought he did. Due to an error in stroke/displacement, he was tossed on final inspection. Running B/SM in 1977, Arlen headed back to Indy and won it all.

The Maverick dominated in 1978 and was the quickest-running B/SM car in the nation. Arlen set low ET at the Gatornationals, Springnationals, Summernationals, Sportsman Nationals, and Grandnationals. A "brain fart" at Indy prevented him from winning class. Apparently, Arlen had switched to a larger cam and 6.20 gears, which he felt might improve his times in the hot and humid Indy air. Recalls Arlen, "We got beat in class by Ed Hamburger. We didn't run on the Friday so some of us went to Muncie, Indiana, to test. We reinstalled the original cam and 5.83 gears and the car came right back. We went back to Indy and made it to the semis on Monday before redlighting."

The ports on the Boss heads are enough to make any brand-X loyalist envious. The Crane roller rockers actuate Manley valves.

The interior, like the rest of the car, has been restored to just the way it ran in the summer of 1977. A Hurst Competition Plus shifter is connected to a wide-ratio Toploader transmission. Ratios are a 2.78 first gear, 1.93 second, 1.36 third, 1.0 fourth with a 1.375-inch input shaft, and 31-spine output. The NOS gauges were manufactured by Auto Meter and were marketed by Ford (they have the Ford Logo on the face). These were donated to the restoration by Jim Aberts.

A worm's-eye view of the meticulously restored undercarriage reveals the large-tube Hooker Headers, Wayne Gapp–fabricated oil pan, and shaved brake drums. The undercarriage has been coated with a black epoxy just as Arlen had done in early 1975.

Arlen recalls that in 1978, the NHRA added weight to the Cleveland-powered Fords. "I went to Indy for the first Division 3 points meet of the season and before the race was rained out, I set the record at 10.17 at 133.50, weighing 9.5 lbs/ci. Right after that race, the NHRA added weight so the next points meet at Edgewater, we had to run at 9.80 lbs/ci. I won that race and reset the record.

"We went back to Indy for the rescheduled points race and because it had started with a 9.5 lbs/ci weight, we were allowed to drop weight. And again we lowered the record." The Maverick eventually ran as quick as a 10.07 at 137 in NHRA trim and a 9.91 in the more liberal IHRA.

Tired of Super Modified and wanting to build a dragster, Arlen sold the Maverick to Mike Edwards at the end of the 1978 season. Mike had plenty of success of his own with the car and won the Quaker State Cup and the final Modified Eliminator Championship in 1981. In total, it's believed the car set or reset class records more than 20 times.

The Maverick passed to Scott Main of MPG Head Service in Colorado before being brought back to Michigan by Ed Bennett. Ed knew the car well as he had been a pit helper for Arlen. Ed's son bracket-raced the Maverick before it was purchased by its current owner in April 2006. Plans from the get-go were to return the car to its original race configuration.

Arlen Fadely was hunted down and proved to be invaluable from the beginning of the restoration. As Mavericks don't enjoy the same reproduction parts availability as their sister, the Mustang, a donor car was purchased and want ads and flea markets were scrounged for needed parts. The hardest parts to find were the Grabber bucket seats that Arlen had initially installed. The original seats had long disappeared and were replaced by Kirkey Aluminum racing seats. A pair was eventually tracked down and, after "paying way too much," the original ginger-colored upholstery was replaced with reproduction black vinyl.

Except for a slightly milder camshaft, the Boss 331 and the rest of the drivetrain are just as Arlen raced it in 1977. The gorgeous pearl orange paint was easily reproduced thanks to a color chip Arlen had saved. House of Kolor provided the candy blue for the hood and tail panel. Dan Danzenbaker laid the meticulously restored lettering. Looking at the restored car today, Arlen says the owner nailed it. It's easy to agree.

The rear, three-quarter view has been a familiar site to many competitors over the years. From any angle, this restored Maverick looks great.

Epilogue: What Goes Around . . .

Do you think that when Dick Kraft built that first rail in 1950 he gave any thought to where it might lead? I believe that all Dick was really looking to do was build a fast car that would tromp the competition. Isn't that the main objective in building a drag car? If we look back on the history of drag racing, the evolution of the sport is plain to see.

In the 1950s, a kid could start with a low- or no-buck beater since cash was always tight, and then rely on plenty of innovative thinking to build the car. The "build" was usually carried out in the family garage using the tools Dad or a buddy's dad had hanging around the garage. No matter where we end up, we all have to start somewhere. For most of us, including today's kids, this was the beginning.

If you talk to any number of famous drag racers, you'll see a similar background and development. Look at the roots of Pro Stock legend Bob Glidden, for example. He started running stockers in Gary, Indiana, during the late 1950s; he graduated to Super Stock and then, finally, Pro Stock.

As the sport continued to evolve, we saw the slingshot rails become mid-engine dragsters and Factory Experimental cars become today's Funny Cars. It was inevitable that we'd have to say good-bye to some of the favorite categories such as Top Gas dragsters, Gassers, Altereds, and Modified Production cars.

The old adage states that what goes around, comes around, and that certainly is true for these early cars. Although the NHRA no longer holds out open arms to these cars, fan support has never wavered and today, interest continues to grow. Along with this revitalization, we have seen an equal growth in nationwide nostalgia events that cater specifically to restored and surviving drag cars.

Cacklefests showcase restored Dragsters and Funny Cars. Restored cars at these events are displayed and fired to the thrill of the fans. And don't think that the owners aren't enjoying it just as much. There is nothing like sitting behind a blown and injected engine with a full respirator in place while the crew ignites the nitro. The owners would love nothing more than to make a full pass in these cars but safety regulations and the fear of wrecking them prevent them from doing so.

For those not content with showing and cackling these original cars, companies such as Neil & Park and Funny Farm Fabrication will gladly build you a nostalgia racer. These guys can piece together a complete rail, Altered, or Gasser for you, if you have the deep pockets.

The Pro Stock category has always had the most appeal for the masses. The love of this class more than likely stems from the fact that, originally, the cars were constructed from showroom models. Unlike Dragsters and Funny Cars, these were cars that the average spectator could relate to and maybe even build at home. More than any other category, Pro Stock gave us heroes. They were characters and had great nicknames: Grumpy, Mr. 4-Speed, Dandy Dick, Dyno Don, and Fast Eddie.

As popular as the surviving and restored Pro Stocks are, they are just too valuable to risk racing. The Outlaw Nostalgia Pro Stock series was created to satisfy those who want to race these older-style cars. Safety requirements are strict but the rest of the rules are pretty basic.

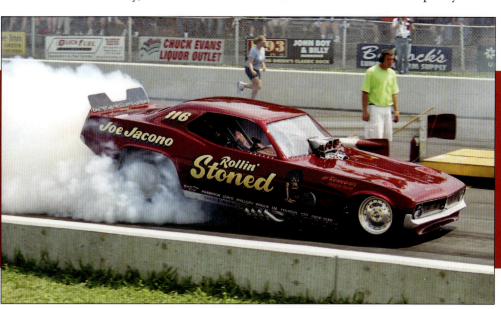

Bob Rosetty restored Joe Jacono's Rolling Stoned '73 'Cuda and put Joe in the seat to produce 7.20 times (no nitro) on the nostalgia trail. Bob's Funny Farm Fabrication will build you a new nostalgia Funny Car, if you have the pockets for it. (Photo Courtesy Bill Truby)

A number of Winged Express cars were built through the years; the latest was a spot-on tribute. The current incarnation, captured here at the Bowling Green National Hot Rod Reunion in 2010 is run by "Mousie" Marcellus and driven by Mike Boyd. The Borsch-Marcellus Fuel Altered was the first to record both 8- and 7-second runs as well as the first over 200 mph. In 1972, the second Winged Express recorded a record time of 7.29. (Photo Courtesy Bob Wenzelburger)

Bodies must be between 1969 and 1982 with a maximum engine size of 711 ci. Watching these cars go down the track is like stepping back in time.

A number of nostalgia events are held across the nation and participation and spectator attendance continues to grow. At some of the larger events, the size of the crowds are starting to challenge those drawn by some of NHRA's major races. It seems that these nostalgia events are offering spectators what the sanctioning bodies are unable to provide: a wide variety of cars, categories, and affordability.

Today's sanctioned drag racing may seem very different from what we remember in the 1960s and 1970s. However, at its root, it is still the sport that we love. Being the eternal optimist, I believe we will continue to see growth; today's youth are slowly learning to appreciate drag racing. Let's hope the NHRA, AHRA, and IHRA recognize the trend and support it.

The Belmont Boys, Jesse and Walt Schrank, took the remains of their 1961 B/FD and built themselves a clone. The former record holder (8.73 at 183.28) was built with the help of grandsons Scott and Kyle. Jesse, 77, and Walt, 80, prove that you're never too old to turn back the clock.

Yesterday meets today in Kyle Marshall's 1957 Chevrolet sedan delivery. The Chevy is a blast from the past: Tim Pogue raced it during the 1960s. The 1955–1957 Chevys ruled the NHRA Stock ranks in the 1960s and are just as popular today. (Photo Courtesy Jim Marlett)

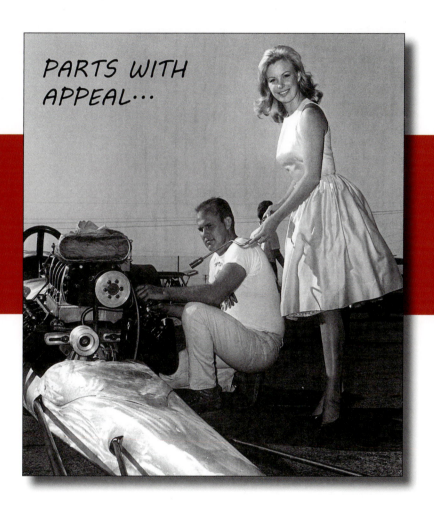

Additional books that may interest you...

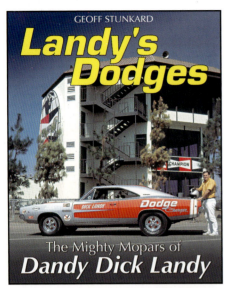

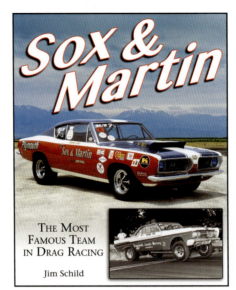

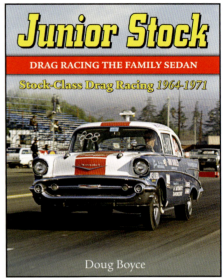

LANDY'S DODGES: The Mighty Mopars of "Dandy" Dick Landy *by Geoff Stunkard* This book takes you chronologically through the cars of Dick's career, from piloting his first mount (1954 Ford Pickup) through his historic years of campaigning Dodges. Chrysler racing historian and author Geoff Stunkard presents a detailed account of Dick's cars, including images from the Landy family's personal archive and modern shots of his restored cars. In addition to coverage of Dick's 1964 S/S Dodge and 1968 Hemi Dart, scarce info about his Ford Galaxies and Plymouth Savoy is included. At no other time has Landy's entire career been chronicled and cataloged in print with this much attention to detail. Sit back in your recliner and enjoy the most comprehensive book on the history of "Dandy" Dick Landy. Softbound, 8.5 x 11 inches, 176 pages, 400 images. **Item # CT561**

SOX & MARTIN: The Most Famous Team in Drag Racing *by Jim Schild* From their humble beginnings drag racing at local tracks in North Carolina to winning the prestigious US Nationals at Indianapolis, Ronnie Sox and Buddy Martin have seen it all. At their peak, Sox & Martin won 9 of 23 NHRA Pro Stock events, won 6 Championships in both AHRA and NHRA, and were invited to the White House. Never-before-seen photographs chronicle the team's Impalas, Comets, Colts, Omnis, Thunderbirds, Probes, etc. The author also includes a thorough examination of the record-breaking Belvederes, GTXs, Barracudas, Road Runners, and Dusters campaigned by the duo. Softbound, 8.5 x 11 inches, 176 pages, 350 color photos. **Item # CT545**

JUNIOR STOCK: Drag Racing the Family Sedan *by Doug Boyce* In the 1950s and 1960s, drag racing was an exciting new sport that anyone with a car could participate in. Based on their equipment, the participants' cars were assigned to specific classes. This class format encouraged amateur participation on a level never before seen. Stock-class drag racing is celebrated in this book, with hundreds of vintage color photographs showing the way it used to be. If you were a fan or participant back in the day, or are a lover of vintage drag cars, *Junior Stock: Drag Racing the Family Sedan* is a book you are sure to thoroughly enjoy. Softbound, 8.5 x 11 inches, 176 pages, 458 color photos. **Item # CT505**

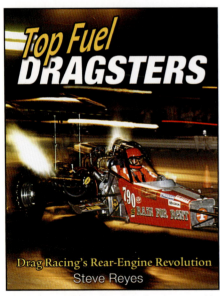

TOP FUEL DRAGSTERS *by Steve Reyes* Over the course of the evolution of technological developments in the late 1960s and early 1970s, Top Fuelers were making enough horsepower so that sitting directly behind the engine, as the "diggers" did in the 1950s through the 1960s, was recognized as a fairly dangerous proposition. Any blower explosion or clutch and bellhousing failure occurred directly in the face of the pilot. Teams and engineers developed the rear-engine layout that is still in use today, where the engine sits behind the driver but in front of the rear wheels. Industry legend and veteran journalist Steve Reyes was there through all the technological changes; he has the photos, anecdotes, quotes, and tales of the era. Join him in the pages of this book where he shares all the stories of this incredible racing era. **Item # CT547**

www.cartechbooks.com or 1-800-551-4754